The

OXFORDSHIRE

Village Book

Compiled by the
Oxfordshire Federation of
Women's Institutes from
notes and illustrations sent by
W.I.s in the County

Published jointly by
Countryside Books, Newbury
and the OFWI, Oxford

First published 1990
New Expanded Edition 1999
© Oxfordshire Federation of Women's Institutes 1990, 1999

COUNTRYSIDE BOOKS
3 Catherine Road
Newbury, Berkshire

ISBN 1 85306 576 5

Designed by Graham Whiteman

Front cover photo of Dorchester supplied by John Bethell
Back cover photo of East Hendred
supplied by Joyce Millward of Harwell W.I.

Produced through MRM Associates Ltd., Reading

Typeset by Techniset Typesetters, Newton-le-Willows

Printed by
J.W. Arrowsmith Ltd., Bristol

🍁 FOREWORD

Oxfordshire is mainly a rural area with pleasant market towns and attractive villages for visitors to explore. The rivers Thames and Cherwell and Oxford Canal offer a variety of water sports and holiday facilities. The Oxfordshire Way, Ridgeway, Thames Path and numerous well marked footpaths cater for those wishing to walk, and the motorways and high speed rail services bring this very interesting county within easy reach of many. Whilst travelling in the area one becomes very aware of the abundance of different building materials available locally over the centuries, from limestone and marl to flint and the lovely silvery blue bricks which were produced around Watlington and Henley.

The county has its share of stately homes. Blenheim is obviously a must for many, but the smaller houses, some still used as family residences, are a joy for the visitor.

With the coming of the motorways a number of our villages have been subject to new and infill housing, bringing new folk to live in the community. This has inevitably changed the face of village life but the central core of the village remains, with the older inhabitants and the new working together.

I know that our members have enjoyed compiling this book and sincerely hope that visitors and residents alike will, after reading their efforts, view Oxfordshire with new eyes. From the open countryside with wonderful views around the Ridgeway, through the Thames-side villages to the edge of the Cotswolds there is much to see and enjoy.

May you return again and again – it is a welcoming county.

Joyce Millward
County Chairman 1985–1990

FOREWORD TO THE SECOND EDITION

We are extremely pleased to have been given the opportunity to update this book about Oxfordshire villages. There may be a few more houses around but the landmarks will not have changed very much. The villages will be a little more mature and Oxfordshire still remains a delightful county to explore. I do hope you enjoy reading about our villages and pay us a visit one day.

Valerie Cantrell
Federation Chairman 1999

ACKNOWLEDGEMENTS

The Oxfordshire Federation of Women's Institutes would like to thank everyone who contributed to the *New Oxfordshire Village Book* published in 1990 and whose work has provided the backbone for this edition of *The Oxfordshire Village Book*. In particular we would like to acknowledge the work of the late Nancy Gieve who co-ordinated the original project, Joyce and Peter Millward, Dr Kathleen Burke, A.R. Dufty, Dr Gerald Howat and the late John Gieve.

We are very grateful to all the W.I.s whose members have contributed to this new edition by updating their original entries and providing some new material, also those who entered the competition for the cover photograph. Thank you to Countryside Books for their continuing interest and a special thank you to Sheila Westall who co-ordinated the project.

Shiplake Lock

County of
OXFORDSHIRE

Adderbury House

🍁 ADDERBURY

'Recent' Adderbury history – for it dates from Saxon times and its mellowed parish church of St Mary the Virgin was started in the early 13th century and largely completed by the 15th century – is of its importance as a Royalist stronghold in the Civil War. The most dramatic episode in village history concerns that war – when the vicar of Adderbury, the Rev Dr William Oldys, was shot by a Parliamentarian soldier near the vicarage. The church has close links with New College, Oxford and was beloved of Sir John Betjeman.

Adderbury House has housed troops from wars as far apart as the Civil and Second World Wars. In the former war Henry Wilmot, 1st Earl of Rochester and Prince Rupert of the Rhine were Royalist cavalry commanders there; in the second, King George VI visited his troops in 1942. During the 17th century the house was home to John Wilmot, 2nd Earl of Rochester (1647–80), a fine lyrical and satirical poet and a notorious Restoration rake. The 350th anniversary of the lyricist's birth was marked by events throughout Oxfordshire in 1997. One of the first celebrations was at Adderbury House, newly renovated to a private dwelling.

Owned at various times by Dukes of Argyll, Adderbury House was in the possession in the 19th century of Major Larnach. When his Adderbury-trained horse *Jeddah* won the Derby at 100-1 and also won at Ascot to complete the 'blue ribbon' of the Turf, the Major gifted the building of the village Institute. This was opened, in great ceremony, in 1898. Seldom have winnings been more happily invested!

Miss Janet Blunt figures prominently in village history. Daughter of an Indian Army officer who settled his family in Adderbury in 1892, she wrote down from word of mouth Morris dance tunes which had for generations been handed down from father to son. Miss Blunt died in 1950 at the age of 91 and it was only the timely intervention of her former maid that saved the manuscripts from the bonfire. It is to these same tunes present-day Morris dancers cavort at their annual Day of Dance around the village inns and on the green on the last Saturday of April, each year. Generously, they are also shared and taught throughout Oxfordshire and, indeed, known throughout the world.

The village green, with its majestic spreading chestnut tree, once held court to visiting magistrates who meted out punishment to miscreants, by way of whipping stool, ducking stool or the stocks. The latter (removed in 1885) were within the memory of one of the earliest members of the WI at its foundation in 1920.

Adderbury has been several times winner of the title Best Kept Village of North Oxfordshire and twice taken the Winner of Winners class. It is clear the judges find its blend of warm honey-coloured stone, beautiful manor houses and cottage gardens brimming over with flowers, incomparable.

🍁 APPLEFORD

About a mile and a half due east of Sutton Courtenay, on the south bank of the river Thames, is the village of Appleford. As you approach the village the eye is taken upwards to the Wittenham Clumps with its crown of trees and below it the spire of the church. If you look to the right, the bulk of Didcot power station commands the view across the fields.

As its name suggests there was once a ford in the village, which made it a good place for a settlement since earliest times. The history of Appleford dates back to the Saxons and the church of St Peter and St Paul originates from then. Nothing is left of the original building, but part of the chancel contains remains from the 12th and 13th centuries and the font is Norman. It has always been a chapelry, with no vicar of its own, but for 500 years has been part of the living of Sutton Courtenay. At the expense of Walter Justice, the church was heavily restored in 1885–86 when the square tower and spire were added.

The village is bounded on its western side by the railway. The halt was closed in 1849 but rebuilt in 1934 and is still in use, linking Appleford to Didcot and Oxford.

Close by the railway line, on its western side, is Bridge Farm, the former home of Mr Arthur Napper who in 1950 introduced traction engine racing. This became an annual event for some time with competitors attending from all over the country. In 1968 a collection of pewter plates and domestic ironware was discovered in Mr Napper's fields. Dating from Roman times, this is known as the Appleford Hoard and is housed at the Ashmolean Museum, Oxford. Other evidence has shown that a Romano-British settlement existed here and two large collections of Roman coins were also ploughed up.

At the centre of the village is the 'Nap' or green. On its north side is Orchard House. This was once the home of Edmund Bradstock, Appleford's principal benefactor. In his will dated 1607, money and land were left to found a village school as well as charities for the aged of Sutton Courtenay and Appleford. These are still administered by the Bradstock's Trust. Sadly the school closed in 1961. It is remembered by the name 'School Lane' and modern houses stand in its place.

East of the village and close to the church is Manor Farm. Parts of it are very old and it was probably the grange of Abingdon Abbey. While the Pullens were at Manor Farm, six or seven skeletons were found, buried in shallow graves, by farm workers. These were thought to have been soldiers who fought in a local skirmish during the Civil War.

The most interesting character to have lived in Appleford appears to have been John 'Jockey' Faulkener. He is interred in Appleford churchyard in an unmarked grave. John Faulkener died in 1933 at the age of 104. He rode his first race at eight years old and his last, in 1903, at 70! Aged 18 years he won the City Bowl at Salisbury and 74 years later watched his grandson win the same race.

John Faulkener had two wives and 32 children, the eldest of whom was the same age as his second wife. His name was Jimmy; he also in turn became Britain's oldest jockey, beating his father by a short head, marrying three times and having 33 children.

During the last 20 years the village has seen many changes. Not only has the village school disappeared, but many of the old cottages as well. The old thatched cottages in Main Road (once called Littleworth), the terrace of cottages built in Napoleonic times and the Black Horse – Appleford's other public house, have all been replaced with modern houses as have the two fields, one called Chambrai Minor and the other in Church Street.

The pre-war cricket pavilion has been skilfully converted to a village hall which stands in the recreation field, and provides a meeting place for village activities. Sadly, the village stores and post office closed in 1988. Very few of the villagers work in the vicinity, but the village spirit remains.

APPLETON & EATON

The village of Appleton, with which the smaller village of Eaton has long been associated, stands on rising ground 100 ft above the river Thames, which is its western boundary.

Woodlands, known as Besselsleigh Common and Appleton Common, still partially cover its eastern and southern boundaries. The Saxon name for the village was Earmundslea or 'Edmund's clearing'.

One can still receive an impression of its old character and charm as a considerable number of stone houses remain standing in the centre of the village, from the Tavern Inn to Charity House Farm. Modern housing exists along the roads in and out of the village, and in recent years a considerable amount of in-filling has taken place. The population of the village is now approximately 1,000.

Most of the inhabitants work away from the village, but there is a village shop and post office, greengrocer's/market garden, and a saddler's shop also, which serves the surrounding area. The village hall, which is a focal point for social activities, was built in the early 1920s. Villagers contributed to it by the purchase of a brick for sixpence – quite a significant figure at that time.

The White family have a workshop in the village and for four generations have practised the rare craft of bell hanging. Their fame has spread countrywide and they service church bells throughout an extensive area. The family form the core of the bell ringers of the ten bells in the 15th century church tower. The 4th of March is celebrated as the bells' birthday to commemorate the installation of the original peal of six bells in 1818. Peals are rung during the day by visiting ringers and a grand dinner in the village hall ends the celebrations.

Church Lane, in the centre of the village, leads down to the 12th century church of St Laurence. A modern primary school has been built in the old manor orchard in the lane, and on the right is the manor pond and tithe barn. The church has a Norman arcade and nave, and has grown during the centuries by additions and restorations, but it is still a homely little church with a feeling of peace and cosiness.

The manor house, which also dates from about 1190, has a moat. This house too has been enlarged and improved by succeeding generations of owners. It is still lived in as a family home.

The lane leading down to the river from Badswell Lane has an ancient well, known as Badger's Well. The water of this well, according to village legend, was a sovereign cure for eye ailments. Before good roads were made this lane was the way by which goods were conveyed for transportation by river.

Another interesting house in the village is The Close, which was originally a plague house. The Thames valley was severely hit by the Black Death in 1348, and many houses were burned down to clear the infection. Those in authority gave the owners the framework for a new home, ie beams, fireplaces etc, and the owners completed the work with lath and plaster or stone.

There are two working farms in the village and two large farms at Eaton.

ARDINGTON & LOCKINGE

Ardington and Lockinge lie two miles east of Wantage, just south of the A417 road. Sheltered by the Downs, they are within easy reach of the grand walking country of the Ridgeway. There is always plenty going on in Ardington, where we are fortunate to have a thriving village shop, tea room and post office. Many of the redundant farm buildings owned by the Lockinge Estate have also been converted into offices and workshops. These include a pottery, a picture framing gallery and furniture making and restoration, all established in a range of beautiful old Victorian farm buildings which once housed a renowned herd of pedigree Guernsey cows. The village school is now a private day nursery but we still have the village pub, and the Loyd Lindsay Rooms provide facilities for village activities.

Holy Trinity church at Ardington dates from the 12th century, and much of the Early English architecture survives. The original doorway is sheltered by a 13th century porch but a doorway in the south wall has recently been replaced by a modern window showing a dove rising above the Downs. The church was extensively renovated in Victorian times and inside is a marble statue of a kneeling woman carved by the designer of Nelson's Column. Nearby is Ardington House, an imposing early 18th century mansion with a fine staircase in two flights occupying the whole of the centre of the ground floor.

The Millennium Stones erected by the Lockinge Estate in a clearing of the recently planted woodland consist of 13 pairs of stones set in a semi-circle, each representing one hour from 6 am to 6 pm Solar Time. A Millennium Stone, through which a hole has been drilled, is set behind the twelve o'clock pair, to catch the first ray of sunlight of the Third Millennium at dawn on 1st January 2000.

11

🍁 ASCOTT-UNDER-WYCHWOOD

Ascott is a pretty little village in the Cotswolds, which has the advantage of being not quite so pretty as other Cotswold villages such as Burford. This means that all is peaceful and tourists pass us by – no acres of car parks, no 'tea shoppes'or antiques shops.

Up until 1874 there was an annual hunt at Whitsuntide in Wychwood Forest, followed by a week of festivities during which the Ascott Morris men danced in the local villages. With the ending of the hunt, their songs and dances began to be forgotten. Early in the 20th century, a Mr Reginald Tiddy who lived in the Priory Cottage in the High Street collected them and taught them again to the villagers, and the stationmaster's wife made the costumes. In 1912 Mr Tiddy had Tiddy Hall built in Shipton Road for dancing, singing and as a reading room. Sadly, he died in action in France four years later, and is remembered by a stone tablet in the wall.

One of the first Margaret Macmillan Clinics in the country was held regularly in Tiddy Hall, providing free medical treatment for the children. In 1915 the Workers Education Association started one of its earliest rural branches there, which kept going until after the Second World War. When in recent years the original Tiddy Hall, a wooden building, fell into disrepair funds were raised for a new stone building on the same site.

On the green there is a tree with a seat round it, planted in memory of the Ascott Martyrs of 1873. The National Agricultural Labourers' Union was attempting to raise labourers' wages to 14 shillings a week, and some men working for Robert Hambridge at Crown Farm, who were only earning eight to ten shillings a week, went on strike. Hambridge brought in two non-Union men from Ramsden, and about 40 local women tried to persuade them not to strike-break. Hambridge took out a summons against some of the women, and they were sentenced to prison with hard labour. Such was the outcry that the women were marched from Chipping Norton to Oxford prison at dead of night, lest the rioters freed them. After questions in the House of Commons they were released. Some say £3 each was collected for them, some say £5, and some say Queen Victoria gave them each a free pardon and a red flannel petticoat. Crown Farm, where the men worked, still belongs to the Crown.

The west end of Ascott is known as Ascott Earl (after an Earl of Worcester) and the east end as Ascott d'Oyley (after Roger d'Oilly who was granted it by

William the Conqueror; Roger's brother built Oxford Castle). Each part originally had a fortified castle, with motte and bailey. The one off Shipton Road was probably wooden, and only earth mounds mark the site. The other, off the Chipping Norton road, was built for defence purposes in about 1129, with a stone tower 35ft square. It was pulled down in 1160 when a garrison was no longer required. The manor house stands within the bailey of this castle, and is partly 12th century.

The church of Holy Trinity is mainly 12th century, and quite small and simple. The six bells in the tower are rung regularly for services. At the back of the church are five wooden pews, possibly the oldest in Oxfordshire. These were for the old and sick, whence may have come the saying 'The weakest to the wall' – everybody else had to stand. The series of round depressions near the priest's door is said to have been made by parishioners sharpening their arrow-heads after the service.

Corner House used to be the Churchill Arms, where stage coaches from Worcester to London stopped to change horses. When the railway came in the 1860s, a new Churchill Arms – now Wychwood Court – was built near the level crossing. The original signal box is of wood and brick – about the only sign of the brickworks that was once in Ascott. It now has closed circuit television so the signalman can control the level crossing three miles away at Bruern.

The Swan is the only remaining pub. On Monday mornings it doubles as a post office, and you can lounge in comfortable seats while waiting to be served your pension from behind the bar.

The school, on the green, was built in 1873, replacing a building of 1833. In 1989 it became the (private) Windrush Valley School – mysterious, because Ascott lies along the beautiful river Evenlode, not the Windrush.

In the grounds of the Old Vicarage up London Lane, there is a pond supplied by a spring which was the source of piped water to the village until 1966.

With converted barns, infill building and council houses, the village has expanded considerably since the Second World War. It now has about 500 inhabitants and around 200 households. But old inhabitants say the population has remained much the same: where large families with lots of children used to be crammed into small cottages, one or two people live now.

🍁 ASTHALL

The village of Asthall was originally a Roman settlement, with Akeman Street passing through it. In the Domesday Book it was called 'Esthale' and was 'held of the King by Roger D'Ivery'.

The church of St Nicholas has played a large part in the life of the village and is architecturally of great interest and beauty. It contains a rare medieval stone altar, an early Norman font and many beautiful features. The 14th century tomb of Lady Cornwall, said to be the wife of Edmund Cornwall, grandson of King John lies under a decorated canopy. In the churchyard a fine wool bale tomb is a reminder of the prosperity that wool brought to this area.

Nearby is the Elizabethan house of Asthall Manor. This was the home of Lord Redesdale and his family ('Uncle Matthew' to all the readers of the Mitford books). The house is approached by a fine avenue of beeches and has a beautiful arch at the entrance.

The Windrush river is a living part of Asthall and a constant source of interest, joy and beauty. A large number of ducks and geese are always to be seen, as well as herons, swans and rare river birds. The blue flash of the kingfisher is always a thrill for those lucky and quiet enough to see him.

Wool and the weaving of it go back to pre-Roman times, continuing through the Middle Ages – the most prosperous times being between 1600 and 1800. The fleeces varied in length and texture according to the breed of sheep. The river was invaluable for washing and cleaning them.

Local industries include farming, and one family has farmed this valley since early in the 20th century. Self-employed industries have been set up by individual people and several country industries – including scaffolding, building, house restoration, dry walling, painting and gardening. The village is very alive now with the comings and goings of these industries and a great feature of it is a feeling of community spirit throughout.

🍁 ASTON & COTE

Aston is a village in West Oxfordshire, situated to the north of the upper Thames and four miles to the south of Witney. Cote is a hamlet about one mile to the east of Aston, and nowadays their names are invariably linked together.

The surrounding countryside is very flat with large open fields. Many elm trees died from Dutch elm disease some years ago but plantings of other species have been carried out. Aston is built round the Square, which is in fact a triangle, in the centre of which is the war memorial. Present day Aston and Cote have experienced many reforms during the 20th century. Gas was piped from the diminutive works in Bampton (a mile and a half away) long before electricity arrived but people were still using wells for water until after the Second World War.

In 1890 Kelly's Oxford Directory listed the following occupations that were based in the village – farmers, masons, brickmakers, shoe-makers, blacksmith, wheelwrights, baker, carrier, grocers and general dealers. The farm wagons built by Longs of Aston were considered to be some of the best in the land, and the works were situated behind the post office. Incidentally, the Long family are still active in the village. In Back Lane a laundry was run by destitute young females who were housed by a charity in the present Westfield House, which is now a nursery school. The site of the old laundry is now used for small businesses, which provides some employment but Aston and Cote is mainly a farming area.

Cote consists mainly of farms, most of which have been turned into private dwellings. The Baptist chapel, registered in 1703, stands starkly surrounded by its tomb-filled churchyard – the plain exterior is contrasted by a unique interior of box pews and galleries. This is now owned by the Historic Chapels Trust. Cote House overlooks the fields to the south-west. This stone manor house was built in the reign of James I but incorporates an older wing. One modern addition to the hamlet are the hatcheries where thousands of day-old chicks are raised and exported to all corners of the world.

Lots of changes have occurred in Aston and Cote over the years with houses and cottages demolished, new estates built, shops closed or changed hands, but the village is still thriving with its two churches – St James' parish church and Cote Baptist church, the school, post office, general stores and lots of organisations from Brownies to a day centre for the elderly.

ASTON ROWANT

Aston Rowant, the Aston meaning 'east tun' and the Rowant after the 14th century Rohant family, is a pretty little brick and flint village lying at the

15

northern foot of the Chiltern Hills. Like all the villages along the foot of the Chilterns it is sited by a stream, the Holbrook, which forms its eastern boundary, the A40 forming its western boundary. To the south of the village the ancient Icknield Way runs below the Chiltern escarpment and to the north the Lower Icknield Way.

The oldest part of the village lies by the 12th century church of St Peter and St Paul. In spring the bank of the churchyard is massed with daffodils and blossoming trees. Elizabeth I, when a princess, rode past on her way to imprisonment at Rycote and the bellringers were put in the stocks for ringing in her honour.

The village boasts a privately owned one and a half acre village green with fine trees and daffodils in spring. Around the green is a farmhouse and cottages which were mainly built in the 18th and 19th centuries. To the east a row of neo-Georgian houses was built in the early 1970s.

There has been a manor house at Aston Rowant from 1352. In the 17th century the house was rebuilt in Haseley stone dressed with Bath stone – a fine house with ornamental staircase and picture gallery. On the death of Edward Dashwood in 1950 the house was sold and used for storage by a grass drying firm – it burned down in 1956. Now 13 ranch-style bungalows have been built in the park and the walled kitchen garden, with its grape, peach and nectarine houses, owned and worked as a nursery until 1986, has been built on.

The village school was built in 1844, much earlier than many in the county. Before that there had been a lace school for girls. Originally pupils spent all their school years in the village, now they leave at nine to go on to Chinnor and Thame. Bucket toilets were only replaced in the late 1960s.

Up until the 1960s most people worked for the 'big house' or on the local farms. Aston House owned the village, it made its own gas for street lighting, etc, the road through the village was swept daily and woebetide a gardener if a weed could be found!

With the coming of the M40 Aston Rowant has become a commuter village, its inhabitants working in London or the larger towns nearby. Two of the farms have become studs, one stallion being the famous *Daring Do*. The village shop has disappeared but the church and school still thrive. The church has a good team of bellringers and a social committee to organise various social events. Unfortunately a lot of money is needed for its restoration.

There is no public house but there is a thriving cricket club, established in 1881, with a pitch so well cared for that it has been used for Minor County games. Twice the team has got to the semi-finals of the National Village Cricket Knockout.

ASTON TIRROLD & ASTON UPTHORPE

The twin Aston villages merge comfortably at the foot of the Berkshire Downs, in the valley below the A417 Wantage to Streatley road. The parishes stretch from South Moreton to Lowbury Hill and have a population of about 550 people. The Ridgeway runs above them to the south. To the west Blewburton Hill, an Iron Age earthwork, has yielded Iron Age, Roman and Saxon relics now in Reading Museum.

Tradition has it that King Ethelred and his younger brother Alfred, later the King, heard Mass together before the first great victory over the Danes at 'Assendune' on the Downs. There is a popular legend that Ethelred, unready as usual, dithered in Aston Upthorpe while Alfred went out and won the battle. The story is erroneous – this was a different Ethelred from the dilatory King known to every schoolchild. Whether the Mass was held in a Saxon church or the royal tent, it is certain that Aston Upthorpe's All Saints' church is built on Saxon foundations, has an 11th century nave, a filled-in Norman door, and a 15th century porch.

St Michael's church in Aston Tirrold dates back to 1080, was remodelled in the 13th century and a tower and south transept added in the 14th century. Both lovely village churches are well worth a visit. The rectory, next to St Michael's, was sold when a united benefice was formed with the parishes of North and South Moreton. The Astons have a tradition of Presbyterianism, and before the Act of Uniformity in 1662, 'Meetings in the Barns' took place. In 1728 the very interesting Presbyterian church was built, making it one of the oldest in England. It is now the United Reformed church.

During the 20th century the Astons have been closely connected with horse racing. At one time there were four trainers in the two villages. Although there is now only one, in Aston Upthorpe, horses can still be seen exercising around the villages.

There is now only one public house left, The Chequers in Aston Tirrold, since the Boot Inn closed. The Chequers serves good food and is an excellent

17

place to meet friends and exchange news, a necessity as over the years other meeting places such as the village school, the library, the shop and the doctor's surgery have all closed. The Astons, however, still have a post office, a well-used village hall and a large recreation ground where football and cricket are played in season and children have a well-equipped play area.

The surrounding land is mostly arable, yielding good crops of wheat, oilseed rape and barley. Carrimers Farm and Upthorpe Farm are the two main farms, and the Astons still remain truly rural villages with well preserved old houses and attractive lanes through which to walk from one village to the other.

THE BALDONS

March Baldon, Toot Baldon,
Baldon in between,
Big Baldon, Little Baldon,
Baldon on the Green.

In fact there are just two villages with a total population of less than 500 and a large acreage of good agricultural land. Both villages have had a close association with the university as Queen's College has owned much of the land, and in time of plague and when the king occupied Oxford in the Civil War, members of the university retreated to the safety of Toot Baldon.

Toot Baldon is on the top of its hill and the name Toot means a look out. It has attractive houses built mainly of local stone. There is a fine old manor house and just over the road the partly rebuilt old court house. Across the field is the delightful little early 13th century church dedicated to St Lawrence, and a little further down the hill is Baldon Row – once called Baldon St Lawrence – a little group of cottages, again mainly stone built. One pair of cottages has a superb thatched roof, the thatch coming to a few feet from the ground.

Little Baldon is now one farm with noteworthy new houses for the farm workers.

Marsh Baldon, formerly March Baldon, is a 'history book' village, centred around the 24-acre gated village green, as the Saxons built it, just off the Roman road with the manor house and church down the road. There are many interesting houses around the green, but the north side has mainly uniform brick built Victorian cottages. A disastrous fire in September 1866 destroyed the thatched cottages; it had been a very dry summer and the five ponds on the green had dried up. The 17th century Baldon House has been extended over the years.

The present church, dedicated to St Peter, was built by the monks from Dorchester. It has a Saxon mass dial, and the east window has some lovely 14th century glass and also the arms of Henry VII when the church was restored.

There is no post office or shop in the village but there is a splendid new village hall for which the small community worked very hard.

Very few people are still engaged in agriculture, most travel to nearby Oxford to work, but there is one employer making use of the fertile soil – in the south west corner of the parish, on an outcrop of greensand, are Mattock's rose gardens, to which has been added a large garden centre. Until recently the farmers used their right to graze their cattle on the village green, now they use it for hay.

🍁 BAMPTON

Six miles from Witney, Bampton lies on a gravel terrace, just above the flat Thames valley. It is an attractive Cotswold village, off the usual tourist tracks, but it is so full of charm that its many special features are well worth exploring.

Bampton's history is intriguing. There was a pre-Christian settlement (a Roman altar was recently dug up in a field) and it grew in Saxon and Norman times. It was mentioned in the Domesday survey, when it already possessed a market, and was famous for its wool trade. In the Middle Ages its administrative area was considerable, and included Witney and Burford. In the 17th century, an important leather trade grew up, and Bampton became famous for its jackets, gloves and breeches.

The chief feature now is the church of St Mary. It is one of the largest in West Oxfordshire. It stands on the site of a former Saxon minster, and is a Norman building, remodelled in the 13th and 14th centuries. It has a noble spire; a gale unfortunately blew down one of the flying buttresses and St John, one of the four figures standing at the corners of the tower.

Around the close and green are four large houses, Georgian in appearance, but of earlier origins. Bampton Castle, previously an imposing and impressive building, now has only the remains of the gatehouse and a stretch of curtain walling, which are incorporated into the farmhouse called Ham Court; however, British Telecom retains the name of Bampton Castle for the telephone exchange. Weald Manor opposite Ham Court, and Bampton Manor to the north, add to the architectural delights; both are set in charming gardens which are open to the public two or three times a year.

The stone cottages, whose roofs were formerly thatched with straw but are now mostly slates or tiles, form terraces leading along three streets to the Market Square, where the town hall and village hall face each other. A corn mill stood at the end of Mill Street, with Mill Green to the south. Old residents remember how the cottages there would be flooded quite regularly, so that the water came up to the third stair indoors; the doctor wore waders, not mere wellington boots, to go through the waters to his patients, who had to remain on the first floor for perhaps three weeks at a time. Now the land has been drained, and the level of the waters controlled by holding ponds at Brize Norton airfield, two miles away.

There are some 2,400 inhabitants, many of whom are concerned at the prospect of further increasing the size of the village. The villagers are a caring group, and are prepared to cherish their inheritance. The traditional Horse Fair may have vanished, but the Bampton Morris dancers flourish; the dancers dress in white, the bells on their leather anklets jingle as they kick and dance to the fiddler's music, and the clown urges them on.

Today, as well as main drainage, electricity and gas, there are other excellent facilities, including a primary school, library, post office, health centre, fire station, six public houses and a number of shops and businesses.

🍁 THE BARFORDS

The two villages, Barford St Michael (or Great Barford) and Barford St John (Little Barford), are a quarter of a mile apart on either side of the river Swere, about six miles from the nearest town, Banbury. A narrow bridge crosses the river which long ago was crossed by a ford, hence the derivation, some think, from the name Barleyford.

After the early 1960s many changes took place, particularly in St Michael.

Before then there were about 80 houses in the two villages. Today there are over 200 houses and bungalows. Probably the most significant reason for this increase in size was the arrival of mains drainage thus removing the inconvenience of cess pits and septic tanks. However, as in many villages, this increase in size has not brought about an increase in amenities. Until it became a private residence in 1957 there was a thriving village school. There were once seven buses a day carrying folk into Banbury to work or for shopping; now there are only three a week. The villages are fortunate in that there is a flourishing post office and stores but sadly the local bakehouse which baked delicious bread closed in the early 1970s and is now, like the forge, a private residence.

Each village has an active church. The smaller one of St John was once a chapel in the Adderbury diocese. The church of St Michael has a uniquely decorated Norman north door, and a Norman tower and font. In days long gone the vicar lived in the 17th century vicarage nearby. The Free Methodist chapel in St Michael was built by local craftsmen in the 19th century and is still in use today.

The Manor Farm of Barford St Michael, mentioned in the Domesday Book, is partially surrounded by a moat which is used by keen fishermen. The farm is also the home of the village post office and stores. There was once a pub in each of the two villages. Today the Crown of Barford St John is a private residence but the George in Barford St Michael is still open and flourishing. The hub of village activity is the village hall built in the 1930s. It is usually fully booked by local groups and organisations and since it has an excellent stage, it is also used by local and travelling theatre groups.

🍁 THE BARTONS

A long, straggling street with buildings of various styles, periods and materials is the first impression of the Bartons gained by the passing motorist. To the discerning eye, to the explorer of half hidden lanes, and certainly to the inhabitants, there is much more to these communities of about 1,700 people.

There are three villages, Middle and Westcote, virtually joined, and Steeple Barton, quite distinct, approached by country lanes. From Saxon times Steeple Barton supplied the royal manor at Woodstock with food and, later, Osney

Abbey. It has a skyline-dominating church and its few houses are pleasingly set in what is now a very small hamlet. The deep-cut narrow road, green lanes and meandering tracks indicate its antiquity. Humps in the fields are remains of a once sizeable village, largely abandoned after the ravages of the Black Death. Traces of the old mill and dried up fish ponds tell of a very different past.

Westcote Barton, another old settlement, has an impressive small church and attractive stone cottages, particularly in Fox Lane, which leads to a ford on the Dorn. The brook was the main water supply, carried by hand to houses as much as a mile away, until the mid-1930s.

Middle Barton (the name Barton means an outlying farm) was settled by post-plague immigrants from Steeple Barton and those taking advantage of the medieval road from Bicester (now the B4030). A population explosion came in the 18th and 19th centuries when enterprising individuals, lacking opportunity elsewhere or unhappy with squire or parson, moved in, erecting cottages and smallholdings on the road verges of North Street, in no particular style and facing in different directions. There are older, attractive stone cottages from the 16th and 17th centuries in the parallel South Street. Never an estate village, but an open village, it was independent of any squire and people enjoyed the freedom to build and live as they pleased.

In the main road there is a farm and adjoining field with grazing animals, of perennial interest to villagers walking by. Here is a reminder of the agricultural emphasis of the past. Few villagers today are farm workers or associated with agriculture and a great variety of professions and occupations is now represented in the population.

Unlike some of its more picturesque neighbours, the Bartons have relatively few weekend-only occupied dwellings and so have retained more of the character of a lively, working community. This is largely due to the development of modern housing estates. Young families have ensured a flourishing primary school and the survival of the village shop cum post office.

The Bartons are said to be known for the friendliness and independence of character of the villagers. Until the recent increase in prosperity, life was very hard for many. Even so the Ruridecanel magazine for 1923 describes Steeple Barton as 'the healthiest parish for many a mile'. Independence of spirit was shown by the small Quaker settlement; the graveyard may still be seen. Methodism flourished and the only church in Middle Barton (far the largest of the villages) is the Methodist chapel in South Street, one of the few remaining village chapels in North Oxfordshire.

Barton Abbey, at Steeple Barton, is the 'big house' (it was never an abbey). In part 16th century but substantially Victorian, it was rebuilt (and named) by the Halls, the brewing family. Since 1925 house and estate have been owned by the Flemings, who have continued the tradition of generous support to the villages.

Nearby is St Mary's church with a fine 15th century tower and interesting memorials and carvings. The smaller Westcote Barton church is unusual in its dedication to St Edward the Confessor and entitlement to the wearing of red cassocks by the choir. Much of the building, on the site of a Saxon church, is 15th century.

Present and past are closely inter-related in the Bartons. Much has been lost but finds are made of medieval pottery and ancient tools in gardens and old out-buildings. Only the old, written records and photographs remain to remind one of the once flourishing Horticultural Shows and Friendly Society activities. The strange and ancient mummers' play of Westcote Barton was last performed about a century ago and only a sketchy text survives. However, a flourishing amateur drama group and programmes provided by a range of clubs and organisations offer a variety of leisure activities.

 BAULKING

Baulking, previously in Berkshire, is a relatively tranquil village with about 85 inhabitants, situated in the lovely Vale of the White Horse and bounded on one side by the river Ock, known locally as Rosey Brook. Long ago it was a thriving market town, its market day having been changed by charter in 1219 from Thursday to Tuesday, and has had connections with the ancient abbey of Abingdon and the manor of Kingston Lisle. Parts of the village were in the past owned by the Earls of Spencer and of Craven. Today, although Intercity trains whizz through the cutting (begun in 1839) and under Brunel's bridge, one can neither board a train at Uffington station (which was built in Baulking parish) nor refresh oneself at the Junction Hotel, both now closed.

The main feature of the village is its large goose green around which stand attractive farmhouses, pretty cottages and the remains of the old village pump. This 18 acre green, in former times controlled by two gates, is now necessarily in three separate parts, the natural 'divisions' being the railway and the church, alongside the latter of which there is presently a cattle grid. Certain adjacent land-holders to the green have grazing rights consisting of sheep commons: so many sheep equal one cow, horse, etc, and whereas in olden times flocks of sheep grazed the green and wool was an important industry, today cattle are let loose annually from 13th May to 6th December. It is good to see domestic geese back after a long interval, but guinea fowl and other poultry are no longer around.

The church of St Nicholas was built in this idyllic spot in the 13th century, and has interesting wall paintings uncovered and restored in 1988–9.

The spacious village green is a favoured meeting place of the Old Berks Hunt, and records show there was a meet of the Royal Buckhounds on 2nd March 1893 when hundreds of folk turned out and there were waggons, 'musicianers', cock-shies and Aunt Sallies. In the 1920s point-to-points were staged on Baulking Hill. Mention must be made of *Baulking Green*, the horse which put the village on the map in the 1960s, bringing many glittering steeplechase trophies back to this corner of England.

Agriculture is still the predominant industry, though today only two of the eight farms have dairy herds, the lush pasture elsewhere being grazed by store cattle, with in places diversification to arable. In the 1970s open cast mining for high quality fuller's earth and the drying thereof on site began, thus providing an ever changing scene: first the creation of bunds, the excavation to great depths even necessitating the resiting of the road to Stanford-in-the-Vale, and after extraction immediate reclamation field by field.

The village hall, brick kiln, shop, pub, school – and alas the splendid elms – are no more, and inevitably some residents now commute elsewhere. The village joins forces with Uffington and Woolstone for many activities, including sport, the WI, MU, Scouts and Guides, but it controls its own parochial affairs through its Parish Meeting.

 BECKLEY

> 'I went to Noke and nobody spoke;
> I went to Beckley, they spoke directly'.

This is an old aphorism, quite probably untrue of Noke nowadays, but certainly true of Beckley. It is the friendliest of villages, where passers-by always speak to each other and newcomers are gathered into the fold and made to feel at home.

In spite of Beckley's close proximity to Headington and Oxford, when you cross the B4027 you enter another world. There has been a settlement at Beckley since Roman times; the Roman road from Dorchester to Alcester cuts the village in two.

Many houses in the centre of the village are survivals from the 16th, 17th and 18th centuries, with only the former school building and a few nearby cottages representing the Victorian era. The 20th century houses are to be found mainly in Woodperry Road, along with the village hall and playing field.

Between the wars many of the tiny stone and thatched farm labourers' cottages became almost derelict as farm work decreased and men took jobs in the Cowley factories. Fortunately their potential for amalgamation and conversion into larger homes appealed to people wishing to move out of Oxford's growing eastern suburbs. Equally fortunate these people wished to retain and even pinpoint the period features of the cottages, so that even when they were practically rebuilt they fitted in with the Beckley landscape. Where two or three cottages were knocked into one larger house, the old door lintels can still be seen through their frame of honeysuckle and roses. One sees with one's physical eyes the pleasing elegance of gracious homes; with one's imagination one sees Beckley's past.

There remains one old Oxfordshire wagon shed and the old smithy is now a garage. Cripps Cottage, where Cripps the carrier lived, is one of the oldest 16th century converted cottages and recalls the time when carriers were Beckley's link with Oxford. Pound Cottage recalls the adjacent enclave in which animals illegally grazing on Otmoor were impounded.

Everywhere one walks one touches history and nowhere more so than at Beckley's glorious medieval church standing on its windswept knoll. Each generation has left its loving mark on the church. There is a treasury of rare 14th century glass, wall paintings, a beautiful timbered roof, a tub font which could be Saxon, one of the oldest church chests in England, a Jacobean pulpit and some very fine Victorian glass in the chancel. There is a modern triptych by Nicholas Mynheer in the Kate Lea Memorial Corner.

🍁 BEGBROKE

Begbroke was mentioned in the Domesday Book when it was valued at 100 shillings, but the name is much older, a possible joining together of two Anglo-Saxon words 'beck' and 'broc', both meaning a small stream. 'Becca's stream' is another interpretation. Rowel brook which runs from Spring Hill and flows under the A44 to join the Oxford Canal, is a development of an Old English word 'ra-wella' or 'roe-stream'. Round Castle, a plateau hill fort, is nearby and may date from the Iron Age.

For nearly 500 years Begbroke Hill Farm was owned by only two families, the Giffords and the Fitzherberts, the present fine stone house being built by the latter in the early 17th century. This is on the site of a previous medieval building, only the cellar of which remains. It stayed in private hands until the middle of the 20th century. During the Partridge occupancy it was known as 'Brewing' or 'Barley' Farm as George Partridge won international recognition for his barley crops. This enterprising man also introduced steam ploughing to Begbroke and was one of the first farmers to advertise the sale of Christmas turkeys. From 1960 until the mid 1980s the farm was popularly known as 'Weeds' because it was the home of the Weed Research Organisation. It now belongs to Oxford University.

The Royal Sun has been a hostelry since the days of Charles II. In 1723 one Hannah Graves, the wife of the landlord, was placed in the stocks for causing a disturbance in the village. Her husband John was ordered not to sell wine, and was fined £40 for being disorderly. Nowadays it is an attractive meeting place for villagers and passing trade alike.

Two of the larger buildings on the west side of the A44, which in effect divides the older part of the village from the newer, are St Philip's Priory and Solid State Logic. The neo-Georgian house occupied by the latter has been used for a variety of purposes – among them a retirement home for elderly clergy, a convent school for 45 years, and now a centre for sophisticated recording systems. The Priory, home of the Servite Order of Friars since 1896, and given to them by Charles Robertson, was the original manor house dating from 1610. During the Civil War it was occupied by Colonel Butler, one of Cromwell's commanders.

It is unusual to find churches of two religious traditions next to each other in a small village – so near the busy A44 yet they form an oasis of peace in their attractive rural setting. St Michael's retains the simplicity and charm of a small Norman church although it was extensively restored in the 19th century.

There is no school in Begbroke today, most children going to Woodstock, but in the hundred years from 1786 there were several of widely differing types, starting with the 'Begbroke Boarding School for Young Ladies' in what is now St Philip's Priory, which lasted until 1819. By this time there was also a dame school and Sunday school for the poor children, and by 1820 the curate had succeeded in establishing Begbroke Free School. To do this he had to 'persuade' an unwilling Widow Parker to become the schoolmistress under threat of eviction from her home! And while encouraging the teaching of reading (and sewing for girls) he believed it would be fatal to teach writing and arithmetic to the poor as 'these accomplishments would raise them above their station'. The school closed by 1884 after running into debt. The schoolhouse was demolished in the 1960s and the school tablet is now incorporated into the wall of a family house built on the site. The next (and last) time Begbroke had a school in the village was in the Second World War,

St Michael's church, Begbroke

27

when St Juliana's Convent was evacuated from Bognor Regis to Begbroke Place, and stayed for 40 years.

Present day amenities on the eastern side of the village include a garage and a small, friendly post office/stores. The five acre playing field was another generous Robertson gift and contains the village hall, home of Begbroke Village Social Club, a bowling green, cricket and football pitches and a children's play area. The land is held in perpetuity for the inhabitants of Begbroke.

🍁 Benson

Benson is a large village beside the Thames, about twelve miles downstream from Oxford. The first official mention of Benson was in the *Anglo-Saxon Chronicle* of AD 571, where it appears as Bensington. This is still the village's formal name, and is written on the name board which stands outside the parish church of St Helen.

Parts of St Helen's church date back to the 12th century. The interior was completely restored and a nave altar added during the 1970s. This can be removed if the occasion arises, and gives a very open and friendly feel to the church. The work was mainly performed by the members of the church, and other volunteers from the community. The church clock is very interesting, as it is in Roman numerals and contains two XI's and no IX. During the Second World War a radio broadcast was picked up that included the message that the German Luftwaffe were going to bomb the airfield near the village with the church that had two elevens on its clock!

Today Benson is probably best known for its RAF station, which housed the Queen's Flight. The airfield was built in 1937, and played an important role during the Second World War as home of the Photographic Reconaissance unit. Many local people work on the station, and the relationship between local residents and service personnel is very good. The RAF fete and the flying displays always prove very popular attractions.

The Thames has played an important and on-going part in Benson's history. Fisheries were mentioned here in the Domesday Book of 1086, and today there is still a thriving angling club. Until about 1934 coal was transported from the Midlands through the Coventry and Oxford Canals, and then down the Thames to Benson's wharf. This site now houses the

Cruiser Station, where boats can be hired, and a holiday caravan park. This also supplies some seasonal employment.

Another thing unique to Benson is the veteran cycle club. The founder, Mr Ned Passey, has a large collection of over 450 antique bicycles in a musem next to his house, and is pleased to show people around. An annual rally is held on the first Sunday of July, starting from the recreation field and going around the surrounding villages, stopping for a pub lunch on the way. The rally began in 1961 and attracts riders from as far afield as America. Most riders dress up in costumes which reflect the age of their cycles.

The village is on the old coaching route from London to Oxford, and the Crown Inn was built in 1709 for travellers to rest, and to change horses. A mounting stone can still be seen on the corner of the building. In those days many villagers would have earned their living building coaches, and would later have transferred to making railway carriages.

BINFIELD HEATH

Binfield Heath lies in the parish of Shiplake and has no official separate status, but those who live there argue hotly that it is a village in its own right. Certainly there is a strong community spirit and a number of residents have roots there that go back many years. The village has in fact more of a core than nearby Dunsden, as most of the houses are near the village shop and recreation ground. At the centre of the crossroads, where the road from Dunsden meets the Sonning Common/Shiplake road, stands a fine chestnut tree which is a well known rendezvous. A smithy stood beside this tree, which must have given rise to many references to the old song. The building still stands but caters for motor cars and has not quite the same charm. It is not difficult, however, if you half-close your eyes and pretend the cars are gone, to imagine you can hear the clatter of hooves and the hiss of steam.

The residence of prime importance in the village is Holmwood. For many years this was owned by the Makower family. Their tradition of involvement in local affairs has been carried on by the present owners, Mr and Mrs B. Talfourd-Cook. Many fund-raising events for charity are held at Holmwood and, unlike the case with many 'big houses', nearly every villager has set foot in the grounds at one time or another.

One of the major events of the year is the Binfield Heath and District Flower

Show which is open to residents of the parishes of Dunsden, Harpsden and Shiplake. The show celebrated its 50th anniversary in 1998 and is held at Holmwood on the last Saturday in August.

In olden days there were several ponds in the area, some of which have since been filled in. One was immediately in front of the New Inn (now a private house), near the blacksmith's, one by the Bottle and Glass, and another by the White Hart. These ponds were essential both to water the farm horses and to provide water for the traction engines which at harvest time used to go from farm to farm, followed by a crowd of children and dogs ready to catch the rats and mice that ran out of the diminishing corn as it was cut. There was also a bakehouse adjacent to the New Inn but this was enclosed and renovated to form a private dwelling.

The brickworks in Kiln Lane provided work for many years and the old road serving the works and some of the houses built for workers are still in use. A few of the houses at the end of Kiln Lane are built of wood and these were donated by Sweden at the end of the Second World War to help the acute housing shortage. These traditional Swedish buildings blend well with the surrounding wooded area.

An unusual covered well stands near Holmwood. Unfortunately the original was completely demolished a few years ago in a motoring accident, but it has been rebuilt exactly as before. In appearance it is a dome on top of a cylinder, built in brick. Various legends surround it, one connected with a ghostly coach and horses which are said to gallop by at dead of night.

It may seem surprising that no church exists at Binfield Heath. Shiplake church is some way distant but that is where parishioners were expected to attend, and a local resident remembers going to church by horse and cart in her childhood. There has been since 1835, however, a Congregational chapel on the corner of Gravel Road and Dunsden Road, a fine site which must have seemed temptingly convenient to local Anglican residents. It is built in an attractive mock-Gothic style and has a pleasantly simple interior.

🍁 BLEWBURY

Aldridge, Caudwell, Corderoy, Grace, Street; some family names of Blewbury past which live on in Blewbury today. Justus Corderoy and Zephaniah Grace, were just two stalwart members of the centuries-old farming community that lived in a cluster of dwellings dependent on the line of springs at the foot of the Berkshire Downs.

Agriculture and its ancillary industries supported the inhabitants of Blewbury well into the 20th century; the farmers, tanners, wheelwright, blacksmith, maltster, miller, harness maker and of course the farmworkers, formed the community. Their tiny cottages roofed with thatch and built of wattle and daub bear witness to their labours. Scattered throughout the village were more substantial farmhouses with their huge barns and pretty orchards.

The village is intersected by streams and footpaths with lovely wide open spaces at its centre. Thatched cob walls still mark the boundaries of the old farmyards. The cavity of one of these walls is said to be infilled with cattle horns from the village tannery and probably they hide more than one lost treasure. A small gate in the cob wall of Boham's farm, its latch dated 1823,

Cob walls at Blewbury

was said to enable the farmer, William Boham, to slip out to the Red Lion unobserved.

For more than a century Blewbury has attracted artists and writers, who found the peace and tranquility of the downs adequate compensation for cold, damp cottages. Marguerite Steen and William Nicholson endured rats and Tudor drains. A. A. Milne declined to rent Boham's, the home of Kenneth Grahame and his wife Elspeth; perhaps the complaint of a former tenant that the larder was mouse-infested deterred him! G. B. Stern lived and wrote in a brick-floored cottage on the edge of the Millbrook. Susan Beatrice Pearce, much loved for her 'Ameliaranne' books, lived to reach her 100th birthday in her tiny 'teacosy' cottage. The village still keeps up an enthusiasm for the arts and painting. The Borlase Gallery has regular exhibitions and every August a group of intrepid amateurs sets off with brushes and paints for Venice.

The coming of 'The Atomic' at Harwell, which replaced the Second World War airfield, changed Blewbury dramatically. It provided employment for villagers and brought in newcomers. New thatch now crowns pristine white cottages and the apple orchards have given way to housing developments. Community life still centres round the four village pubs and here plans are made for the annual Shakespearean or other production which is performed in Blewbury's open-air amphitheatre at Orchard Dene, or for the commissioning of the triennial community opera, or for the summer festival.

The changing structure of society brought new needs, in particular homes for the elderly. One of the very first co-ownership societies providing homes for the over fifty fives was formed here at Dibleys where an estate of well-designed bungalows was built. The accommodation is now leasehold under the management of Dibleys Heritage Ltd.

At one time strings of race horses were a common sight in the village but they have moved onto the downs nearer the gallops. Riders these days are from the busy local riding school, whose comings and goings were viewed from next door by Dick Francis as he wrote his racing thrillers. The former stables of Steve Donoghue have been converted into a house and many farm outbuildings and barns have become houses or are leased to small business enterprises. Where Cavaliers and Roundheads once took shelter and cart horses stamped their feet, the only sound is the whirring of computers.

A terraced prehistoric settlement looks down on the village from Blewburton Hill but from its summit only the tower of the church can be glimpsed, half hidden by trees. The charity school and the almshouses beside the church present a view little changed with time. To see Blewbury you must leave the main road and explore its maze of footpaths.

🍁 BLOXHAM

Situated about three miles from the town of Banbury on the A361 route to the heart of the Cotswolds, Bloxham is one of the principal ironstone villages of North Oxfordshire. The main road has not always followed its present route, but formerly passed along Old Bridge Road, where the village war memorial now stands, to the Elephant and Castle public house, where the old coaching arch still forms the entrance to the present day car park.

Since the early 1960s there has been substantial growth to accommodate newcomers who work in Banbury, Oxford and other towns farther afield. However, in times past there were several farms, a brickyard, sawyard and blacksmith's forge to provide local employment. Ironstone was mined by men who were paid 7d per ton and the record is said to stand at 14 tons hewn in four hours. The ore was then pushed in trucks along to the village railway station, once said to be the prettiest in Oxfordshire.

A village with a range of schools, shops and other services vital to modern day living naturally attracts growth. However, the heart of the old village, designated as a conservation area, with picturesque cottages set in narrow lanes, remains unspoilt by the development of new estates on the perimeter. St Mary's church dominates the village and its spire, said to have been commissioned by Cardinal Wolsey, soars to a height of 198 ft.

To the south of the church is a small thatched building known as the Court House. Built in 1689 on the site of the former Town House, it now serves as a village hall. The building is owned by the Bloxham Feoffees who for centuries have been the custodians and administrators of various village charities. In the past this body of men has been responsible for roads, bridges, street lighting, drainage and even the winding of the church clock. The Local Government Act of 1894 saw the creation of the parish council which assumed some of the Feoffees' responsibilities, but they still retain an income to be distributed to those in need. The undercroft of the Court House is home to the Bloxham Village Museum, which is open on Sunday afternoons.

The village school was formerly housed in what is now part of Bradford

Court and one parish councillor can recall when coal fires burned in the school room and Horlicks and milk was served to pupils at break time.

In the second half of the 20th century rural communities everywhere faced increasing threats. Small villages witnessing the closure of the school, shop/post office and withdrawal of public transport predict an uncertain future. Such a prospect has never been Bloxham's lot. Most new families experience a warm welcome and that sense of community concern which is more common in rural England than some people imagine. The needs of all are catered for from the baby clinic to the Lunch Club, Day Centre and meals service for the elderly, all run by volunteers and certain indications that Bloxham will thrive as an old village with a modern identity for many years to come.

🍁 BODICOTE

Journeying north on the A423 from Oxford one could perhaps be forgiven for missing Bodicote village as it is not on the main road. However, why not turn into the village at the first sign and enjoy both the old and new parts. A number of stone cottages and several of the large old mansions still exist (one of the latter now houses part of Cherwell District Council). There is no village green as such but there are lots of green open areas, including a large playing field.

The children are served by the Bishop Loveday school. The church is dedicated to St John the Baptist and each year villagers celebrate the patronal festival. It is a church that is very much part of the village.

There is a very active WI, Mothers Union, church choir, drama group, Scouts, Guides etc. The senior citizens are not forgotten, bungalows and flats supply good housing and a community centre at Dillon House provides some entertainment on a regular basis. There is also a residential nursing home.

To the south-west of the village the delightful Sorbrook flows, and just above on farmland overlooking Bloxham is an attractive windmill.

🍁 BOTLEY

It is difficult today to imagine that Botley was once a peaceful place. Lying between Oxford and Cumnor and roads to the west it seems now to be just a

34

*Anskill pays his annual fine or 'bot' for the mill-place
that he seized at Botelea, c1090*

busy highway. But up until the 1920s it was a really pretty village with its rustic
look of grey stone walls, thatched cottages and farms, a lovely old bakehouse
and corner shop, all surrounded by fields and footpaths and lovely trees. A
quiet and serene place it seemed, but all is now lost beneath the
encroachment of bricks and concrete, concealing an origin which goes back
to the days of the Saxon invaders who gave the place its name.

During the Civil War the mill suffered much damage; it is claimed that
unknown rebels came from Abingdon and set fire to the mill, destroying it,
but tradition has it that Cromwell rebuilt the mill for the use of his men. A
sword about a yard long and a cannon ball were fished from the stream years
later. Further downstream, towards North Hinksey, which is in our parish,
there was a ford where cattle used to cross and from which Oxford got its

name – we are very proud of that! As Botley Mill has a long history, playing an important part in the lives of the people, so did Seacourt which was also a village in those far-off days with a church and a manor of considerable value.

Botley stayed small and remote until a causeway with bridges over its seven streams was built early in the 16th century, bringing an important road into the hamlet for the first time. Along this stony pathway villagers and travellers had shorter journeys into Oxford and the surrounding areas with views of lush meadows and pastures.

It was not until much later that an improvement was made to the road and a toll gate was set up to help pay for repairs. Although this made travelling easier there were other dangers to contend with, as the roads around Oxford became infested with robbers and highwaymen and Botley Road was no exception: it is recorded that one February night in 1784 the Bath coach was held up at the foot of Cumnor Hill and eight passengers lost £28 between them!

As time passed the village of Seacourt was abandoned and by 1722 there was just an old farmhouse with a few cottages and inns – there had been 24 of these at one time! It is likely they were provided to accommodate and refresh the pilgrims and travellers who journeyed to Oxford and to the shrine of St Frideswide at Osney. Botley, it is said, was famous for its beer and was a popular place to stop for a drink.

Sadly, the last two cottages at Seacourt were demolished to make way for redevelopment in 1964. Now Botley is a thriving suburb with its shops, banks and offices, good nursery and primary schools, social clubs and an excellent library, not forgetting its places of worship. We have a Catholic church, a Baptist chapel, and the modern red brick church dedicated to St Peter and St Paul which links with its twin parish of North Hinksey, just a mile away. There the pretty little Norman church of St Lawrence, the thatched cottages, old stone walls and village green remain a place where residents and visitors can wander in peace and tranquility.

 # BRIGHTWELL-CUM-SOTWELL

The main part of the village is bounded in the north by the A4130 Wallingford to Didcot road, and as the name suggests, Brightwell and Sotwell, also Mackney to the south, were once separate settlements. The parishes were not united until 1948, bringing to an end the bizarre situation of the parish clerk of

Brightwell writing letters to himself (as parish clerk of Sotwell).

A Roman road ran from north to south from the Sinodun Hills down Mackney Lane (a section of the Alchester to Silchester road), and from east to west a Saxon highway ran from Slade End to Haddon Hill. Village footpaths now follow these routes. A 1st century gold coin (minted in Colchester) was dug up in Mackney Lane in 1873 and is now in the British Museum.

In the older parts of the village, houses are situated along narrow twisting roads, where large trees, high hedgerows and high walls (including a rare thatched cob wall) are characteristic. There are three smallish estates: Greenmere, the council estate, built in 1948 and more recently King's Meadow and Monk's Mead. The recent amount of infilling has reached saturation point and rather altered the landscape.

In 1086 in Brightwell there were 48 families, plus a mill and a church; in Sotwell 22 families and a mill. The 1938 population was 850, a figure now

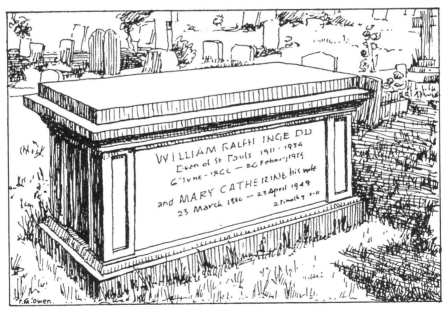

Dean Inge's tomb, Brightwell-cum-Sotwell

37

almost doubled to approximately 1,400. There is a post office/shop and those essentials of modern life, two garages and one pub, the Red Lion, the only one remaining of five in pre-temperance days. Other assets include the village hall and an excellent village magazine. The hall is a handsome brick building with clock tower which, in 1975, was converted from its original use as the 1869 village school after the latter was moved to a newer part of the village in 1961.

Less than a century ago the main work was provided (outdoors) by many small farms, orchards and large gardens and (indoors) by domestic service at the big houses. Here, as elsewhere, the farms now form larger units, with some disappearing entirely. The picture of employment has radically changed. The proximity of laboratories such as Harwell, Rutherford-Appleton, JET, Howberry Park and Didcot power station, attracts engineers and scientists, but the range of occupations is as diverse as one could find anywhere.

There is a wealth of old buildings in the village, including many thatched cottages. The most architecturally important house is Smalls in Mackney, built for a burgess of Wallingford of that name in about 1580. It is an unspoiled Tudor house with the unusual distinction of being listed Grade I, a category usually reserved for large stately homes. Other houses dating from the late 16th century include Woodleys, Middle Farm, The Old Priory and Abbot's House, all near St Agatha's church.

Of several moats in the village, the most complete is at Sotwell House, where the stream provides a favourite place for feeding the ducks, and where the lovely garden for many years has hosted the village fete. The moat at Brightwell Manor is partly dry now. This house is not strictly a manor and for part of its life formed part of a group of farms with The Old Priory and Middle Farm. It stands behind St Agatha's church and is chiefly Georgian, but an older part dates from c1605. It is thought to occupy the site of a wooden castle delivered up by King Stephen after the civil war and possibly demolished at that time, c1150.

The parish church has the rare dedication to St Agatha; perhaps a relic of this Sicilian martyr was once brought here from Winchester. The oldest parts of the present church are 12th century, possibly on the site of a church mentioned here in Domesday Book.

The smaller church of St James in Sotwell, of ancient origin, had an early history connecting it with churches in Wallingford, but in 1868 it was attached to Brightwell. The 1884 rebuilding in Early English style (celebrated joyfully in 1984) included several features from the old wattle and daub building it replaced. The most impressive of these is a magnificent open roof of oak timbers.

The registers of St James begin in 1684. An entry in 1886 records the first burial of a member of the Free Church, a custom which continued for any dissenter. Brightwell Free Church was founded by Miss Augusta Fairthorne, member of a village family well known for their benefactions. This lady, who disagreed with the High Church attitude of the rector, persuaded her brother to allow services to be conducted in a marquee in his garden at The Red House. A small wooden church was built there in the 1870s and later replaced by the present Free Church building.

Until the advent of the Second World War the children of the village observed the quaint custom of greeting Shrove Tuesday by serenading the gentry with a song begging for pennies to provide the pre-Lenten feast of pancakes: 'Pit pat the pan's hot, And I be come a-shroving'. On May Day they paraded their garlands, and small money prizes were awarded to the most attractive. Christmastide saw the Mummers offering their unique version of St George killing the Turkish infidel.

🍁 BRIZE NORTON

Brize Norton may be a small village but its name is known throughout the world. The RAF base which is called after it and carries servicemen and women to theatres of conflict and overseas postings, was officially opened on 13th August 1937. At that time it was home to No 2 Flying Training School, but with the start of the Second World War it became operational. The Resistance movements in occupied Europe received personnel and supplies through RAF Brize Norton and in June 1944 it was the base for parachute and glider operations over Normandy.

After the war the USAF came in with their B36 and B47 bombers, but in 1965 Brize Norton returned to RAF control and became the Transport Command station which it still is today. RAF Brize Norton is now one of the largest operational stations in the RAF.

This may be the Brize Norton that the world knows. But to those who live here it is their home village, and the glamour of faraway places and international statesmen has little effect on their lives. It is true they hear the planes taking off, but very few service personnel live in the village.

Parochial questions have probably concerned the inhabitants of Brize Norton since there was a first settlement here to the north of Bampton, or Nortone, before the Norman Conquest. In the 13th century a Brun or Brown was added to the name and that in turn changed to the Brize of today. The church, dedicated to the unusual St Britius, dates from the 12th century and contains an effigy dated 1346 of Sir John Daubyngy. Another person of note who is buried in the church was Thomas Greenwood, said to be descended from a daughter of Henry VIII's Chancellor, Sir Thomas More. The Greenwoods, who were connected with the Manor of Brize Norton for some 300 years, remained Catholics throughout the 17th century, but one member of the family was nominally Church of England to avoid paying the taxes imposed on Catholics at that time. One wonders what the 'man for all seasons' would have thought of such behaviour.

Most of the inhabitants of the village were not famous and little record remains of individuals. But Brize Norton does have in its past a curious story which centres on an area to the west of the village called Stonelands.

In the 17th century there was a house called 'Sworn Layes Great House' in this area, which through ecclesiastical oversight was not designated as belonging to any particular parish. This meant that people living there could get away with activities that would not have been tolerated by the clergy within a parish. As a consequence, when King Charles I and his court were at Oxford from 1642 to 1646 it appears that Sworn Layes was used by the ladies of the court for the delivery of illegitimate children.

This custom continued certainly into the 18th century when there were references to 'Sworn Lanes, commonly called the Bastard School' and Shilton church records payments to 'poor afflicted lying in women' at Stonelands.

By 1801 these matters were obviously more acceptable and could be referred to more directly. An advertisement in the *Journal* reads: 'Private lying in notice is hereby given, that Sworn Lays in the County of Oxford is a house belonging to no parish, well situated to receive lying in women privately, and such may be treated with on reasonable terms by applying to James Hart, at Sworn Lays Great House, near Burford, Oxfordshire'. The children born here were, if lucky, trained for service or labouring but local tradition has it that many were killed in infancy and buried in the grounds. There was reputed to be the ghost of 'a horrible old woman carrying a screaming naked baby'.

The lying-in ceased around 1836 as the new Poor Law came into effect and the workhouses began to look after such activities. Sworn Lays, which had also served as a pest house during outbreaks of the plague, lost the advantage that its geographical position had given it and by 1906 it was a ruin. Today no trace of it is left.

🍁 BUCKLAND

From the 16th century until the late 20th century nearly all the houses and land in Buckland were in one ownership. Up to the Second World War most people who lived in the village worked on the estate in one way or another. Now that so many houses have passed into other hands, with inhabitants commuting or only there at weekends, village life has changed, but there is still a nucleus of families who were brought up in the village and whose names can be found in the parish records which survive from the late 17th century, eg Goodman, Carter, Shewry.

In 1997 the last remaining post office/general stores closed, but there used to be another general stores, butcher, bakery and drapers. The drapers, as recently as the 1920s, sold bales of cloth to be made by women into garments for their families, the only made-up goods being men's boots and corduroy trousers. There were also a blacksmith and wheelwright, two shoemakers and a brewery. However, the Lamb Inn survives and is thriving. Buckland still has a Roman Catholic church as well as the parish church, and until recently a Baptist chapel. The village school serves several other villages besides Buckland.

Buckland Manor became known as Dukes' Manor because for a time it was owned by the Dukes of Suffolk. In 1544 the Crown sold it to John Yate of Charney, Merchant of the Staple at Calais. The Yate family remained Roman Catholics after the Reformation. As with most Roman Catholics, the Yates took the King's side in the Civil War and in a survey of 1647 (Sir) Edward Yate was said to be 'beyond the seas and all his estates sequestered'. A stone table in the Old Vicarage garden is inscribed:

'Charles 1st, King of Britain spent the night at the house nearby and when he was hungry was entertained by the Vicar of Buckland who brought the King to eat at this table so that the altar and throne might forever be united in friendship.'

41

When the last male heir died the great-granddaughter of Edward Yate, Mary, inherited Buckland. She married Robert Throckmorton of Coughton Court, Warwickshire.

Buckland House was built in 1757 by Sir Robert. It stands to the west of the old manor house, which was then turned into stables and grooms' quarters. The surrounding grounds were landscaped by Richard Woods and several stone buildings which are still standing were built at this time, including an ice house, still complete, close to the lake which was formed at this time.

In 1811 Sir John Throckmorton wagered 1,000 guineas that it was possible to make a coat from wool off the backs of sheep between sunrise and sunset. On 25th June two sheep belonging to him were sheared by his shepherd, Mr Druett, and the wool given to Mr John Coxeter at Greenham Mills, Newbury who 'spun the yarn, spooled, warped, loomed and wove burred, milled, rowed, dyed, dried, sheared and pressed' – in eleven hours.

The cloth was then given to Mr Isaac White, tailor, who cut the coat out and had it made up within two hours and 20 minutes. Mr John Coxeter, the master manufacturer, presented it to Sir John, who appeared with it on before an assembly of 5,000 spectators who had come from near and far to witness this performance, completed in 13 hours and 20 minutes.

In 1908 the estate was sold to Sir Maurice Fitzgerald who, with his architect Romaine Walker, enlarged the house and built many new buildings in the village. Queen Mary and Sir Winston Churchill were entertained during the Fitzgerald's time. Their grandson, Richard Wellesley inherited the estate from them and to him fell the task of bringing it from near feudal conditions to modern farming methods. The estate remains a woodland and arable unit and is now managed by his son, Charles.

🍁 BUCKNELL

Just a short drive from the urban sprawl of Bicester lies the tranquil village of Bucknell. A cluster of beech trees to the west of the village probably gave its original name, which was Buckenelle (Beech Hill). Always predominantly a farming community, Bucknell once boasted a coach house, forge, bakery and village shop. Many of the old thatched cottages remain and the village shop is now situated in what was the old coach house. A large pig farm which produces most of its own feed, the herds of Friesians and Herefords and the surrounding arable land ensure that the village farming traditions carry on.

The history of Bucknell and its church dates back to Saxon times. St Peter's church is unusual in that it has a Norman tower between the chancel and the nave; this formed part of an earlier church. The tower is 12th century with the exception of the crenellated belfry which was added in the 15th century. Behind the church stands the manor house, dating back to the 17th century. It has a chequered past and is supposedly haunted. It was surrounded by a moat and has a ha ha. In 1709 Samuel Trotman took over the estate. He was very eccentric and known locally as 'The Mad Trotman'. At one time Bucknell had no public house because the Trotman family would not allow a licence to be granted in case the poor people of the village spent too much time and money 'tippling'. In more recent tmes the manor house was used by Oxfordshire County Council as an old people's home but it is now once more privately owned and has been extensively restored.

The stone houses opposite the church appear to have changed little over the years, although many alterations have taken place internally. It is here that the blacksmith's shop was situated and is the spot where a Mr Ally killed himself whilst making gunpowder.

There is evidence of two local charities. The Trotman will of 1600 left an amount of money for a 'small portion of meat to be distributed to the poor of the village each December'. Dr Gauntlett's Charity was also distributed in December, one year to ladies, the next to men. The women were given warm woollen cloaks with hoods. After receiving them they were instructed to put the name of the charity on the inside of the collar. The lady of the manor would then check that this had been done. Eight pairs of strong leather shoes were given to the men and the name of the charity was written on the instep of the sole. This would be seen when the men knelt down to pray in church.

The Trigger Pond public house was originally three cottages and then a butcher's shop. In the early 1900s it was owned by a butcher named Golder, a very large man. When he died it was found he was too large to be removed from the shop. A window was taken out and an improvised bier had to be made to carry away the body. The shop later became an off licence. A dartboard was hung on the wall outside and it soon became a meeting place for the locals. At this time it was called the Twigger Pond, the pond being on the opposite side of the road with a well in one corner. The pond is now a very attractive feature of this village. Beautifully landscaped, it contains many plants and fish and is a breeding ground for ducks and moorhens. The Trigger Pond public house has also been extensively restored, retaining many original beams and a straight chimney fireplace.

🍁 BURFORD

Enter Burford from the A40 roundabout and one is struck by the wide street, descending the hill to the bridge over the Windrush. The houses are in a variety of styles and dates, but the use of local stone throughout maintains the special Cotswold appearance.

Burford church spire can be seen from afar as you approach the town up or down the Windrush valley or by roads from the North. Too vast to be a convenient parish church for the dwindling congregation, the church is also used for concerts and large meetings which cannot be fitted into the hall across the green.

In earlier times Burford was a flourishing market town dependent on the sheep of the Cotswolds, the local industries being fulling, tannery, saddlery, glove making, and two bell foundries at different times; all that was necessary could be purchased locally.

In 1990 Burford celebrated the 900th anniversary of its first charter. It may seem strange that a community of barely 1,200 people should have a Mayor and Town Council (the population is probably smaller now than in the 18th century at the height of the coaching era, and much the same as at the end of the Middle Ages). The present arrangement only dates from the reorganisation of local government in 1974, but is a reflection of Burford's earlier history when it was ruled by an Alderman and Burgesses, elected from the Guild Merchants. The Burgesses' roll is to be seen in the local museum at the Tolsey, the 15th century building where the tolls were collected from the traders. It is also still used for the Town Council meetings.

Burford has grown very little because of stringent planning restrictions which ban any expansion outwards, and insist on any new building being done in local materials. This means that the cost of housing in the town is exceptionally high, so that there is very little chance for first time buyers to obtain property.

The two 'big houses' were the Great House, an imposing castellated edifice built in 1685 right on what was once the main road through the town; and the Priory, originally a monastic hospice, which came into private ownership after the Dissolution of the Monasteries, changed ownership several times and has now come back to housing a religious order of nuns and monks. Another striking building is the Methodist chapel, originally built as a private house in the 18th century.

The grammar school was founded by local men of property in 1571 and stayed at the lower end of the town until 1957, when the new comprehensive school was built on the main road above the town. The old buildings have been retained as boarding houses.

When the school celebrated its quatercentenary in 1971, an ancient custom was reintroduced. This is the dragon procession on Midsummer's Eve, said to commemorate the victory of the West Saxons over the Mercians about AD 750. The dragon is a large tent-like stucture with an impressive head, carried by some 20 children, whose legs are the only part of the human form to be seen. It goes from the top of the hill to the bottom accompanied by Morris dancers and finishing with dancing on the green in front of the church.

There was another small school run by a couple called Huntley at the top of the hill. Mrs Huntley, as well as her school duties, made biscuits and sold them to coach travellers; eventually one of her sons moved to Reading, went into partnership with a Mr Palmer, and this is the origin of the famous biscuit manufacturers.

In the distant past Wychwood Forest was only a mile away, and there was a royal hunting lodge on the outskirts. The men of Burford were allowed one deer per annum, but the story goes that this did not satisfy them, and a lot of poaching went on; the carcases would be hidden in one of the 'bale' tombs in the churchyard, and woe betide you if you were found to have one in your larder!

The first private owner of the Priory was Edmond Harman, barber surgeon to Henry VIII. His successor was Sir Lawrence Tanfield who upset the local people by removing (quite legitimately) all the rights and privileges of the Guild Merchants. His wife was even more unpopular and after their demise, they were said to haunt the town, riding in a coach and four over the rooftops. Eventually seven clerics were called upon to exorcise them, which they did by shutting up the spirits in a bottle and dropping it into the river. Rumour had it that if the level of the river dropped below a certain point, they would escape; so, until the 19th century, in time of drought the older inhabitants used to pour water over the bridge to keep the level up!

During the Civil War, a group of soldiers rebelled against Cromwell and were rounded up in Burford. Three hundred were imprisoned in the church as the only building large enough; after three days the three ringleaders were taken out and shot. In the mid 1970s a tablet was erected to them outside the church, and each year since then a great meeting has been held on the church green, followed by a procession round the town.

🍁 CARTERTON

Carterton was named after a man called William Carter, who bought up a lot of land locally. He then sold it off in plots, for smallholdings and market gardens. People even came to settle here from London.

The original bungalows were built of wood with outer shells of tin. One family also had a very deep well where they kept their milk and butter in a bucket, dangling on a rope.

Carterton has become best known for the growing of tomatoes, the soil here seems to give them a flavour all of their own. Sadly though, many local nurseries have disappeared over the years, the families not carrying on the business and greenhouses making way for housing development.

Carterton was once part of a parish with Black Bourton, using St Mary's church. A small wooden building, St John's, served as a church until the present day brick-built one in 1965. There are Catholic and Methodist churches for the community here as well.

Royal Air Force Brize Norton came into being in the 1930s. Carterton was to have been the name of the airfield but it was changed to avoid any confusion with Cardington in Bedfordshire. In the 1960s the United States Air Force was stationed here. To take their larger bombers the runway was extended, thus cutting the parish into two, and later Black Bourton became a parish on its own.

There was once a railway station. The line had been there for years from Fairford to Oxford. A platform and buildings were hurriedly built in 1944 during the invasion of Europe to transport troops to the airfield, and it was later used for carrying the tomatoes and mushrooms from a nearby farm. It was then cut off from Carterton when the Black Bourton road was closed with the building of the new runway, although a footpath and cycle way around that side of the airfield is still in use. What a pity that the entire line was eventually closed – it would have helped to ease the present day congestion of getting into Oxford by road!

Over the years a lot of caravan sites were allowed to spring up and Carterton has been called a 'shanty town'. But now only a few remain, being replaced by newer estates and roads. The famous crossroads area has been developed, though not into everyone's ideal centre! The selection of shops and services and the Thursday open air market have helped the surrounding villages to survive.

CASSINGTON

People have been visiting Cassington since the last Ice Age, and even before the use of pottery and domesticated crops and animals, hunter-gatherers

Cassington village green with war memorial

47

(Mesolithic people) passed through the area on hunting parties, leaving behind the flint tools that they made.

There were three Iron Age settlements in Cassington, one at Purwell Farm, another to the south-west of the village near the present A40 junction, and another to the east of Bell Lane. An Iron Age hill fort was built to the north-east of the present village on Bladon Hill, and just before the arrival of the Romans a large earthwork fortification was begun at the confluence of the Evenlode and Thames.

Cassington today is a small village of some 800 inhabitants, situated on the gravel strata between the ancient forest of Wychwood and the Thames. The centre of the village is the green, unchanged through centuries, with attractive old cottages, the 18th century Red Lion, the former Victorian vicarage and the primary school, along with the old post office. An avenue of lime trees directs the eye across the green towards St Peter's church. The Village Fete is held on the green on St Peter's Feast Day.

The war memorial, now dedicated to those who gave their lives in two World Wars, was commissioned in 1919 by the vicar, who lost three sons in the First World War.

The ancient Norman church of St Peter was built as a private chapel by Geoffrey de Clinton, Chamberlain and Treasurer to Henry I. The Cartulary of Eynsham Abbey records that the church was consecrated in 1123 and four of the original consecration crosses are still visible. The magnificent Norman arches survive. The faded remains of a Doom painting were uncovered over the chancel arch and await restoration. The church retains many of the original 15th century bench pews, said to be among the oldest in the country.

The largest among the old houses is the farmhouse which stands on the site of the manor house of the de Clintons and still retains its moat and a rectangular dove house. It is known as Reynolds Farm, after the family who owned property in the area in the 15th and 16th centuries. They were Roman Catholics, and during the religious troubles of the 16th century Cassington became a refuge for recusants from Oxford. Later, during the Civil War, Royalist sympathisers who had been deprived of their posts gathered at Cassington.

Bell ringing has always been one of Cassington's energetic activities. The sound of our bells was favourably commented upon by John Betjeman.

Cassington Mill on the Evenlode, mentioned in the Domesday Book, continued to grind corn into the 20th century and the buildings still stand. In the surrounding grounds there is a flourishing caravan site, visited by holidaymakers from all over the world.

The village is the proud possessor of a modern playgroup and primary school, situated at the centre of the village in a large playing field where conservation work has been carried out to preserve a pond and encourage its wildlife. Cassington also has outstanding sports facilities.

The last shop in the village closed some time ago and the post office now operates from the Red Lion two mornings a week. An influx of young families into the village over the past two years serves to provide encouragement as we enter the 21st century.

🍁 CHADLINGTON

Chadlington was first mentioned in the Domesday Book in 1086 as Cedelintone. It is said to have been named after St Chad, who came from Northumberland and lived in the area for a while.

Chadlington is reputed to have two ghosts. College Farm was once farmed by Mr Gardner, whose ghost is said to have walked the passages carrying a red handkerchief. The other ghost is an old gentleman wearing carpet slippers who walks across the upstairs hall of Langston House.

There is another story relating to College Farm. Many years ago the farmhouse was broken into and a robbery took place. The robber escaped with his booty, but because he was disturbed dropped his hat. This clue was used in quite an original way and resulted in his eventual capture – a man could be recognised by his hat in the 18th century! The Chadlington robber's hat was taken to a fair at Chipping Norton and put on top of a stick. When someone from Duns Tew came along and said without thinking 'That is so and so's hat from our place,' the game was up and the robber caught and dealt with.

Langston House, a large imposing house in the east end of Chadlington, was originally built by Squire Langston MP as a rectory for the Rev Carpenter, who paid a nominal sum of £1 per annum rent. Many years ago it was occupied by Colonel and Mrs Schofield. Mrs Schofield use to ride around the village on a large tricycle with her two pug dogs in a basket on the back. She would also try to keep the verges clean and picked up any rubbish, only to throw it over the wall into the nearest garden she was passing!

Sir Henry Rawlinson, the diplomat and expert on Assyria, was born in the manor house in 1810 and was the owner of the horse *Coronation*, which was trained in Chadlington and won the Derby in 1841. One villager's grandmother in her young days was a 'stillroom' maid at the house and used to tell how she sometimes went to Chipping Norton on a donkey led by one of the stable lads. The roads were made of white stone and were very dusty.

Squire Langston also built the reading room, which was used originally as a school. In addition, from 1840–50 there was a private school at the Baptist chapel. Children used to enjoy the annual village fair on Easter Monday when processions of horse-drawn vehicles came to the village with their roundabouts, swinging boats, coconut shies etc. The procession, led by the village drum and fife band, went first to a service in the parish church, and this was followed by a dinner in the Malt Shovel for the band.

It is said of one of the former butchers in the village that when his mother died the undertaker asked if he would like her buried in a double grave with his father. After a little thought the butcher said, 'Well, they never got on well in life so they're not likely to now. Maybe we'd better have separate graves!'

🍁 CHALGROVE

Although not a large stream, Chalgrove Brook was once powerful enough to turn five mills, as is revealed in the Domesday Book. Meandering across the fields to the south of the village, it flows on through Stadhampton and then to Chislehampton where it joins the river Thame, a tributary of the Thames. During the 19th century a sluice gate was constructed at the eastern end of the village and from the original stream (the back brook) water was diverted to run alongside what is now the High Street. This artificially created loop (the front brook) has become an attractive feature in Chalgrove.

Flooding was apparently a regular occurrence and is strong in the memories of Chalgrove folk. Written accounts, dating from the late 19th and early 20th centuries, indicate that stilts were popular among the young as a means of getting about in such conditions. However, even stilts were rendered useless when, in January 1881, the temperature dropped sharply overnight and the floodwater turned into a thick sheet of ice.

If excessive amounts of water could play havoc with everyday life then so could an extreme lack of it. In 1921 a severe drought reduced the stream to a trickle and for a long time the mill wheel never turned. As an emergency measure a steam threshing engine, borrowed from a local farmer, was connected to machinery inside the mill in order to grind the corn. More recently, in 1976, another drought left the stream bed dry in places and surrounding land became hard, cracked and almost impossible to cultivate. An interesting by-product of the last mentioned drought was the discovery, by aerial reconnaissance, of filled-in moats and earthworks next to the back brook. Apparently such features are more easily identified in hot, dry conditions. Subsequent archaeological excavation at this location revealed the remains of an impressive medieval moated manor.

The brook is also a source of entertainment. Generations of boys have learned their fishing skills here and, even now with a greatly reduced flow, it is possible for a lad to surprise Mum and Dad with a lively trout. In the early 1970s an enjoyable, but sadly short lived, custom known as the Chalgrove Brook Race was an annual event. The race was contested by several teams over a three quarter mile course from the top arch to the Lamb public house. Teams ran in relays carrying a ball and had to scramble under or over each of the 40 or so bridges.

The importance of the brook to Chalgrove should not be underestimated. Its presence was undoubtedly the reason for early, possibly pre-Roman settlement here. The stream provided water, motive power for mills and probably a good number of fish. Even today the intrusion of massive housing development cannot take away the pleasing aspect of the High Street and its brookside cottages. Yes, the brook has shaped Chalgrove's character and, as the old saying goes, 'You don't belong to Chalgrove until you have fallen in it!'

🍁 CHARLBURY

The name Charlbury is of Anglo-Saxon origin, from the old English 'burgh', a fortified place or earthwork, belonging to 'Ceorl', possibly a personal name but more likely meaning that it was inhabited by freemen.

In the 8th century it belonged to the Mercian kings and in 1094 it was given by the Norman Bishop of Lincoln to Eynsham Abbey. When the abbey was dissolved by Henry VIII, there were two claimants to the manor of Charlbury. One was Sir Henry Lee of Ditchley, who had installed his mistress, Ann Vavasour at Lee's Rest, the other Sir Thomas White, who founded St John's College, Oxford in 1555. Eventually the courts found in favour of the President and Scholars of St John's, who leased Charlbury to Sir Henry Lee and his descendants for the term of three lives. In 1857, by exchange, the property passed to the owner of Cornbury Park. St John's College still appoints the vicars of Charlbury.

Cornbury Park was an important part of the history of Charlbury. An Elizabethan hunting lodge, the gift of Queen Elizabeth I to the Earl of Leicester, it was demolished and a beautiful house built in its stead by Lord Clarendon in the reign of Charles I.

Spinning and weaving went on in many homes, and in the early 1800s the gloving industry was revived by leading Quakers to help alleviate the poverty resulting from the Napoleonic Wars. Gloving continued as a cottage industry and then in small factories until the early 1960s and the glove-makers Fownes, whose crest was a falcon, built Falcon Villas in Hundley Way for their employees. Charlbury was mainly a self sufficient agricultural community, served by its own craftsmen and shopkeepers, its own corn mill (pulled down in 1935), several malt-houses, inns and many beer-houses, its own water supply and gasworks, until after the Second World War.

In 1853 the Oxford, Worcester and Wolverhampton Railway was opened. In 1977 heavy lorries were banned from the town centre, a one-way scheme was devised and a ring-route for through traffic designated.

❧ CHARLTON

Until the middle of the 20th century this small settlement had existed as a separate entity from the market town of Wantage, a mile away, since at least the 11th century, when it was mentioned in the Domesday Book.

Since the Second World War Charlton has been almost swallowed up by housing estates and is now firmly joined to Wantage. The 'Atomics' came first and built their well-landscaped estate along the Humber Ditch on part of the old Charlton House estate. Palmers Farmhouse still stands in the middle of a cul-de-sac and Truelocks and Barnards Farms have become Charlton Heights estate, although the farmhouses are still there. Sadly, Truelocks Farm lost its old barn in a spectacular blaze one Friday afternoon in 1989.

The Victorian church of Holy Trinity, which was built as a chapel of ease, stands near the old stone school house with its rolls of honour of prize winners proudly displayed on one wall. Many families bearing these names are still to be found nearby.

The new Charlton primary school and adult training centre are across the road and Maude House for the elderly now stands on the site of Chestnuts Farm – or Pococks – where Charles I is reputed to have had 'supper and bed' with Sir George Wilmot in 1643 and again in 1644. This farmhouse and several thatched cottages disappeared as recently as the late 1960s and a well-loved pony – *Smokey* – almost came to grief in the old well soon afterwards.

Charlton is still a community, somewhat larger than the 40 to 50 households of years gone by, and hopefully the remnants of the original village will survive for many years to come.

CHARLTON-ON-OTMOOR

A sleepy village in the heart of the country, Charlton is one of the seven towns of Otmoor, where the village folk know the main priority is a pair of wellington boots! The wetlands of the moor attract all kinds of wildlife. On a winter evening flocks of geese and swans are seen travelling from some unfortunate farmer's field back to the moor.

This is a place where villagers in the past have fought for their rights to graze livestock and enclose their strips of land. Today visitors come to see the wildlife, enjoy the quietness or walk the Roman road where Joseph's Stone can still be found. Some say this is a Roman milestone but others think it is more likely to be a horseman's mounting stone. Fog and storms still engulf the moor. Years ago a curfew bell would be tolled at 8 pm to guide the traveller back home. It was this bell which was heard by Thomas Tryte when he lost his way crossing the moor to Bicester. There is a poem written about his famous walk and Tryte's distressing time while lost on the moor.

This bell has long since ceased but the bells of St Mary's, known locally as the heavy five, still ring out and fundraising efforts are being directed to add a new bell for the year 2000. Many generations have rung the Charlton bells. The Hayneses, the Millers and the Maycocks are all familiar names in Charlton tower. Quite a character was Old Tom, one of the Maycock brothers, known so well for their thatching skills in the county but otherwise working a smallholding in the village. Old Tom was rarely seen without his bike, which he rode mainly in the middle of the road. With his shock of white hair, two or three days' stubble on his chin and the inevitable pipe, Tom was known to everyone in the village. Besides ringing one of the bells his strong baritone voice led the church choir and for a funeral he donned pin stripes and bowler to act as bearer, that was after giving a hand to dig the grave. His greeting in the street would almost certainly be 'Ello Gel', so long as you were of that sex. Tom now lies in St Mary's churchyard and Charlton has lost a real character.

The farms which provide much of the work in the village are fast disappearing. Farm barns are being converted to houses. However, there are some farms left. One farmer still draws water from a black water well. The black water spring runs right through the village and in olden days farmers used the water to treat sick cattle. Village folk used it for eczema. That same farmer also uses a fresh water well to water his stock. The wells are beautifully built, mainly of stone and some are bell shaped. One well, obviously designed to serve two households, is built under a dividing wall and pumps are set up each side of the wall. Most of the old cottages are built from the lovely mellow stone, some of which was dug locally. A few thatched roofs remain and many of these old houses have cellars, in some cases still in use but when the water level rises some are known to flood.

May Day celebrations are still held in Charlton. Many years ago the villagers used to carry their May garland across the moor to Horton-cum-Studley. Now the school children process from the school to the church, each carrying a floral cross. A long rope garland is at the head of the procession, colourfully decorated with flowers and ribbons. The children make several stops to sing the May Carol. A service in church follows and every year the cross on the rood screen is redressed in box for the occasion. Afterwards the children give a display of country and maypole dancing in the Main Street. This happens on 1st May every year no matter what day it falls on.

Charlton does not have a country mansion or a famous person within the parish but it still boasts a village pub, its very own bus service and a community spirit next to none.

🍁 CHARNEY BASSETT

Roughly in the centre of the triangle formed by Abingdon, Faringdon and Wantage, lies the village of Charney Bassett, nestling on the north bank of the river Ock. It is believed that the river, in Celtic times, was called the Charn, from which the name Charney is derived, and Bassett from Ralph Bassett who held land hereabout and died in 1127.

A small compact village, its dwellings number just about 120, the only large house being the manor, which since 1947 has belonged to the Society of Friends and is used by them as a Meeting House, and also a guest house and conference centre. In the Middle Ages the manor, or Grange as it was then called, belonged to the Benedictine Abbey of Abingdon and it contains some fine examples of medieval building, still in constant use. Village organisations are encouraged to use the manor, and such events as the harvest supper and biennial church fete, to name just two, are always held there.

Hard by the manor stands the church of St Peter, plain and simple, built mainly in Norman times but probably on the foundations of an earlier Saxon place of worship. Its main attraction is a very fine example of a Norman carved tympanum, re-set in the north wall of the chancel above the entrance to a squint passage; there are only a few of such examples to be found in the country.

Close by the manor and the church is a water mill and records show a mill was here when the monks occupied the manor. Obviously rebuilt over the centuries, the present day structure was in constant use for grinding corn until the First World War, when the miller's son, James Douglas, went off to war and his father eventually had to cease milling. The building stood almost intact until visited by a local industrial archaeological group in the 1970s, who were so fascinated by their find, they have toiled to restore it to working condition and open it to the public.

On the village green, which is opposite the Chequers Inn, stands another medieval relic – a stone shaft on three steps. It is thought this may have been a market cross, where goods could be offered for sale at certain times of the year. A sundial was added to the top later and this would have been used as the village time-piece. After the First World War the centre step was replaced with a dressed stone as a memorial to those whose names are carved thereon.

One mile to the south of the village, but still in the civil parish of Charney is Cherbury Camp, believed to have been built about the beginning of the 1st century AD. It is similar to the better known Uffington Castle on top of White Horse Hill, although slightly larger, but unfortunately is not protected so well, and consequently is being quite considerably eroded. There is a legend that the tribe or army camped in Uffington Castle moved out towards Cherbury to do battle, but a shepherd boy lying out in the fields saw them coming and sounded his horn, so warning the Cherbury occupants, who were then able to go out and meet their enemy and win the battle. Hence it is said the area around the crossroads midway between Charney and Buckland is where they 'gained the field' and it became known as Gainfield. The shepherd boy was supposedly given all the land within the sound of his horn for his part in this, and this eventually became the Pusey estate.

True or legend, there is a Pusey Horn in the British Museum, and another inn in the village, which was closed during the Second World War, was known as the Horn Inn. Cherbury Camp and other land to the north-west of the parish is still the property of Pusey estate, but in 1908 a large portion of the houses and many hundreds of acres east, south and west of Charney were sold to Berkshire County Council, who divided it into many smallholdings, of about 40 acres, which were worked by tenants. Today the ownership has passed to Oxfordshire County Council, who have sold off a majority of the dwellings, and the dozen or so smallholdings in Charney parish have been converted into three small and one large farms.

The village school, which closed in the early 1980s, was always known as the Bouverie Pusey School. It was built in 1871 by the Pusey family of Pusey House, probably at the same time as the New Road was made and the six pairs of houses were built on the east side of the road. These houses are of a most unusual design with stone mullioned and arched windows and high pitched roofs, often described as similar to small churches. The only other houses similar to these are to be found at Black Bourton on the road from Faringdon to Burford, probably by the same architect.

🍁 CHECKENDON

Checkendon is a rambling unspoilt village 600 ft above sea level, eight miles north from Reading. Entering the village from Reading you pass the Four Horse Shoes, the old village inn, the older portion thatched as it has been through the years.

The fine old Norman church of St Peter and St Paul stands in the centre of the village. There are two Norman arches in the chancel. On the wall of the apse are fresco paintings of the 13th or 14th century, which have been painstakingly restored. The brasses on the sanctuary floor are of interest, the larger of John Rede being early 15th century. The many monuments are worth a study, and say much of Checkendon's notable forebears.

The drive to Checkendon Court runs by the church. This estate dates from 1030. Beside the church is its own primary school. In front is the village green on which the children have their maypole dance. The old forge still stands but is no longer used as a smithy. At the rear is a flourishing agricultural supply company. A group of interesting houses and cottages nestle around the village green. The village hall was built in 1913; there the children have school meals. The play group and all the village events are held here. The main development has been one road, and here is the post office and stores.

The village is surrounded by beech woods, with bluebells in the spring, and the rich colour of the autumn leaves. There are a few public footpaths in the woods. Farming goes on around the village and the fields reflect the passing seasons.

🍁 CHILTON

Chilton has been in existence since before the Domesday survey and its present church since a few years after that time. Over the centuries many changes have taken place.

Church Farm, the pride and success of old Jo Church back in the 1800s, is now an estate of desirable residences. Likewise, Lime Tree Farm no longer feels the warm breath of calves on a frosty morn, but the rattle of 'Clean-Your-Own-Seeds' machinery setting out on its perambulations. The old, red-brick barns of Manor Farm, once the first welcome to the village, have long since given place to chalet-type houses. Opposite, where fields and trees once formed the entrance to Dane Hollow, an estate of new houses now stands, called 'Limetrees'.

By the side of the Bargeway, there used to be famous orchid nurseries which despatched their patiently-cultivated treasures as far off as Japan. The nursery site, too, is a new housing estate, commemorating its famous origins only in its name.

Lime Tree Stables, Chilton

Racehorses no longer ballet-dance along Main Street since both training establishments closed. The field where the horses once grazed in Lower Road is now yet another housing estate, albeit somewhat up-market, called 'The Paddock'.

From time beyond memory the unofficial emblem of Chilton has been the rook, perhaps stemming from the ring of 'immemorial' elms round the churchyard, which are now, alas, no more. But Chilton's rooks are faithful and there stands now on Harwell airfield's old bomb-dump a grove of sycamores with one of the largest colonies of rooks in South Oxfordshire. And they, and all wildlife, have fair fling on the beautiful country park which was, until 1990, the prefabricated estate, for workers at AERE.

The tiny Methodist chapel in South Row (surely one of the smallest in the country with a capacity of 25) would have been crowded out 50 or so years ago, when the 12th century parish church had fallen into disrepute under an unpopular rector. Now the chapel languishes almost invisible in a losing battle against the elements and a large holly tree.

Chilton appears regularly in the media as the home of the Rutherford Appleton Laboratory, whose scientists gather information on outer space with their spectacular microwave dish which forms a landmark, purely white by day and eerily green by night, at the foot of the downs. They have collaborated with France in the *Ariane* rocket explorations and in NASA's *Ampte* project, increasing our knowledge of the formation of stars and galaxies. The laboratory supports university research in physics and is Britain's centre for academic computing since its merger with Atlas.

Hard by the runway from which the RAF glider-spearhead took off for Normandy on D-Day (which event is commemorated by a plaque and granite plinth near the A4185) is the National Radiological Protection Board, selected to lead European research into all aspects of radiation.

🍁 CHINNOR

Chinnor is situated at the base of the Chiltern Hills, 18 miles east of Oxford and just five miles from the M40. There has probably been a settlement here for many centuries because of the proximity of the ancient Icknield Way running from Lincolnshire down to Wiltshire, which is thought to be pre-Roman and was certainly used during the Middle Ages for driving cattle and sheep.

Still standing in the village today is the mostly 14th century church of St Andrew, although parts of it go back to the 12th and 13th centuries. The wooden screen is reputed to be the sixth oldest in England and a splendid collection of wall-mounted brasses include a foliated cross from about 1338. The stained glass windows date from 1350 through to modern. The bells link the Elizabethan reigns, the tenor having been cast during Elizabeth I's time and the sanctus in 1965. The 14 large pictures in the church have been identified as Thornhill's designs for the rose window in Westminster Abbey.

There is also a Congregational church built of brick and flint, the local building material, opened in 1805, the year of the battle of Trafalgar. The Methodist church is the most recent of the three places of worship, having been rebuilt in 1873 after blowing down the previous year two months after opening.

Industries based in and around Chinnor included lacemaking, chairmaking and agriculture. There were four lace schools in Chinnor in the early 19th century. Among the 268 lacemakers there were many children working to supplement the very low agricultural wages. Timber for chairmaking was known to be stored in the barn at Chairmakers, a 16th century property in the High Street. 'Bodgers' were the men working the beech woods in the surrounding hills.

In more recent times, the cement works opened in 1908 which brought facilities to the village earlier than in surrounding areas. The village is the centre today for several small industries.

Nowadays Chinnor, with its population of approximately 8,000, serves as a base for people working virtually anywhere in the Central Midlands/South corridor. Expansion in Chinnor began with new housing estates being built around the village from the 1960s onwards and it now supports various playgroups and two primary schools, one of which has a special unit for autistic children. There are two village dentists, an optician and two doctor's surgeries, one of which won a design award in 1967. There is sheltered housing for the elderly in Leverkus House and a private nursing home at Hempton Field.

The Village Centre, built on the site of the Rectory stables, provides a coffee shop, a day centre for the elderly, a youth centre and public toilets. There is a branch of the county library next to St Andrew's School, a thriving evening class programme, a cricket field, football pitches and playgrounds in the village centre and Mill Lane. For entertainment there are many societies locally, including the Chinnor Players and Chinnor Operatic Society.

🍁 CHIPPING NORTON

Chipping Norton is a small, hilltop market town as compact as a village; everybody meets in the High Street. It is built mostly of hard, grey limestone, has no urban sprawl and is picturesque enough to be under several conservation orders. It is still a working agricultural community with whiffs of pig manure and bedding straw. Even the dozen antiques shops don't affect its everyday rural busyness.

Approach roads are lined with trees, and the High Street manages to be both cosy and spacious; cosy because it is completely enclosed by 18th century stone frontages, spacious enough to hold the September Mop Fair with its swings, roundabouts and flying boats.

It has nurtured only two nationally famous figures, and is rather shy about both of them. One was Charles Stewart Parnell, the Irish politician who came unstuck politically over his relationship with Mrs O'Shea. He went to the vicar's school down Church Street. The other was Charlie Hind, as notorious a highwayman as Dick Turpin. After his hanging, his head was stuck on the Bridge Gate in Worcester. He was a High Street butcher's boy. Another poor boy, Henry Parish, found himself pressed into the Oxfordshire Militia during the Napoleonic wars. He was shot on Brighton downs for stealing flour, which he wanted to eat and the army wanted to use to whiten his pigtails. The scandal led to army dress reform.

Few national figures, then, but plenty of local characters. Reg Johnston, for instance, used to support Hospital Sunday by stalking through the town on stilts. He kept a leather shop, now the Indian restaurant, and one morning a lady asked if he had any good plastic handbags. 'There ain't any good plastic handbags,' said Reg very loudly. 'Next customer.'

Some of the clergy were as forthright as the townfolk. One was sentenced to be hanged from the church tower for refusing to use Cranmer's new prayer book. A cherished item in the town's museum, run by members of the Local History Society, is a school register of the 19th century. Against one of the names the headmaster has written 'kidnapped by the curate', an echo of the friction between the Church and National schools. The National school, at the top of New Street, is now a recording studio.

Travellers westward along the Worcester road never fail to notice in the valley the palatial stone building with its great Tuscan-style chimney piece. It is Bliss Mill, where at one time hundreds of Chippy people worked producing its famous tough tweeds. It has been converted into luxury flats with views over the old weaving shed. Not everyone who once worked there was sorry at its demise. There was often 'trouble at t'mill' and during the great strike of 1913 there was a huge gathering on the town hall steps addressed by students from Oxford and much ill feeling about 'scabs' who had to be escorted home by the police.

Chippy claims fame for the discovery of aspirin as a pain killer. In the middle of the 19th century a clergyman living in the town, Rev Edward Stone, followed up a local story that the bark of the willow trees which line the banks of the Common brook yielded a juice that eased rheumatics and fevers. He tested it and confirmed the countrymen's remedy. Much later pharmaceutical chemists followed up the clues and in 1899 marketed aspirin to their great profit.

While not particularly wealthy, Chipping Norton people are well provided for from the cradle to the grave. The War Memorial Hospital and maternity unit are cherished institutions. The two medical practices are models of friendliness and efficiency. There are four churches and the public library maintains a list of more than 50 recreational organisations. What annoys some of the older native inhabitants is that Chipping Norton seems to get no credit for the startling claim that, after the First World War, it ran three baseball teams and introduced the game to the United States!

🍁 CHOLSEY

The prehistoric road, the Ickfield Way, crosses the river Thames here at Cholsey. The people who settled and farmed in the village, well after earlier Roman occupation, must have found Cholsey attractive with its mixture of arable land, pasture, marsh and woodlands. By the 7th century the people had been brought to Christianity by Birinus, the Abbot of nearby Dorchester.

The pride of the village is the church of St Mary, founded in AD 986 on monastic land donated by Ethelred the Unready. The present attractive building of stone and flint was erected in the early half of the 12th century and has a fine dog-toothed Norman doorway and a sanctus bell cast in London between 1290 and 1310. Henry I gave the church lands to the Abbots of Reading, who also owned a summer residence at Cholsey. A walk around the churchyard reveals a wealth of wild flowers, especially in the spring. Buried in the north-west corner is Agatha Christie, author of over 100 crime novels and stories.

Cholsey's focal point is the village green, long known as 'The Forty'. Dominated by magnificent horse-chestnut trees, it has been the centre of Cholsey since the Middle Ages. There are several local traditions about the origin of the name, but the most likely explanation is that it is Saxon in derivation, meaning 'island in the marshland'. An estate map of 1695 clearly shows water around 'The Island'.

Take a walk round the village to see the many interesting properties; attractive flint and brick houses, thatched cottages and barns. Follow the footpath from Cholsey to Aston Tirrold to see Lollingham House, built in 1516 and the former home of John Masefield, the Poet Laureate. There are many fine walks around Cholsey, with a bird sanctuary between Bow Bridge and the river Thames. The handsome Cholsey Viaduct, designed by the 'little giant' Isambard Kingdom Brunel, forms a distinctive feature in the landscape.

CHURCH HANBOROUGH & LONG HANBOROUGH

The Hanboroughs lie between Witney and Woodstock, the boundaries formed by the river Evenlode to the north and east unchanged since medieval times. Much of the area was wooded and Pinsley Wood survives to this day. Both villages stand on a T-shaped ridge, from which they take their names: Hagena's or Hanna's Hill.

King Henry I (son of William the Conqueror) stayed in Hanborough briefly in 1105, Charles I and his army drew up on Hanborough Heath, and in January 1965 a train bearing the body of Sir Winston Churchill for burial in Bladon churchyard came to Hanborough station. J. B. Priestley lived in Church Hanborough and more recently the novelist Penelope Lively. Lewis Carroll wrote several chapters of *Alice in Wonderland* while staying at The Long House in Long Hanborough.

The first evidence of settlement dates from the Bronze Age and there are signs of early Iron Age and two early Roman pottery kilns. The parish church of St Peter and St Paul, in Church Hanborough, now mainly dating from the 15th century, was certainly in existence in 1130. Substantial parts of the Norman structure can clearly be seen. Additions and alterations throughout the centuries have resulted in a building of outstanding beauty.

A 'mission' church was built in Long Hanborough in 1893 and a school, still in use for the little ones, in 1879. A Methodist church has flourished since 1895. There is a modern County Primary School.

From 1751 to 1870 the Witney-Bicester road was a turnpike. The railway station, still much used, opened in 1853. There was no post office until 1877, electricity came in 1932, mains water in 1935, and main drainage in 1963.

Agriculture, glove-making and quarrying were formerly the main sources of employment but in modern times these have been superseded by technology.

The population has fluctuated: in 1801 it was 655, by 1851 it had nearly doubled to 1,153, but then fell to 216 in 1921. Since then Long Hanborough has grown rapidly as a dormitory for Oxford. In 1991 the census showed a resident population of 2,626 living in 975 households.

Church Hanborough is designated as an area for conservation and is still, for much of the day, a quiet and peaceful village, the houses mainly mid to late 18th century, built of local stone with slate roofs. There are in fact lovely old Cotswold stone houses in both villages. The oldest are in Long Hanborough – the Malt House, mid 16th century, the Manor House, later 16th century, and others typical of the Cotswolds.

The Hanboroughs are served by a Co-op, a post office with newsagent and sweetshop, a butcher, two hairdressers, an antiques shop, a cycle shop, a nursery, a photographer, three garages, a dentist and five pubs. There is a large medical practice with its own surgery and its own dispensary – a great boon.

🍁 CHURCHILL

Leaving Chipping Norton along the Churchill road, the magnificent tower of All Saints' church soon comes into view. This is a slimmer version of the tower of Magdalen College, Oxford (reduced by a third in size) and a much loved landmark in the area surrounding Churchill. It is from the tower that a local choral group greet the dawn with joyous singing on May Day each year.

There is impressive history here. Warren Hastings was born in the village in 1732. At the age of 17 he sailed for India. During a colourful and at times tempestuous career he became the first Governor General of India in 1773. He eventually returned to England and spent his last days at nearby Daylesford, where he died in 1818. A commemorative plaque on the wall marks his birthplace in Hastings Hill.

William Smith was born here in 1769. He became a well known civil engineer but his main preoccupation was the preparation and production of a series of detailed geological maps of England, for which he is rightly regarded as the Father of English Geology. He died at Northampton in 1839. In 1891 the Earl of Ducie erected a monment in Churchill of oolitic stones from the district to the memory of William Smith. The name oolite was given by William Smith to the rocks that form the higher grounds in the locality.

The handsome fountain was erected in memory of Squire Langston who died in 1863. He was a great influence in the life of Churchill, responsible for building the church, in 1826 and the school. Through him farmhouses, barns and cottages were built or renovated. Neglected land was taken over and cultivated.

The remains of the original church nestle at the foot of Hastings Hill. In 1986 the Old Church Preservation Society was formed to repair and maintain the building and there are plans for a local history museum. The well tended burial ground surrounding the old church is still in use today.

The Methodist church in Kingham Road was completed in 1927 and stands on land given by the Crudge family who still farm in the village today. There is a very good relationship between the members of both churches and joint services are always well attended.

The village has had an enthusiastic cricket team for many years, a flourishing WI now in its 75th year, a thriving play group since 1972 and lively amateur dramatic activities. Many events take place during the year, the biggest of these being the biennial Classic and Vintage Car Rally which attracts much interest from a very wide area. The proceeds of this are distributed to local charities and the church. In November a huge bonfire and carefully organized display of fireworks delight the residents of Churchill and neighbouring villages; followed in December by the lighting of the Christmas tree on the green, when everyone gathers around to sing carols by torchlight.

Inevitably, there have been changes. Reduced roll numbers at the school (attended by both Warren Hastings and William Smith) led to its closure in 1981. However, its conversion to five houses has been attractively achieved. Elsewhere in the village other developments and conversions have taken place – most have blended well with existing buildings.

🍁 CLANFIELD

The village of Clanfield lies on the flat expanses of the Upper Thames Valley, not far from Radcot Bridge. Clanfield was mentioned in Domesday Book as having 14 villagers, 13 smallholders and four slaves. There is a much ploughed-over barrow on the outskirts, which must mark the grave of one of its earlier inhabitants. Perhaps the most interesting approach is from the south over Radcot Bridge. Here in the meadows on your right you will see Friars Court, built on the site of a previous building that belonged to the Knights Hospitallers. Part of the moat and fragments of early masonry remain. Here lives a farmer who is also a pioneer conservationist. He and his late wife planted trees and shrubs, created a lake for wild fowl and a farm trail for visitors.

The church is dedicated to St Stephen and on its 14th century tower is a statue of the saint, holding in his hands the stones of his martyrdom. Above the Norman doorway is an early mass dial. Near to the church stands Chestlyon Farm, where once lived a wealthy family of that name. The present house dates from the 16th century, but it has at one corner what could have been a small Norman chapel.

The village has a Methodist chapel, still in use. Methodism once flourished in Clanfield. Camp meetings were held on the green, where the preacher would address the crowd from an old farm wagon. These early evangelists were often pelted with rotten eggs. There is a story of one such preacher, a Clanfield man, who while marching at the head of the procession towards the chapel, was jeered at by the local lads. 'Thee bist afraid to preach now,' they yelled, whereupon the old man stopped in his tracks, carefully removed a clean red spotted handkerchief from his top pocket, laid it on the ground (to save his Sunday corduroys) and knelt down and prayed for their conversion!

A stream runs through the village towards the Thames, its banks in spring bright with daffodils. This stream is crossed in several places by perfect little stone arched bridges, which cannot be properly appreciated unless you walk along 'the causeway' under the weeping willows. This path may be part of the ancient trackway that led from Clanfield to Radcot. It would have been above the flood plain, very necessary when in the old days the Thames frequently flooded in winter. The old records tell us that it had to be kept clear, which was something not always adhered to, as more than once a local scallywag was fined for dumping a load of manure on it!

There are two village greens, and 'the causeway' links them. One is overlooked by the Plough and the Tavern, the two village inns, and also by a group of attractive cottages. Here too, the village cross once stood. In 1826 there were 102 houses and the inhabitants numbered 490. Today the population stands at around 1,000.

Clanfield is a friendly village and its residents are drawn from all walks of life. There are retired folk and there are young families, fortunate in having a fine post office cum newsagent and general store, and a thriving primary school. There is an agricultural engineering repair shop, and on the site of what was once 'Knapps' is an agricultural engineering implement agency. 'Knapps' was an old Clanfield firm: L. R. Knapp and Co Ltd, established in 1745, 'Makers of Drills, Distributors and Hayloaders'. They employed as many as 40 Clanfield men at one time. Today agriculture employs about 20 and that includes the four farmers.

The football club is well supported. Clanfield holds a very popular annual Produce and Craft Show and an annual Horse Show which raises magnificent sums of money for local charities and village needs.

❀ CLEEVE

Cleeve is sometimes considered part of Goring village. However, Cleeve has a number of buildings and amenities in its own right. The name of the hamlet of Cleeve refers to a cliff or clift, i.e. the cutting of a channel by the force of the stream. Cleeve clusters round the crossroads, half hidden in the hollow.

Goring Fire Station is in Cleeve. The Volunteer Fire Brigade was formed in 1890 and in April 1976 a new fire station was opened in Icknield Road.

Elvendon Priory is a beautiful and interesting house on Elvendon Road. It dates from the 12th century and has a colourful past. A tunnel is said to exist between it and Goring Priory.

Cleeve Mill was built mostly of wood in the late 16th or early 17th centuries. Corn was last ground there in 1888 and the mill is now residential property. Cleeve Lock was built of timber in 1797 and rebuilt in stone in 1874. Cleeve presents itself as a busy and colourful scene.

❀ CLIFTON HAMPDEN & BURCOT

Clifton Hampden is noted for its delightful riverside cottages, bridge and church high on a cliff of lower greensand which here forms a solid bed to the Thames. After a visit to Oxford in 1862 the Lord Mayor of London's State Barge embarrassingly ran aground here, and in 1891 the river was so thickly frozen a sheep was roasted on it. From the church porch there is a fine view down to the elegant six-arched bridge built in 1864 using local bricks, to a design by Sir George Gilbert Scott for the then lord of the manor, later 1st Lord Aldenham.

In 1843 and 1864 the same eminent architect rebuilt the derelict church. Now pretty and Victorian in aspect, it retains features back to the 12th century or earlier. There is a stone carving of a boar hunt, possibly from a Norman tympanum. A small stone cross near the porch marks the grave of young William Dyke, reputed to have started the battle of Waterloo too soon by letting off his musket by accident before the order was given. He was eventually a sergeant in the Grenadier Guards – Wellington forgave him. An English flank officer's sword, probably picked up by Dyke on the battlefield, is kept by a village family.

The village, well-known to anglers and river-users, has three hospitable thatched inns: The Barley Mow on the south bank, featured in *Three Men in a Boat*, The Plough at the crossroads, and The Chequers in Burcot. The red phone box outside the post office below the church is a listed building, the famous design of George Gilbert Scott's renowned grandson Giles. The school clock on its little tower was constructed by the makers of Big Ben and is identical in movement. A narrow gap at the foot of a declivity to the left of the post office was once the coach road from Dorchester-on-Thames.

The European Atomic Energy Community's JET Project (Joint European Torus) is partly within the parish and researches safe power from nuclear fusion with temperatures equal to that of the centre of the Sun. Its laboratories stand on land formerly a Second World War Naval Air Station though far inland, HMS *Hornbill*. Two land mines which fell in a field near the Barley Mow did little local damage but by a quirk of geology broke windows and brought down chimneys miles away in Cowley.

🍁 COMBE

Combe is an unspoiled village on the fringe of the Cotswolds, centred around a delightful village green, which has a public house on one side and a church on the other. In spring daffodils grow all around the green; these were planted by the WI on their 50th anniversary.

The 14th century Anglican church of St Laurence is reputed to have been moved by the monks of Eynsham Abbey from the old village, which was down in the valley – near the site of Combe Mill. One of the main features of the church is the Doom painting above the chancel arch. There are also several other wall paintings, a lovely stone font and pulpit and some old stained glass.

Across the playing field is the Methodist church dating from 1893 and refurbished in 1988. This replaced a smaller building dating from 1835.

The playing field, which was opened by the Duke of Edinburgh in 1949, has a children's playground and is used for various sporting activities throughout the year. The field is very well kept and the views across the Evenlode valley are marvellous.

The Reading Room which was built in 1890 at the instigation of Miss Adela Brooke of Combe House, provides a centre for much of the social life of the village.

Combe Feast is one of the main social events of the year. A fair is held on the village green, an open air service takes place on the Sunday evening, cricket matches are played on the two following days and there is general fun and games at the fair.

May Day is celebrated by the school children who parade around the village carrying flowers and singing May songs. The children congregate at school for tea. After tea everyone gathers on the green for the crowning of the May Queen and maypole dancing. School records show that this tradition has been carried out in Combe since 1870.

Although the village remains unspoilt, there has been careful development and this has helped to keep the community 'alive' by ensuring that there is a good mixture of age groups. There is a good local bus service and a railway halt just outside the village on the Cotswold Line (Oxford – Worcester). The village has one shop/sub post office.

Combe Mill, which is situated between Combe and Long Hanborough, as well as being a commercial saw mill for Blenheim estate, houses a Cornish beam engine which is 'in steam' on special week-ends. There is a museum in the same building.

The village has retained much of its truly rural character, although gone are the days when cows wandered through the village at milking times; there used to be five farms in Combe, but now there is only one, which is highly mechanised.

🍁 CROPREDY

The village is situated at a crossroads in a valley through which meander the river Cherwell and the Oxford Canal. Cropredy became famous during the Civil War when King Charles' army was travelling north from Oxford. Parliamentary troops under General Waller intercepted the Royalists by the river and a battle took place. Charles won the day and was able to cross Cropredy Bridge. Some of the soldiers who were killed in the battle were buried in the churchyard. There are, to this day, bloodstains on the vestry floor, where a young messenger was killed. The lectern was thrown into the river for safekeeping and was not recovered for some 30 years after the

Cropredy Lock

battle. A foot in the form of a lion was missing and this was replaced in bronze, but when the lectern was cleaned it was found to be made of brass. The lectern to this day has one bronze and two brass feet. Armour from the battle was left on display in the church. School children would polish the armour and learn all about the battle, up until the mid 1980s when the armour was stolen.

Many years ago a gentleman was walking home across the fields when a fog came down and he was lost, then he heard Cropredy church curfew bell and realised where he was. So thankful was he that he gave the land now known as Bell Land so that the rent from it could pay the Cropredy bell ringer. The curfew bell was always rung at 6 am to awaken workers, at 12 noon calling the workers in from the fields for dinner and at 8 pm. One story tells how the poor ringer on a very frosty, slippery morning crawled to the church with the aid of sacks tied around his legs only to find he had left the key behind. Cropredy is one of the very few places in England where the curfew is still rung regularly. This is on Tuesday, Thursday and Saturday evenings.

The canal opened in 1790 when barges carried coal, corn, stone, bricks and other items. There were two wharfs. Today the canal has a new leisure use for numerous pleasure boats, a canoe club and, of course, fishermen. Competitions take place and children can still get much pleasure from fishing in both the river and canal. When winters were colder and the canal used to freeze, many workers and school children would skate on the canal to Banbury. The last time when the ice was thick enough for this was in the winter of 1963/4.

The village has two greens. The main one at one time stretched down to the river and was surrounded by a manor house and thatched cottages. A red horse-chestnut tree stands in the centre and this was planted to commemorate Queen Victoria's Diamond Jubilee.

In addition to the two inns, the Red Lion and the Brasenose, there is a tea and coffee shop close by the green. The Old Coal Wharf by the canal has become an Arts and Film Society venue and also a place for refreshments. The village store stands by the canal bridge, opposite the pavilion and sports field.

The Methodist chapel built by Thomas Cherry over 100 years ago is still there, but his descendants have moved their builders' premises to Great Tew.

The beautiful church of St Mary the Virgin, parts of which date back to the 11th century, was known as the Mother Church for Wardington, Great and Little Bourton, Mollington and Claydon until the 1860s. Next to it stood the

17th century vicarage. This was sold in 1964, and several houses, bungalows and flats were built in its place. Another estate of 25 houses has been built on land which was once part of Poplars Farm. The farmhouse itself has been much restored and renamed 'The Eagles'.

For over 30 years, Cropredy has played host to the thousands of fans who attend the music festival called the 'Fairport Convention', held one weekend every August.

CROWELL

Crowell parish covers some 996 acres extending from the Lower Icknield Way approximately three and a half miles in a south-easterly direction up onto the Chiltern ridge, reaching a height of 800 ft at one point. Nowhere is the parish more than half a mile wide. Crowell Hill is covered in the main with beech wood and lower chalk slopes. The lowland is mainly arable. It is thought that the name Crowell comes from crow's well, spring or stream as the village grew up at the source of the Pleck, a tributary of the river Thame.

Ellwood House is the only remaining farmhouse north of the B4009, of which there were four in 1839. The house dates from the 16th century, the front of which is of timber-frame construction concealed by chequer brick. There still remains a raised granary to the rear of the house. In the late 19th century the house and land were bought by Joseph Hill of Kingston Blount and the house restored as a farmhouse. It still remains in the Hill family today. Ellwood House was named after Thomas Ellwood, a Quaker and friend of John Milton.

The village used to be larger than it is today and according to the 1851 census there were 16 lacemakers, three chairmakers, a chair bottomer, a wheelwright, a carpenter, a victualler and a number of farm labourers. Today although there are a couple of houses in the village housing farm workers and a farm at the top of the hill, the majority of people work either in Oxford or towards London. One of the longer established village families runs a funeral service business, the mortuary and chapel of rest being situated close to the church and village pub.

The Catherine Wheel public house was used by drovers in the last century herding their cattle from the west country to the eastern counties. There was a lean-to shelter with an earth floor to the rear of the pub where they slept. This area now forms part of the bar. In 1859 a great part of the village was destroyed by fire including the pub, which was one of the first buildings to be rebuilt.

John Bunyan is said to have stayed at the Catherine Wheel between his spells in gaol. He entertained the locals on his flute and there was until recently a copy of the chair that he used in prison in which one of the back struts was in fact his flute. Rumour has it that the prison officers never discovered the hiding place and so he was able to play his flute when alone in his prison cell.

The parish church of St Mary the Virgin serves Kingston Blount as well as Crowell. There is evidence to suggest that the church existed in the 12th century though the first documents only date back to 1231. The church was almost totally rebuilt in the 1870s, using as many of the original materials as possible so as to keep its 14th century appearance.

There is no longer a school in Crowell though records show that there was a writing master here in 1713. During the 1830s there was a day school teaching 30 boys and girls, supported by the rector and payments from the children's parents. By 1854 the older children were going to school in Chinnor at the rector's expense and by 1878 the school in Crowell had closed, the children attending school in Aston Rowant or Chinnor as they do today.

🍁 CROWMARSH GIFFORD

This village, which now includes Newnham Murren, lies on the eastern bank of the river Thames, across the bridge from Wallingford. The name Crowmarsh can be taken literally and the Gifford part comes from Walter Giffard who was given this land by William the Conqueror. Walter had been Standard Bearer to William in Normandy.

Many of the houses straddle the busy main road to Henley. There are pleasant rows of old cottages as well as small estates of more modern houses. The wide street in the centre of the village for centuries held an annual fair. It was said in the Middle Ages to be the most considerable in Oxfordshire. The horse fair, as it later became, died out at the end of the 19th century.

Much of the village's history is linked to that of nearby Wallingford. For instance, during the 12th century King Stephen constructed a series of wooden forts close by the bridge, opposite Wallingford castle where he was laying siege to Empress Matilda who contended the throne. No traces of these buildings remain today, unfortunately. The parish church of St Mary Magdalene was apparently used during the siege as a fortified post, and desecrated. Later, during the Civil War of the 17th century, some of King Charles' troops sought refuge in the church when Cromwell's men marched on Wallingford from Henley; the vestry door, which was formerly the west door of this Norman church, has supposed bullet holes in it. A leper hospital, with its own chapel, was established in Crowmarsh by the burgesses of Wallingford in the 12th century and was closely associated with the hospital of St John the Baptist on the southern side of Wallingford. But in times of plague Wallingford tried to keep Crowmarsh people out of the town by posting wardens on the bridge.

A foundry was set up in the village about 1865 by one of the local Wilder family. Walter Wilder's made castings, mainly for agricultural machinery but also for, amongst others, street lamps and drain covers. Have a look for them as you go around South Oxfordshire!

The foundry and some of the old farmhouses have gone now. One row of cottages next to the foundry was once part of Howberry Farm which at the beginning of the 18th century was tenanted by a farmer of national repute – Jethro Tull; he was a pioneer of mechanized agriculture, producing the first seed-drill that really worked. Today the names of two small housing estates on the site recall the past.

A hundred years ago the village had more small shops than it has today, and included a baker and butcher, as well as two grocers and a post office. There is still a post office and general stores but the other present businesses are mainly concerned with the building trade. There used to be two beerhouses in addition to the two public houses that are still open, the Queen's Head and the Bell. The Queen's Head is the oldest secular building in the village. It was originally a 14th century aisled hall of a kind which was usually the dwelling of a man of considerable status. The elaborate design is still evident in its timber frame. The Bell has been much altered as well as enlarged over the years, but has been an inn since at least the mid 18th century.

Crowmarsh Gifford has a modern primary school which also takes in children from Mongewell and North Stoke, having outgrown two former school buildings that have since become private houses. One cottage, next to the Bell, and some land, was left to the village under a charity set up by one William Emery. There is a tradition that Emery had a lot of money because he had found a buried hoard on a plot where he farmed in nearby Ipsden. The cottage became known as the Poor's Cottage and the land is now used for allotments.

South of the village are meadows and farmland, while on the north side the 18th century Howberry Park now houses Hydraulics Research Limited, the Institute of Hydrology and headquarters offices of the District Council. Visitors to Crowmarsh may choose to stay at the Bridge Villa camp site which is close to the river south-east of Wallingford bridge. Watery Lane, the bridleway which runs alongside it, sometimes lives up to its name!

CUDDESDON & DENTON

Cuddesdon was once known as the 'Holy Village' and differs from other villages because it has an Anglican theological training college and also used to be the official home of the Bishops of Oxford at the Old Palace. A small number of houses and an extra accommodation block for the college are the only new buildings in the parish since the 1970s.

The college was founded over a century ago. During the Second World War it was taken over by the government as a hostel for Irish girls who worked in the Cowley factories. Until 1996 the principal of the college was also vicar of the parish and over the years practically all who have held this post have become bishops – notably the Archbishop of Canterbury, Dr Runcie, who held the post between 1960/69.

The Old Palace as it was known, opposite the college, stood in twelve acres of trees. Over the centuries it has a history of fires, the last being four decades ago when it was burned to the ground. In the 1960s part of the woodland ground was sold for executive-type houses – in the kitchen garden four staff bungalows were built and a modern palace/house for the Bishop was also built. The Bishops have since preferred to live elsewhere.

The village has a hamlet known as Denton on the south-west side which has 27 houses. The big house has windows built in its surrounding garden wall which were purported to have come from Brasenose College, Oxford, in days gone by. There are two picturesque timber-framed black and white thatched cottages, and a small brook running through.

Denton has a large spring which in years gone by supplied the hamlet with its water. Because of its quality the water was collected by the then Oxford Eye Hospital and used for eye treatments. Now of course it is all mains water.

Like other villages most people go outside to work – the only employment now being three farms, the college and a public house. Public transport is a thing of the past. There is still a village hall and a recreation ground, but no sports club which was flourishing years ago. The event in the year is the annual church fete which involves the college, church and village all getting together.

 ## CUMNOR

Cumnor is an extensive parish three miles to the south-west of Oxford. The village itself is situated on high ground, rising in Cumnor Hurst to 825 ft. The name signifies 'Cuma's hill-slope', Cuma being an 8th century abbot of Abingdon. Housing connects it with the former hamlet of Chawley and in the valley are two other rapidly growing settlements, Farmoor and Dean Court. The name Cumnor is first found in a medieval copy of an Anglo-Saxon charter of AD 982 granting land to Abingdon Abbey, and it was mentioned in the Domesday Book.

Until recently agriculture was the main occupation. Today Cumnor is almost a suburb of Oxford, but still maintains a village atmosphere. The village has a church which is well worth a visit, St Michael's, with an interesting graveyard. Visitors should see the tomb of William Godrey, who fought with Charles I in the Civil War, and notice a slab marking the grave of Dr Benjamin Buckler, vicar from 1755–1780. The church bells were first rung in the 17th century. In July 1989 these bells were rehung and six old bells and the sanctus bell were rededicated; in addition two new bells and the frame were dedicated.

The field beyond the church was for many centuries part of the park belonging to Cumnor Place. The remains of Cumnor Place have long gone, apart from a small wall beside some steps and what was probably once a hearth for a fire. The house was made famous by the mysterious death of Amy Dudley, wife of Robert, Earl of Leicester, better known as Amy Robsart; she is buried in Oxford. In September 1560 the whole household went to Abingdon Fair, leaving Amy behind. When they returned they found her lying dead at the bottom of the stairs in the hall. This story was used by Sir Walter Scott in his novel *Kenilworth*.

A hill leading out of the village towards Farmoor is called Tumbledown

Hill. The story is told, and as far as residents know it is only a story, of Dick Cromwell, son of Oliver, riding back after a battle – or was he returning from hunting? – and falling off his horse on Tumbledown Hill. He was known as Tumbledown Dick.

In 1997, Cumnor Old School was finally converted into The Old School Community Centre revealing the hammer-beam roof, and a minstrels' gallery was built in the main hall. The nearby Old School House was converted into a local shop and post office. In the High Street is a 16th century farmhouse with a knot garden.

A tradition in the village is Pumpkin Night (Halloween), arranged now by the Bear and Ragged Staff, a public house in the Appleton Road, for the best and heaviest pumpkin from the villages of Cumnor, Standlake and Bampton. The proceeds of the party go to charity. According to stories it is also the night when the Mayor of Cumnor gets ducked in the village pond nearby. The Bear and Ragged Staff is a very old building – about 400 years old, and was for several centuries an old farmhouse.

There is a physic well off the footpath through the fields on the way to Bablock Hythe: difficult to spot now as it is overgrown, though it can be found if you know where to look. It is said to have healing properties for eye ailments.

DEDDINGTON

> Aynho on the hill,
> Clifton in the clay,
> Dirty drunken Deddington
> And Hempton high way.

Deddington is an old village sitting on top of a ridge overlooking the Cherwell valley between Oxford and Banbury. Here the wind comes straight from Siberia, say the old residents. Part of the church and some of the houses date back to the 13th century.

In its time the village was an important stage between its neighbouring towns and had a flourishing trade in cattle, sheep and horses. Old records show that at the November 'Pudding and Pie' fair as many as 600 or 700 horses changed hands. The old street-names like Bull Ring and Horse Fair are still in use. The fair marked an important day in the village in the 18th and 19th centuries. It offered villagers a fine day out with a band playing, and a chance for them to buy clothing, linen and household goods. After the Second World War it turned into a fun fair. Otherwise Deddington was self-sufficient and supported the usual trades like glove-making, a forge, candlemaking and clock making. The old industries included a paper mill and a beaver hat factory at Clifton. It was also known for good malt, hence the third line of the rhyme.

Today, Deddington is still a beautiful village of some 2,000 inhabitants. The older houses are built of golden Hornton stone and some of them are of considerable architectural and historical interest.

The village is big enough to offer all sorts of amenities and small enough to be a sociable community where people know and trust each other. There are plenty of shops and one of the pleasures of living in Deddington is to go shopping on a Saturday morning.

The village has a hall on the Hempton road, the Windmill Centre. Scouts and Guides use it as a venue, and major events and big meetings are staged here. There are adult education classes and the grounds of the centre have tennis courts, a bowling green, children's play areas, and football and cricket fields.

The village has three churches, the old handsome parish church of St Peter and St Paul, the Congregational church and the Wesleyan chapel. And how many villages still have a real live set of bells? Deddington does, and the residents are lucky to be able to hear the chimes on practice evening and the ringing by visiting bell-ringing groups and for Sunday services and weddings. On special occasions the Tower Captain opens up the bell tower and visitors are allowed to climb up and up, gasping as they reach the top, and are given an interesting insight into the art of bell ringing and a breathtaking view over miles of Oxfordshire.

Deddington also has an elusive ancient monument. In recent years English Heritage put up a sign directing tourists to Deddington Castle. Alas, a moat and a couple of stones are all that represent what was once a castle.

Deddington was granted its own coat of arms in 1993. The citation is displayed on the north wall of the parish church and the coat of arms is on the south wall of the Town Hall.

In 1996 'Daeda's Wood' was planted as a community project, the first in the Woodland Trust's 'Woods On Your Doorstep' project backed by the

Millennium Commission. Deddingtonians helped to pay for it, planted the trees and sowed wildflower seeds on the site. A stretch of path provided by Cherwell District Council allows access for all.

DORCHESTER ON THAMES

Travellers north on the busy A4074 from Shillingford can see across the vast ploughed field to the sturdy crenellated tower of Dorchester Abbey; they leave the bypass and enter the village over the long curved bridge spanning the willow-lined river Thame as it winds its mile long way down to join the Thames.

The river and the abbey have been the main influences in the history of this beautiful village.

In AD 635 the king was baptised in Dorchester. The Christian King Oswald of Northumbria wished to marry the daughter of the king of the West Saxons, King Cynegils. Cynegils became a Christian having been converted by Birinus, the 'Apostle of Wessex'. The two kings gave Birinus land on which he built his first church, probably this first Dorchester Cathedral was timber-built. (Soon after he dedicated a church in Winchester which later became Winchester Cathedral). In the abbey is a reconstruction of the original shrine to St Birinus, a stone from which was placed in a silver processional cross, carried on a pilgrimage to Winchester in 1979 and presented to the bishop.

Following the Danish Invasion, the Dorchester diocese stretched from the Thames to the Humber. After the Norman Conquest, Dorchester's importance decreased. Remegius, the new Norman bishop had his seat transferred to Lincoln. Later a house of Augustinian canons was set up and during the next three centuries they built the magnificent abbey. At this time Wallingford, Oxford and Abingdon were the flourishing market towns, and Dorchester, apart from the abbey, was just a village.

There are no traces of the monastery buildings, destroyed on the orders of Henry VIII. Only the Guest House survived to become a grammar school in 1652, the gift of Sir John Fettiplace.

There have been many restorations of the abbey over the years. The last major effort was in 1970 when there was another 'royal occasion' when the rededication was attended by the Queen Mother.

The main road through the village, called the High Street, has many

79

interesting houses, some dating back to medieval times, but over the years they have been repaired, refronted, or reroofed making their study fascinating. Cruck construction, thatched cob walls, Elizabethan jettied houses, herringbone noggins and many other architectural features can be found.

Near the bridge, built in 1815, is the little toll house, for this road through the village became one of the first turnpike roads in Oxfordshire and two of the 15th century coaching inns still remain, the George with its gallery and external staircase and the White Hart which had its coach yard at the back.

A hundred years ago the population was just under a thousand. Many of the men were agricultural workers and the village had many small shops and ten public houses; there were butchers, millers, carpenters, a tailor, baker, blacksmith, wheelwright, undertaker, grocers, carriers and coal merchant – a typical self sufficient village. There was one unusual employer, a Missionary College where young clergy were trained for work overseas.

Twenty men were killed in the First World War. After the war the first council houses were built, rehousing some of the families living in primitive one up, two down cottages. Dorchester was not affected by the Depression, for there was plenty of work in the new Morris Motors and Pressed Steel factories at Cowley, and also at the Ordnance Depot at Didcot. New houses were built on the Abingdon and Oxford roads. There was a flourishing school which included one of the new senior schools.

After the war the character of the village changed completely. Mains water and drainage were laid on and then any spare bit of land was built upon including the two small farms; small cottages were bought and improved and it became a much sought after village. (The population is still just about a thousand.) Luckily young people came in as well, so there is still a flourishing primary school; the senior school became a comprehensive moving to a larger site in the new, mainly council built, development on the disused airfield in the north of the parish now named Berinsfield after our first bishop, St Birinus, and which became a separate parish in 1964.

Today, it is still a lively friendly village with clubs or societies catering for all ages and for all tastes. The lakes of the old gravel pits support sailing clubs and other water sports and are a paradise for birdwatchers with their enormous flocks of winter migrants. Throngs of visitors come to enjoy the village and the river and to be uplifted by the splendour of the abbey. The old grammar school is still a place of learning as a small museum and weary travellers can be refreshed in the tearooms of the abbey's Guest House.

 DRAYTON

Drayton is two miles from Abingdon on the old A34, once in Berkshire, now in Oxfordshire. It is the centre of an agricultural area, and was once famous for its walnuts. On the village green stands a stone cross in commemoration of Queen Victoria's Golden Jubilee.

Drayton has several fine houses, including Lime Close, parts of which are Elizabethan, which was visited by the diarist James Woodforde in 1763. Other houses of note are the Grange, Sutton Wick House, Gothic House and the Manor, opposite which is the only six-bay cruck cottage in England.

Gothic House has a mural on the gable-end of St George killing the Dragon painted by Charles Sykes in 1949, the design taken from the original, smaller mural inside the house. Drayton people used to perform a mummer's play of St George and the Dragon annually at one time. Charles was an artist and sculptor, and in 1911 he designed the 'Spirit of Ecstasy' for the Rolls Royce motor company.

St Peter's church contains some fine carving done by Rev F. E. Robinson, who worked on it each day from 5.30 am until his parochial duties took over. He was also a renowned campanologist, and was the first Master of the Oxford Diocesan Guild of Bellringers, and claimed to have rung in every belfry in England. A brass plaque above the pulpit states 'In every work that he began, he did it with all his heart'.

In 1870 the casual act of throwing away hot ashes started 'The Great Fire of Drayton' which wiped out half the village and caused a national appeal to be launched. Drayton bricks made of Kimmeridge clay, dug, shaped and fired behind the Wheatsheaf, were used to rebuild the village.

In 1957 a Beverley aircraft came down near the village with some loss of life. More recently in 1989 a Tornado jet crashed on the outskirts of the village after flying into a flock of starlings.

One well known village lady was Mrs Marion Caudwell. Mrs Caudwell died in 1987 at the age of 93, after a lifetime of community work as area organiser of the WRVS, 25 years on the Abingdon RDC and eight years as a County Councillor. She gave a piece of land and raised money for housing and a day centre for the elderly which bear her name, and opened her garden each year for the church fete, an idyllic setting.

The busy Abingdon-Steventon road passing the green follows the line of the old toll road through Drayton used by the Oxford-Southampton stage coach in the 18th century. Whatever transport you use, Drayton is worth a visit!

 DUCKLINGTON

Ducklington is situated one and a half miles to the south of Witney, close to the river Windrush. It is on the A415 road to Abingdon, but the village is fortunate in having a bypass which relieves it of much traffic.

St Bartholomew's church, commenced in Norman times, was once plundered by Cromwell's men and some of the damage can still be seen. They cut the heads off eight statues, only those that stood in the shadows escaped. Present day parishioners embarked on mammoth fundraising to rehang the bells which now ring out over the village.

In a nearby field grows a rare plant, the Snakeshead Fritillary. These are depicted in a stained glass window and on the altar cloth, and their flowering is celebrated each year on 'Fritillary Sunday', usually the first Sunday in May. The church is open to visitors with many interesting things to see and

St Bartholomew's church, Ducklington

refreshments are available in the nearby village hall. An elderly villager relates that, as a lad he and his friends were paid to gather these beautiful flowers and send them to market at Covent Garden. They are now protected and must not be picked.

The village hall was once the church tithe barn. It was used for many years as a meeting place and was known as the 'Parish Room'. In 1974 the room was purchased by the village, and much fund-raising and hard work resulted in a 'new' hall with modern facilities. It is now in great demand by all organisations, from playgroup to pensioners.

A small book titled *Living and Lifestyle in Ducklington 1640 to 1740* was published by the village History Group who studied records from the period, giving new insight into life at that time. The majority of 140 or so villagers worked on the land but there were a few craftsmen who plied their trade such as weavers, tanners and blacksmiths. It is very different today with only one working farm in the village and a population of over 1,000. Most people go much further afield to work, and all trades and professions are represented.

When the post office and shop closed, the building was converted into a bungalow. An enterprising villager seized the opportunity and has reversed the process, converting his bungalow into a post office and shop! This is the fourth or fifth location of this business in living memory. This, together with a garage and two congenial public houses are the only traders in the village.

There has been little crime in the village, although one notable exception was the theft of the post office safe. It was wheeled away in the early hours on a trolley. Several people were awoken by the noise as it was trundled down the road but although they saw two men pushing something, they did not seem to think it unusual and went back to bed. The booty was later recovered from a ditch and except for a broken handle was none the worse for its outing.

Author and broadcaster Mollie Harris spent her childhood in Ducklington, her book *A Kind of Magic* depicts life in the village in the 1920s. Many of the places she mentions have changed little since that time. The footpaths, streams and rivers are a constant source of pleasure to us, as they were to her then.

 DUNSDEN

Like many areas near the Thames, Dunsden has poorly defined boundaries. Situated on the uplands rising from the river between Caversham and Shiplake, the area was apparently used from early times as a passageway between the low lying, often flooded river valley at Sonning and the higher ground at Sonning Common where safe grazing could be found.

The name appears in Domesday Book as Dunesden. Much of the land was wild heathland and belonged to the Bishops of Sarum, whose influence was considerable as they owned the manor of Sonning and huge tracts of land in Berkshire. Bishopsland Farmhouse still stands at the northern end of the parish, commemorating the connection.

For many hundreds of years farming has been the main activity. The names of more than ten farms are commemorated by farmhouses which are now in private hands. The lands have been amalgamated and form part of Phillimore Farms operated by the Phillimore Settled Estates. The Phillimore family have been benevolent and conscientious landowners for over 150 years. Members of the family still live at Coppid Hall and are much respected; it is largely due to their careful husbandry that Dunsden remains a rural sanctuary even though only a few miles from the town of Reading.

Although not strictly in Dunsden, the brickworks in Kiln Lane at Binfield Heath must have provided local employment. A resident remembers the explosion when the works were blown up and demolished in around 1932. Ancient bricks can still be found and many people have used them to build garden walls or incorporated them in their houses.

Chalk quarrying was another activity, and a small quarry is still in use near Playhatch.

Playhatch House is a fine old building and one of the most gracious houses in the parish. Several houses and two pubs make up the hamlet of Playhatch around the foot of the steep hill that leads to Dunsden from the main Reading to Henley road. This hill road is of comparatively recent origin. The original road, known as Foxhill Lane, still exists, as does the old drovers' road from the Flowing Spring public house, going up the hillside and coming out at the George and Dragon pub, now a private dwelling. There are probably more footpaths and old roads in the area than macadamised roads and walkers are well rewarded by peaceful scenery and spectacular views. Another pub now turned into a house is the Old Black Boy at Dunsden Green. This was also a post office but now customers must travel to Binfield Heath for their stamps and pensions.

An old covered well stands at a fork in the road near the top of the hill by the village green. This was opened for use in June 1878 and is 150 ft deep but has been closed off for safety. It was provided by Miss Susanna Palmer and Mrs Isabella Crawshay. The Crawshays were ironfounders from Wales who owned Caversham Park, the the local 'stately home', and the Palmers were part of the famous Reading biscuit family. The two families also founded the village school in 1846 which was described at the time as 'superior to anything hitherto seen in that rather wild and inaccessible country'. The school closed at Christmas 1973, the remaining children being transferred to Shiplake Church of England primary school, and the building fast fell into disrepair. Eventually the descendants of the owners were traced, the building was renovated and it has now become a village hall of considerable character, retaining its raftered ceiling and high windows, no doubt designed to prevent idle pupils being able to stare out at the view of the valley spread out below.

The church was built in 1842, the architect being John Turner who also designed Rugby school. The land was given by the Crawshay and Palmer families and lies a mile away from the village green further to the north. It is a fine example of Victorian simplicity, built of grey and pink brick with a slate roof. Inside is a memorial plaque commemorating the First World War poet Wilfred Owen who lived for a time at Dunsden vicarage as assistant to the vicar. The graves of his parents and sister can be seen in the churchyard. After Wilfred's death they came to live in nearby Emmer Green.

An interesting feature of the area is the incidence of swallow holes or 'swillies' as they are known locally. These are apparently bottomless ponds and streams that surface only intermittently and then are 'swallowed up'. An impressive example of this occurred in 1955 when a pond formed in old clay workings collapsed into a pit 100–150 ft deep, taking four mature trees with it. During heavy rain, water will collect for a time in certain areas and then disappear suddenly overnight.

🍁 DUNS TEW

A name like 'Duns Tew' cannot fail to excite curiosity and its origin is the subject of considerable speculation. It is thought that Tew means 'ridge', and the village does lie on the North Aston fault, separating limestone and sands in the south from the clay of the north, but there is not a ridge in the usual sense of the word. Duns might come from an Anglo-Saxon called Dunn, perhaps a landowner, and possibly living after the Conquest, as the full name does not appear until the 13th century. Perhaps there is some connection with the names of the other 'Tews', Great and Little Tew, but these villages are some four and five miles distant.

Duns Tew is a very attractive little village with its stone cottages and winding roads. It is well-loved and well-cared for, as is demonstrated by the fact that it has several times won the Best Kept Village competition, including the Best of the Winners category.

The church of St Mary Magdalene is an important centre in Duns Tew. Set in its beautifully cared-for churchyard this medieval church has a healthy congregation of all ages and has a thriving Sunday school. An army of flower arrangers, cleaners and gardeners ensures the church itself is looked after.

The closure of Duns Tew village shop was a great loss, particularly to people without transport, and also because another meeting place has disappeared. People shop in Banbury or Deddington or from the various mobile shops that come to the village, which is in stark contrast to how things were in 1841 when there were a family of stonemasons, five carpenters, five wheelwrights, four shoemakers, four tailors, three blacksmiths, two slaters, two grocers, two bakers, one butcher and one joiner – all in Duns Tew! Fortunately the White Horse pub still survives, so all is not yet lost. But this survey does underline how occupations have altered. Although the village does have two building firms, a soil and sand specialist, a kitchen joinery firm and a children's clothing company, most people do not work in Duns Tew, but commute to another nearby town, or even to London.

There are still people in the village who remember going to the village school. It was eventually closed due to lack of pupils, and in 1965 the Parish Council bought the building for the many organisations in the village to use. One of these is the Duns Tew Drama Group, which has been in being for about 20 years. All proceeds from their performances are donated to worthy causes such as the church appeal or the children's play area. In 1996 a farmer, Mr Johnnie Rae, donated two acres of farmland for the use of the village children. The children serve on the fund raising committee, and enough money has been raised for, amongst other things, basketball, skateboarding and roller blading! Duns Tew has a great community feeling which travels through all its people, young and old.

🍁 EAST CHALLOW

The village lies at the foot of the Downs, about five and a half miles from the famous White Horse Hill. It has expanded over the last few years, growing from a village, which consisted of houses dotted either side of the main Faringdon Road, west of the nearest town of Wantage, to a fairly large area populated by about 1,500 people.

Not many of the buildings are of a great age, except a farm called Woodhill, whose deeds date back to the 1400s, and one or two old cottages situated alongside the village green, where the now defunct water pump still stands.

Opposite the green stands the church, which has had restoration work done to the exterior over the years and has some interesting features inside, such as a Norman font, 13th century arches and a window which dates from 1100. The chancel screen was erected in memory of four villagers who drowned in the North Sea in 1905.

Originally the main industries were farming and foundry work, which took place in what was an old coaching inn before being altered by Nalder and Nalder to house the equipment for making office grinding machines. These were exported all over the world.

This building was on the banks of the old Berks and Wilts canal which thrived by means of shipping coal, hay, coffee machines and other goods throughout its length. A former village resident, a Mr Hiskins, used to ply his coal barges from Wantage Wharf past Challow and on to Swindon and beyond.

Now with the closure of the foundry, smaller industrial units are housed on the site, making various components for use in other products.

The old school, which was designed by C. E. Street, has been converted into a residential home without losing its original charm of grey stone. Villagers have a choice of social activities. There is a thriving cricket club and British Legion, both of which are situated up the hill, the village hall, and at the lower end of the village is a newly built country club with a sports complex.

The village pub, the Goodlake, so named after a benefactor who lived in nearby Letcombe, was run by members of the Lovegrove family for 130 years until the death of the last member of the family in the 1970s.

🍁 EAST HENDRED

East Hendred is a lovely old village lying at the foot of the Berkshire Downs, surrounded by farms and orchards. It is four miles from Wantage and to the south of the A417 trunk road. Its name is derived from the Anglo-Saxon 'Hennerithe' or 'rill of the waterhens'.

Like many another English village its roots go deep into the past, to Saxon times and beyond. After the Norman Conquest, Norman knights and abbots were given land in Hendred. The village was divided into five manors and names like King's Manor, Abbey Manor and Framptons are reminders of those feudal days. King's Manor still retains a Crown Stewardship last exercised in 1901.

The manor of Arches or Hendred House has been occupied by the Eystons since 1453 and this gracious house is a focal point in the village. Incorporated into the house is the little Saxon chapel of St Amand. In 1688, when William of Orange was marching to Oxford, some of his soldiers desecrated the chapel. The Eyston family were related by marriage to Sir Thomas More, Chancellor to Henry VIII. They have two precious relics; the drinking cup of Sir Thomas More and the staff used by the aged John Fisher, Bishop of Rochester, as he climbed to the scaffold at Tyburn to be executed with More.

The chapel of Jesus of Bethlehem stands on what would have been the centre of the medieval village. With its priest's cottage attached, it was built in an unusual design by the Carthusian monks of Sheen in the 15th century. It now houses a small museum, open on Sunday afternoons, showing different aspects of village life. The Parish Council also meets there.

There are Anglican and Roman Catholic churches in East Hendred with a good record of ecumenism over the past years. The ancient parish church of St Augustine stands on a slight rise. Its architecture is Early English and it has a fine peal of bells. The faceless clock, with its wooden workings still intact, plays 'The Angels' Hymn' every three hours. Inside the church there is the 13th century nave and a Crusader lectern thought to be unique. The Victorian-Gothic Roman Catholic church was built by the Eyston family in 1858.

'Pit pat, pan's hot,
Here we come a'shroving

88

With a batcher up my back
A halfpenny is better than nothing.'

This is the jingle sung by the children as they converge on Hendred House at midday on Shrove Tuesday accompanied by parents and teachers for the traditional bun and a halfpenny ceremony. The centuries-old custom is enjoyed by the children, each of whom, after chanting the song, is given a bun and (today) a penny by the Squire, Mr Eyston.

Another custom which still prevails is the distribution of flour to 24 old people on St Thomas' Eve. In the old days this was given as corn which was then taken to the mill in Mill Lane to be ground.

For many years East Hendred has been associated with racing stables and a common sight is that of a string of fine racehorses going to and from the gallops on the downs. A Grand National winner came from the Turnell stable.

Most age groups are catered for in the village. Football, cricket and tennis are played on a fine sports field used by young and not so young. Although the forge is no longer in use, other crafts are practised here, from pottery to hand-carved furniture. There is also a small vineyard where the MacKinnon family grow, press, ferment and bottle their grape harvest.

The village is especially fortunate in having two schools, three pubs, a shop and post office and an hourly bus service to Wantage and Didcot. Snells Hall, the former Church of England school, serves the village as a community centre and has been extended as part of the national Millennium programme. The village also has its own website.

Originally an agricultural community, mechanisation has meant the loss of many jobs on the farms. Fortunately the siting of the Atomic Energy Research Establishment, the Esso Research Centre and the JET Project, in the neighbourhood, has meant an influx of people into the villages around, including East Hendred, whose numbers have swelled to 1,300 with the arrival of scientists, engineers and other staff.

🍁 ENSTONE

As motorists rush through the village of Enstone on their way from the Midlands, to London or the South, probably their only concern is whether the speed-camera situated in the centre of the village is in operation? If they would slow down, or even stop and venture from their cars, they would find a thriving community of about 1,000 inhabitants, made up of villagers whose names can be traced back to the earliest records living close to neighbours who have settled in the village, mostly in the last 30 years.

Enstone has the second largest Parish Council area in Oxfordshire and is made up of the villages of Church Enstone, Neat Enstone and hamlets Broadstone Hill, Chalford, Cleveley, Fulwell, Gagingwell and Lidstone. Although these hamlets now only provide homes for small numbers, they have in the past been flourishing communities, with prosperous residents living in substantial houses.

Enstone is mentioned in the Domesday Book as Henestan, and is believed to take its name from Enestan which was the Saxon word for 'giant stone'. It is not known if this refers to the Hoar Stone which stands at the Fulwell crossroads, and is believed to be part of a prehistoric burial mound. This ancient site has become neglected and overgrown over the years, but is now being purchased by the Parish Council from private ownership.

Church Enstone occupies the northern side of the peaceful Glyme valley, through which the stream meanders silently from its source at Chipping Norton, towards the lake at Blenheim Palace and then onwards to the river Thames at Oxford. As the church is dedicated to St Kenelm, we can deduce that a religious building has stood on this site since the early 9th century. The present church, with its Norman and Early English architecture, was probably added to the original building from the 11th century onward. Just below the church stands the impressive tithe barn built by William of Wynchecombe in 1382, and in the valley there is an 18th century water mill, which although no longer in use still retains its water wheel.

The word Neat is added to Enstone to distinguish it from Church Enstone and signifies the black cattle or oxen which grazed the land before the Enclosures. It is through this part of the village that the busy A44 road passes, reminding us that before the railway era, Enstone was on the main coach road from the Midlands. It was to service the passing coach trade that the many inns became associated with the village, though sadly only the Crown at Church Enstone and the Harrow on the main road remain as public houses.

Near the Harrow, on the north side of the river Glyme, Enstone's most famous feature was situated. It was during the 1620s that Thomas Bushell constructed a water garden and grotto, by making use of an existing rock and a prolific clear spring, known as Goldwell. For a relatively short period, there was a banqueting hall, fountains and cascades of water, which would suddenly change direction and drench unsuspecting onlookers. The gardens reached the height of their fame in the 1630s, when Charles I and Queen Henrietta visited and enjoyed a programme of 'speeches and songs'. Bushell died in the 1670s, the gardens fell into a state of neglect, and any remains were finally destroyed in the mid-19th century. Nothing is left of this part of Enstone's history; even the yew tree, under which the 'band played', was blown down in the gales of the 1980s.

More recent history has been described in Sheila Stewart's book *Lifting the Latch*. This transcribes the words of Mont Abbot, who for over 80 years lived and worked on the land around Enstone. Many of the smaller village organisations still use the Parish Hall, whose opening in 1922 was described in *Lifting the Latch*. But there is now a much larger Youth Hall, and a vibrant Sports and Social Club, which provide much of the varied social life in the village.

Enstone is lucky to still have a village grocery shop and a post office, but there is little new industry to replace employment lost from agriculture and other traditional rural occupations. One interesting change of use, on the site of a former stone quarry, is Whiteways Technical Centre. Here, Formula One racing cars are researched and constructed, to compete in Benetton's racing colours at Grand Prix around the world.

However, an active primary school ensures that the next generation are not only being provided with the technological skills for the future, but are also learning to value the best traditions of the past.

🍁 EWELME

The school at Ewelme is reputed to be the oldest building in the county to be used as a primary school, with about 40 children attending now. The roof in the upper class room is of the same style as the roof in Westminster Hall in London.

The church, dating from 1436, bears many resemblances to those in East Anglia, built in flint, stone and brick. It was built by William and Alice de la Pole, Countess of Suffolk and said to be modelled on Wingfield Church in Suffolk. There are still families in the village by the name of 'Winfield'.

There have been about 30 new houses in Ewelme in the post war period and many of the older ones have been modernised. Luckily there is still a shop-cum-post office and a bus service runs to Wallingford three times a day. A car service is run to Benson Surgery two days a week and people with cars kindly transport those without. This service is much appreciated by the doctors and patients.

The Almshouses, built in 1437, were modernised a few years ago, and in order to do so the 13 had to be reduced to eight. Alice, Duchess of Suffolk, ordained that there should be 13 almshouses and a Master's house so, now the odd five have been built in the main street. The Master is the Regius Professor of Medicine at Oxford and he and his family can use the 'lodgings' whenever they wish and many make full use of them. The snag to the almshouses for the elderly is that whichever way they are approached there is a slight hill or steps to get up. Not very thoughtful of Alice?

The famous watercress beds are in limbo, which is sad after being a well-known feature throughout the years. Ewelme watercress was highly sought after in London and Birmingham.

You are not considered a true Ewelmeite unless you have fallen in the brook which runs all down the street and through the watercress beds on its way to Benson and the river Thames. Otters have been seen at the Benson end, and kingfishers are often seen near the bridge at Ewelme, plus many other water birds.

🍁 EYNSHAM

Over the centuries the name of the village has changed no less than 13 times. The 'old 'uns' used to refer to it as Ensam, spelt Ensham, its last spelling before the present one which has been in use for most of the 20th century and is not likely to be changed again.

A Benedictine Abbey was founded here in 1005 and became very wealthy, owning land throughout Oxfordshire. The abbey was surrendered to Henry VIII in 1539. The ruins stood for a couple of centuries and then, as they began to deteriorate, the land became a quarry. The only remains now are carved pieces of stone built into many of the cottages and garden walls. Perhaps the villagers were encouraged to cart it away and build their own dwellings, some of which still remain today.

The abbey also owned the flour and corn mill, the yearly rent payable by the miller being ten shillings and 450 eels. Many years later it became a paper mill supplying fine paper for the bible presses, and it was there that experiments were carried out to make paper from grass. During the early part of the 20th century it became a glue, rag and flock mill. Rags were turned into cheap flock mattresses. This all came to an end in the late 1920s, but the old mill buildings had a further use. The rubble from them was used as ballast when the nearby A40 was built in 1935. The lovely mill house still remains.

One fly in the ointment for the people of Eynsham, and of course further afield, is the toll bridge at Swinford, which has been here since the 18th century. Apparently one day King George III was travelling through to Burford, but at that time there was nothing but a ford across the Thames. The river was high, and the King's coach and horses almost foundered in the river. It was because of this that the owner Lord Abingdon was granted, by Act of Parliament, the right to build a bridge and charge a toll on everything that passed over, the takings to be tax free for ever. This of course still holds today. But the owners have to keep both the bridge and roadway over it in good repair. Now only mechanical vehicles are charged to drive over.

Eynsham villagers were, and still are, proud of their Morris dancers. There has been a side here on and off for over 125 years. They are known as The Eynsham Morris, their dances differ from any other group and are renowned for their speed and vigour. Before the First World War the dancers used to perform at all the big houses at Christmas time, including Blenheim Palace. One of the members of the Eynsham Morris was called 'Feathers' Russell, because he always wore pheasants' feathers in his hat. He was a tall and very good looking man. He must have impressed the Duke of Marlborough, because he commissioned a painter, William Nicholson, to paint a portrait of Feathers in his Morris dancing outfit. The portrait called 'Chairing the Dancer' now hangs in Cecil Sharpe House in London.

War broke up the Morris men, but in 1980 Keith Green, a member of an old Eynsham family, formed a new group. Now they dance all over Great Britain and are often invited abroad to dance at big festivals. A delightful song called The Eynsham Poaching Song is often sung at their gatherings.

Eynsham has, like many other places, changed dramatically over the years. Once an agricultural village, now there are only a couple of farms here. At one time many of the menfolk went off to work in the car factories at Cowley, now

93

there are several new factories on the outskirts of Eynsham, employing both local men and women.

 FARMOOR

Farmoor is a small village to the west of Oxford and is a part of Cumnor parish. Wytham Wood is to the north-east and due west is the river Thames and Swinford toll bridge.

The history of Farmoor goes back to when it was a collection of farms. The landowner was the Earl of Abingdon and in the 1920s the Earl sold his estates and many of the farms came into private ownership. The Franklin brothers, local farmers, bought ex-army huts and erected them in the village. They were occupied mostly by railwaymen. The huts remained in Farmoor until the 1950s when Dean Court Estate was built and the families moved into the new houses.

In 1929 a start was made on building bungalows in Mayfield Road and on the Oxford/Eynsham road. Also in that year a march by the unemployed Welsh miners came through the village on their way to London. Some found work in the car factory at Cowley.

In 1935 a summer camp was organised in Farmoor Meadow for unemployed Welsh miners by the University Labour Club and Balliol College. Open-air services were held because Farmoor had no church. In the autumn a prefabricated wooden hut was erected and this was used regularly for services for the next 62 years. In 1986 a fund was set up with the intention of building a new church. Residents and friends helped in various ways and, with the aid of generous grants and donations, over £50,000 was raised. In 1998 the building was refurbished with the addition of a committee room and facilities for the disabled.

Wimpey built the Meadow Close estate of 80 houses in the 1970s, thus doubling the size of Farmoor. This was on land where cattle had grazed, and filled in between the Oxford Road properties and the reservoir.

In 1962 the village hall was built to replace a wooden hut. There is a village shop with post office, a florist and a garage and workshop. A good bus service operates between Oxford and Witney and the Mobile Library calls alternate weeks.

From 1926 a small Bedford bus, provided by Farmoor Garage, took children from the age of five years to Cumnor school. In 1935, due to the increase of children attending the school, Mr Franklin adapted an old hearse for school transport, which led to headlines in a Paris newspaper: 'English schoolchildren go to school by hearse'. 1938 saw the opening of Botley school which accepted children from Cumnor school at the age of eleven years. Since 1958 they have attended the Matthew Arnold school at Cumnor.

The first stage of Farmoor Reservoir was commenced in 1962 and the second stage followed in the 1970s. Excavations revealed bones of prehistoric animals, as well as the remains of mud villages. Recreational facilities, fishing and sailing are available at the reservoir. Pinkhill Meadow between the reservoir and the river Thames provides six Wetland Habitat Zones. Permits may be obtained from the Warden's Office for birdwatching, and residents of Farmoor can claim passes to walk the footpaths round the reservoir.

❧ FERNHAM

Fernham is a cluster of houses, two farms and a pub, clinging onto a bend in the B4508 road. It was frequently used as a short cut by Oxford/Swindon traffic. Now Faringdon has a bypass the road is slightly more peaceful.

The village presently consists of 75 homes. At one time mainly agricultural, it is now very varied with most people working out of the village and a high proportion of retired people. The part time post office and stores housed in an old stable at the Woodman Inn was closed by the Post Office without warning a while ago. Thankfully for a country village, there is still a bus service. The village hall and youth club is no more, the old chapel is now a house and the parish business is conducted in St John's church. The church, consecrated in 1861, was built at the instigation of Rev John Hughes, vicar of Longcot with Fernham, and still serves the faithful with at least one service almost every Sunday.

The village green is just a name only since the council laid a tarmac road across it as access to the sewerage pumps. Left with two wide grass verges, no longer do the villagers congregate at the village pump on the green to gossip or play at tossing horse shoes at an iron pin. The pump cover erected over the well has recently been restored but the pump is a symbol only, although the old eight foot deep stone-lined bottle well is still intact underneath, safely capped off. The bakehouse behind the original manor house, which was justly famous for its bread and cakes, is gone, the site cleared and three large houses erected on it.

At one time Fernham could boast three general stores, one with a post office, a shoemaker's shop, a coal, oil and candle merchant, a smithy, a hurdle maker, a small market garden, a wagon builder and undertaker, and the obligatory pub. Before that there were two pubs; the house now known as Forge House and previously as The Red House, is thought to have been the Black Horse pub. It's the only house in the village with a cellar! There could also have been a rope maker, with his premises in Baganetts Alley perhaps? Sad to relate now, all that is left is a pub, the Woodman Inn, a free house dating from the early 1700s and a very popular haunt summer and winter.

Fernham residents could look forward to an annual flower show, harvest suppers, a Christmas party for the children and old people at Ringdale Manor and the summer spent cheering on the village cricket team. There was a dame school by the church, the children paying 1d on a Monday for a week's tuition – no penny no admittance! Now the only organisation is the Women's Institute, supported by the neighbouring village of Shellingford.

Fernham has some outlying guardians at 'Nightingale' along the Longcot road, the community of Benedictine nuns at the priory. At one time this was the original Ringdale manor house, but it is now overlooked by the later Ringdale manor, built on the edge of an ancient British camp similar to the one on White Horse Hill.

🍁 Filkins, Broughton Poggs, Langford & Kencott

Filkins, Broughton Poggs, Langford and Kencott are all small villages built in the local stone, bound together by a twisty ribbon of lane, and if you walk across the fields, by the old paths none is more than 15 minutes apart.

Each village has a very definite character of its own. Kencott is so quiet and tidy, the grass so green, the flowers so brilliant. It is no surprise that over and over again it wins the 'Best Kept Village' award. Look a little closer and find a more mysterious side: the dog sees a friendly ghost walk to and fro through a door that was blocked up in 1690; the church was dedicated in the 12th century to St George and on the tympanum and the village sign are figures that most take for St George slaying the dragon – not so, it is Sagittarius the Archer shooting into the mouth of the hound of hell. Hens still wander in the road and the whole street comes alive when the gardens are open in the summer. Then you can wander from cottage to cottage, from stall to stall and buy best home-made produce.

At Broughton Poggs, aeroplanes may roar overhead but inside the thick stone walls is the sweet music of bell ringing. The Old Rectory is said by some to have inspired Trollope to write the *Small House at Allington*. Queen Anne Boleyn may glide down the Ladies' Walk – who are we to argue? It is certainly a creepy spot – much more pleasant to sit on a sun-warmed tombstone by the small Norman church, remembering the monks who looked after the fishponds, and puzzle over the bumps on the field, which are all that remain of the old village.

Langford is the lucky village with a thriving primary school and an enthusiastic cricket club. The highlight of the year is the dance held in a large modern barn, when the caller gets young and old on their toes to the country and square-dance music. All the money goes to charity.

Filkins has a quarry that produces stone slates, and Saxons Close has been listed by the Dept of Environment because they were the first houses to be built by the district council using vernacular materials and traditional skills. It was argued at the time that the small extra initial cost would be outweighed by low maintenance costs, and so it has proved. Next door is the Centre: the doctor's surgery, the community post office (once the village hot baths), the swimming pool and the bowling green. In August the Bowls Club organise the annual flower show in the Carter Institute with skittling on the paddock opposite. Step inside and admire the Edwardian portrait of Mrs Amelia Carter draped in a fur stole. She funded the hall as a reading room for young men – to keep them out of the pubs! – from the profits made in the development of Carterton. No alcohol was allowed but there were two big open fires and a fine billiard table. At the top of the village the Crosstrees farmyard has been redeveloped. Woollen cloth, smocks and shrugs, pictures, furniture, green rushes and stone trefoils have replaced sheep, calves, hens and bulls.

✹ FINMERE & MIXBURY

Finmere and Mixbury are located on the borders of Oxfordshire, Buckinghamshire and Northamptonshire, rich in history and spectacular scenery of outstanding beauty.

There has been a church on the hill at Finmere since 1287. The present St Michael's, built in the 14th century, is well worth a visit. The carvings on the pulpit, pew ends and reredos were done by Rev Seymour Ashwell (1866–1902) who also farmed the Glebe himself; he must have been a very busy man!

In the lane just below the church gates is the old village school built by the Duke of Buckingham in 1824, closed in 1948 but recently tastefully restored to serve as a residence.

The old rectory, built in 1867, replaced the original which was destroyed partly by a violent storm, then three years later by fire. The beautiful gardens were laid out, or rather improved by 'Capability' Brown when he was working on the grounds of Stowe, just a few miles over the Buckinghamshire border.

Finmere House was granted by Henry VIII to four of his Queens in turn. Guess which one with 'her head tucked underneath her arm' is reputed to have been seen in the past drifting through the gardens at night. Some villagers can remember the late King George VI and Edward, Prince of Wales using the Finmere House stables for the hunting season in the 1920s.

The former manor house or court house, now called Bacons House, was owned by the Duke of Buckingham, lord of the manor. Standing on the bank of the Ouse, it had a watermill but the Duke destroyed this, pulling down part of the house at the same time and reducing it to its present size. In 1858 all of the land north of the parish church was sold to Merton College, Oxford.

In the mid 19th century there were two blacksmiths, several butchers, a baker, carpenters, shoemakers, a cattle dealer, cooper, a brickmaker employing three labourers, an innkeeper-brewer, and 98 women and 48 girls above the age of ten made lace. How different now when there is just one shop at the Finmere Garage and the King's Head public house, with hardly anyone working on the land.

During the Second World War there was an aerodrome at Finmere, now this has become the site for what is said to be the largest Sunday market in the country. There is a recently built village hall on the northern outskirts of the village, abutting on the playing field.

Mixbury is a small quiet village now, but you can walk through to the old jousting ground and visualize the Knights of Old fighting for the honour of their chosen damsels. Many ancient relics have been excavated on the site of the old castle.

There is an ancient 11th century church and an old school building (now the village hall). It has been said that at dusk on summer nights children can be heard singing, though it has not been used as a school since the 1950s.

Monk's House Farm is also reputed to be haunted. This contains a bricked-up room and at one time a tunnel led to the church.

Like Finmere, this village has changed considerably. In the 19th century there were five farms (these remain), two carpenters, a mason, a baker, a tailor, a blacksmith and a shopkeeper. Now a number of new houses and bungalows have been built, inhabitants working further afield.

Horse riding is popular in both of these villages and the disused railway provides an interesting nature reserve.

A tributary of the river Ouse runs through the adjoining hamlet of Fulwell which links the two villages.

🍁 FINSTOCK

Finstock is the sort of place you've been to without noticing. People in cars on the B4022, along the ridge of high ground between Witney and Chalbury, may be briefly aware of a road sign and a scatter of houses as they race past, without realising that they are missing Finstock itself which straggles down the eastward-facing slopes of the ridge, overlooking the Evenlode valley. Turn off at the crossroads at the top of the High Street and you will probably pause a moment to admire the view over rooftops and rolling fields into such a far blue distance that at least one awestruck visitor has been known to suggest that you must be able to see to Moscow. You can certainly see the John Radcliffe Hospital and the Beckley Mast. As you follow the bends of the High Street downwards, you will look in vain for any signs of commercial splendour which the name might suggest and it was presumably so called simply because it was higher than the rest of the village. There is a certain dogged obviousness about Finstock street names. High Street, therefore, leads, inevitably, down to The Bottom from where the road curves up again to flatten out into School Road.

Apart from a school, Finstock also boasts a post office, which used to be in someone's garden shed but is now incorporated into the shop, a recreation ground, a village hall, two pubs, a church, marooned by itself on the main road, a railway halt and a bus service, of sorts. The village hall, which started life as a gloving factory, is the meeting place for various village organisations and with the seasonal round of parties, summer fetes and bazaars one always has the impression of something happening in Finstock.

In days gone by, as 19th century census returns show, the inhabitants of Finstock would have earned their living entirely in or around the village, the men mostly as labourers on the farms of the large estates of Cornbury, Blenheim and Wilcote, which surround it, and the women engaged in gloving to eke out the family income. Probably many people would hardly have left the boundaries of the village in a lifetime. Today, however, only a handful of villagers work locally on the land and most commute by car or train to Witney, Oxford, or even further afield to London.

The churchyard, which is carpeted with primroses, violets and lesser celandine in the spring, is a sunny place to sit and contemplate the view over the village, but although Finstock, with the smoke curling lazily upwards from its chimney pots, may appear tranquil enough now, many a lurid tale tells of a more violent and boisterous past. In fact, at one time Finstock must have resembled a frontier town of the American West as it was on the route of the drovers' road from Wales and the West Country to the London markets and at regular times of the year was invaded by gangs of strange men with their bellowing, trampling herds of cattle, looking for a watering-place.

Today, the great forest of Wychwood only marches up to the line of the B4022 but centuries ago Finstock was still within its borders and the forest was a dangerous place. Footpads, vagabonds and highwaymen haunted its coppices and thickets and any well-to-do farmer unwise enough to set off for Charlbury with his pockets stuffed with money was liable to end up thrown in a ditch with his throat cut. The Crown public house, which dates from the 14th century, seems to have been particularly notorious as a rendezvous for thieves, who frequently had to make hasty exits from upper windows, one step ahead of the law. Apart from the incidence of serious crime, there seems to have been a great deal of unruly behaviour in the form of drunken brawls and gang fights between rival villages. Even within living memory, Finstock had a reputation for being both tough and rough and an elderly lady in an adjoining village still recounts with a rueful smile how in her childhood a walk through Finstock often meant risking a hail of stones from hostile urchins.

Anyone walking about in Finstock must also have been aware of the constant sound of running water as several streams, fed by springs high up on the hillside, cascaded down the valley. At least one ran down beside the High Street cottages, which had little bridges across to their garden gates. It must have been a picturesque scene worthy to rival the well-known Cotswold tourist traps of today. In 1928, however, the streams were enclosed in pipes and covered over and like them Finstock seems to have been gradually quietened and tamed.

🍁 FOREST HILL

With a population of about 700, Forest Hill (administratively part of Forest Hill with Shotover) lies on a hillside just to the east of Oxford. Stone houses cluster along the three roads making up the village, and together with one remaining pub and a Norman church form a central conservation area, while Shotover House and its surrounding parklands lie to the south, separated from the village by the main A40. In the centre of the village, the former King's Arms public house has been turned into a private house, the owners of which believe the building was once a standing tower used as a hunting lodge in Tudor times.

The road system, which still exists, was fundamental to the primitive hamlet of Forst Hyll (Old English meaning 'hill ridge'). At the bottom of the hill ran a road to Oxford, to the west went the Roman road from Dorchester to Alchester, and a Saxon track ran to Brill. But the most important of these routes was the one to Islip (birthplace of Edward the Confessor) and now the B4027. This ran on to Woodstock, with its royal palace, and in stagecoach days was part of the turnpike to Worcester and Holyhead.

In more recent times, the M40 was finally finished in 1991, running a few miles north of the village on a route that avoided Otmoor. The closing of the gap on the Oxford-London A40 has made the road safer and has dramatically reduced the through traffic in the village, but has meant a long detour for villagers and visitors.

The village appears in Domesday Book as the manor of Fostel. It passed to those great Oxford landlords, Oseney Abbey and the monastery of St Frideswide, while the adjoining manor, held by the prioress of Littlemore, is still remembered in the modern Minchincourt Farm. The parish church, originally a chapel of the church at Stanton St John, was dedicated to St Nicholas the Confessor.

The best known of the tenants of Manor Farm was Richard Powell, a spendthrift Royalist who had borrowed £500 from a John Milton of Stanton St John. Interest on the loan went to Milton's son John, the great Puritan poet and pamphleteer. While in pursuit of his money the poet met and in 1642, to general astonishment, married Powell's daughter Mary, then aged 16. It was an unhappy alliance and Mary soon returned from London to a happier life in Forest Hill. She bore Milton four children, but died in 1652 aged 25. There is a stone seat opposite the church, called Milton's Stone, where the poet reputedly sat to wait for Mary.

In the late 18th century Manor Farm again had literary associations when William Julius Mickle lived there and translated the Portugese epic, the *Luciads*. Mickle was a considerable poet, a friend of Boswell and Johnson; he was buried in the village churchyard. But perhaps the most colourful individual of this period was the Reverend John Mavor who in the 1820s ran into debt over the building of a new vicarage. He spent some time in Oxford gaol, from where he managed to fulfil many of his parish duties, even apparently being let out on Sundays to conduct services.

Later in the 19th century, the village changed rapidly. Manor Farm was demolished and rebuilt in 1854 by Lincoln College, red-brick houses were built and, important to daily life, a post office opened in 1882. Standpipes in the streets supplied water from the village well. An austere Methodist chapel was built at the end of the century and facing it an equally austere village hall. Most villagers were still employed on the land while the local woods enabled hurdle makers to follow their craft.

The First World War changed all this. Sixteen men did not return, a large number for a small village. New agricultural techniques meant fewer men were needed on the land, but above all the motor works at Cowley became the main employer. The first council houses were built, the telephone was available for the prosperous, and electricity and street lighting arrived in the 1930s. Transport was much improved – buses made the shops and cinemas of Headington and Oxford accessible and the vigorous social life of the pre-war village was to some extent replaced by more urban pleasures.

Since the Second World War many new houses have been built and the village remembers its brushes with literary history in Milton Crescent,

Powell Close and Mickle Way. Apart from members of the families, employment on the two highly mechanised farms has almost disappeared. Work in the motor industry has waxed and waned with the fortunes of Cowley. The almost universal ownership of cars has made the large supermarkets around Oxford available and there are no shops, not even a post office, left in the village. Deep drainage has made even the oldest houses more pleasant and recently mains gas has become available.

Many of the villagers are now newcomers, finding Forest Hill pleasant and convenient. The Methodist chapel has been converted into a private house but the village hall is still put to good use. The church is now part of the combined Wheatley Team Ministry but still attracts a significant congregation.

🍁 FREELAND

Freeland is a village not on the way to anywhere. It straggles along a road between the Oxford-Witney and Witney-Woodstock roads. On approaching the green, splendid with daffodils in spring, the cluster of cottages and pond with ducks make a typical village picture, and on going past the pond to take in the view towards Oxford, one can sometimes find a shoot of bracken – a defiant relic of the old heathland.

Freeland began as a squatter settlement on the outer reaches of Eynsham as early as 1650, and after the enclosures of the 18th century the settlement grew. Squatter cottages were built with the narrow wall by the road, thereby using the minimum frontage.

One of these cottages in the centre of the village is now the Oxfordshire Yeoman pub. In 1973 the brewers, Morrells, wanted to rename one of their public houses after the old county regiment. As the site of the New Inn, Freeland was acquired in 1842 by one William Merry, yeoman, it was the one chosen. At the other end of the village, on the Witney-Woodstock road is another public house with a long history. Although not quite in the Cotswolds the area provided grazing for sheep. By the drove road was an inn providing all the shepherds needed, and it became known as the Shepherds All. In later years, someone who evidently thought the locals were unable to speak properly added an 'H' and Shepherds Hall it remains to this day.

Back on the main road through the village is a cottage which can answer a common question asked by strangers about the unusual name of the road –

Wroslyn. This ivy-covered cottage was once an inn (suitably far from the centre of the village) where wrestling bouts were held. In this part of Oxfordshire wrestling was pronounced 'wrosling' so when road names were requested the Parish Council preserved this little part of our history. The cottage is called Wrestlers and the bungalow built on the field where the bouts took place, Wrestlers Mead.

The little stone Methodist chapel was built in 1805, to the 'greatest mortification' of Thomas Symonds, then curate, later vicar at Eynsham. It is the earliest of such buildings in the Witney-Faringdon Circuit. Through the members' long friendship with New Zealand hymn writer Colin Gibson, there is now a hymn tune called *Freeland*.

With the completion of the building of the church in 1869 Freeland became a separate parish. Since the population of the hamlet was only about 200 at that time, it is perhaps an unexpected place to find a 'gem' of a small church designed by one of the greatest Victorian church architects, John Loughborough Pearson. This virtually unchanged Tractarian church was built thanks to the generosity of the Taunton family and other benefactors from the Oxford Movement. The stained glass and interior decoration are by another leading Victorian firm of Clayton and Bell. The chancel is decorated with 13th century-style wall paintings which are echoed on the pulpit and font. Pearson later added a carved alabaster reredos. The parsonage and a school were designed and built as one group of buildings with the church.

At the end of the 19th century there were some brick kilns which used clay from North Leigh common, and the row of houses at the north end of the village known as Red City are made of these local bricks. A number of villagers were employed as out-workers by the Woodstock glove factories. Now, in common with many Oxfordshire villages Freeland has a 'light industrial complex'.

🍁 FRITWELL

Fritwell in the Elms the old books say, though alas most of the elms have gone now. It is L-shaped, divided into two parts by the brook, the source of the Little Ouse. The east-west road now runs to Somerton and crosses one of the few stretches of the Portway that remains north of the Thames. A number of the stone-built houses date back to 1636.

The church, situated by the village green at the northern end of the village, is 11th century, dedicated to St Olaf. It has many interesting features including a fine tympanum with ball and chevron over the south door. Over the north door is cable moulding ending in grotesque animal heads. There are traces of a small monastery nearby.

The school opened in 1872 is still thriving and now serves five villages. May Day used to be a big day in the school calendar. A king and queen elected by the children paraded round the village, followed by the scholars singing traditional songs and carrying a garland of spring flowers. After a scrumptious tea, the day ended with dancing round the maypole. This event is still held each year, but takes place at the school, as the village has become too big for the children to visit each house.

The playing field was established in 1973. This is used mainly by the local football team and has facilities for children. To get the field in good condition a sponsored stone pick was organised.

After the Queen's Silver Jubilee celebrations in 1977 when the whole village united for a carnival day, it was decided to carry on the fun and have an annual carnival, all organisations in the village participating.

In 1908 *Rubio*, owned by Mr Bletsoe of Dove House Farm and trained by Mr Withington, won the Grand National horse race. Prior to the race, it was shod by local blacksmith Mr Gibbs. The forge has now been replaced by a road of houses called Forge Place.

Each end of the village had its own manor house. The older one at the southern end is now Lodge Farm. The Elizabethan manor at the northern end dates from 1596 and is reputedly haunted. Sir John Simons (Chancellor of the Exchequer) lived in this one during the 1930s. During the time he lived there, a magnificent stone water tower was built which is still used, also a substantial villa in the gardens along with a recreation hall.

Transport has changed, not for the better. In the 1930s buses ran from the village garage to Banbury and Oxford very frequently and a good train service existed from Fritwell and Somerton station. The carrier's cart went to Banbury several times a week and the driver would make purchases and deliver them for a small fee. Now buses run to Banbury and Bicester two days a week – very infrequently, and the station is closed.

Two public houses survive, one shop and a post office. Dew's stores opened in 1885 and in its heyday almost anything could be bought there. People were employed there and at the butcher's and slaughterer's, garage, post office, blacksmith, bakery, farm, railway and laundry. The blacksmith, bakery and laundry have gone but the others still serve the community well. Individual craftsmen covering a wide range of skills offer employment. We now have a small development of 19 houses and another one to be built consisting of 12 houses.

Fritwell, on the edge of the Cotswolds, is still unspoilt. It is easy to take a walk in solitude with views of idyllic countryside, or if you favour progress watch the M40 carving a swathe across the Cherwell valley.

🍁 FULBROOK

Fulbrook village is to be found on the north-eastern outskirts of historic Burford Town. It starts from the river Windrush boundary at Burford bridge and continues for about three-quarters of a mile to the Shipton Downs. It contains a church, two public houses and a small hotel.

The name Fulbrook comes from two sources. The brook starts as a spring on farmland to the north of the village, and runs mostly underground into the Windrush. The 'Ful' part comes from a shortening of the name 'fuller', a person who washed and shrank their wool and cloth in the local brook. A source of fuller's earth was also found in the same area and it was used to absorb grease from the woollen fleeces. Fulbrook was known to be a prosperous area for sheep farming, and to have connections with the wool markets of surrounding towns such as Burford and Chipping Norton. Several 17th century wool-staplers' tombs can be seen in the churchyard.

Fulbrook has always been a separate entity from Burford, and had its own religious settlement on the site of the present church – St James the Great – in Saxon times. There is a massive English yew tree in the churchyard, with a girth of $19\frac{1}{2}$ feet, known to be nearly 1,000 years old, and thought to have been planted at the start of the last millennium. It is registered with the conservation foundation.

Fulbrook was recorded in the Domesday Book of 1086 as having five manors in the village, and was originally held by the Earl of Winchester. Examples of at least two manors can still be found at Westhall Hill and Pytts House, near the church. The original village was sited behind the church on land which adjoined the famous Wychwood Forest, an ancient royal hunting estate from Saxon times onwards, known to harbour gypsies, miscreants and poachers. During Saxon and Norman times, when the church was rebuilt, the open field areas were used for jousting tournaments and houses built in the area of Upper End have names such as 'The Roarings' and 'Knightspill' which bear testament to this activity.

The village is mainly made up of attractive honey-coloured stone houses, greying with age, and with stone slate roofs. The majority are tucked away in pretty lanes off the main road. Many of the properties overlook the cultivated rolling fields leading to the Windrush valley. The water meadows of the river attract many varieties of birds such as herons and swans, and other species of wildlife.

GARSINGTON

About five miles east of Oxford lies the village of Garsington. It is mentioned in the Domesday Book but its origins date back well before that time.

The lovely parish church of St Mary, situated on a hill top, is visible for many miles around. The site commands magnificent views. The Norman tower of the church is the oldest part dating back to 1160, the nave and chancel having been added later in the 13th century.

Garsington boasts many splendid houses of historic value. Although dating back to the early 16th century many appear little changed from the time of construction. The most famous of these is the manor house built about 1625 on an earlier site. It is thought to be one of the most beautiful of the smaller period houses throughout Oxfordshire, set in superb grounds which are open to the public twice a year. The garden incorporates two yew hedges which are said to be the highest in England.

During the First World War when Philip Morrell, who was the MP for Oxfordshire South, and Lady Ottoline took up residence, the manor became much celebrated. Firstly for its use as a refuge for conscientious objectors and later because of the many famous people entertained there, among them Bertrand Russell, Aldous Huxley, D. H. Lawrence and Virginia Woolf. A small two-storey cottage contained within the manor grounds, known as the Bakehouse or Monastery Cottage, was used by artist friends.

Another prominent building, a Tudor Gothic-style school house was opened to its first pupils in 1840 and was used until a modern primary school was built nearby in 1982. The old school house still stands resplendent in the centre of the village and in spite of being converted and modernised for dwelling purposes, the exterior is little changed.

Near the end of the old school wall stands a medieval village cross, recorded in 1240. A new head and shaft was needed but the base has survived the passage of time. This cross held pride of place on the village green many years ago, but the green is now sadly depleted.

The Gizzle, meaning a field or spring-fed pond, should surely be mentioned. Until modern pumping equipment was installed, many people from the village drew water from the Gizzle in buckets, using wooden yokes to carry it home. Recently cared for by the Garsington Scout troop, it is a pleasant corner to rest awhile, if rather tucked away. It can be approached via a footpath from the church or by road passing the manor.

With regard to footpaths, it is said that Garsington has probably more than any other Oxfordshire village. The fields are criss-crossed with them, probably due to the fact that during the 19th century many of the villagers earned their living on the land with so many farms and market gardens nearby. Some of the old stones, placed upright as stiles, can still be seen.

Whilst farming dominated, a flourishing brick works at Kiln Farm was started about the middle of the 19th century. This provided alternative employment for the villagers and as well as being used locally, the bricks were transported to other nearby villages.

The population could not have been large at the time of the 18th century, nonetheless six victuallers were then licensed. Today the number has been reduced to three.

The close proximity of the motor industry starting up in the 1920s, and the ease of travel, has made Garsington a popular village in which to live. Many modern houses have been built, and the population has almost doubled in recent years, numbering 2,000 or more.

A wide and varied programme of traditional activities is enjoyed, incorporating the church, village hall, public houses etc. Splendidly situated in a field on the outskirts of the village is a sports club much used for sporting and social events.

🍁 GOOSEY

The manor of Goosey was given to the monks of Abingdon Abbey and a cell was established here in the 12th century. Abbey Farm still serves as a reminder of the monastic connection, and legend tells of an underground passage used by the monks leading from the farm to the church, but it has never been found. The monks wore long black serge robes and are remembered today, with their geese, on the altar cloth in the tiny 13th century church which stands at the south-east corner of the spacious and open green.

The former village inn, The Pound, now a private residence, stands at the western entrance and was the setting for music and dancing at the Goosey Feast held every November in the 18th and 19th centuries. This Feast has been revived and still takes place on the village green each year, but at the beginning of September and in a rather different form.

Five beautiful old farmhouses and the village school, now a private residence, surround the green. Goosey mere stands in the south-west corner and is now somewhat overgrown but was once used as a skating rink by the villagers and also supplied the water for their domestic chores.

Geese no longer graze on the green but villagers still retain grazing rights and its character has remained unchanged over the centuries.

Church Farm, Goosey, dated 1670

🍁 GORING

Goring has developed as a rural community on the east bank of the river Thames in the Goring Gap. It lies in one of the most attractive reaches where the river flows through an area of outstanding beauty.

Here, long ago, the Icknield Way, one of the great early highways, crossed the river by means of a ford and joined up with the great Berkshire Ridgeway. Today these two ancient ways form the basis of the modern Ridgeway Path running from Ivinghoe Beacon in Buckinghamshire to Overton Hill near Marlborough.

The two highways were used extensively for driving sheep from East Anglia to the great fairs in the west. This unfortunately attracted the attention of sheep rustlers who proved difficult to contain.

From Saxon times Goring had a corn mill which was of great benefit. From Norman times until the 15th century it was owned by the prestigious Abbey of Bec in Normandy. Later, the mill provided electricity for the village but it is now a residence.

The church of St Thomas of Canterbury is late 11th century and was probably built by Robert D'Oyley, the first Norman lord of Goring. In the 12th century a small group of Augustinian nuns founded a priory adjoining a church, which building they shared with the parishioners. Later, the nuns built their own church to the east of the parish church, separated from it by an interior wall.

The parish church has an interesting brass of Hugh Whistler and his family. Hugh's age at his death appears to have been '216' years according to the inscription. This is probably a careless engraving of the more likely '46', too great a flourish being provided to the first downward stroke of the '4'.

The church also has one of the oldest bells in the country, cast about 1290 by Richard de Wymbis. It hangs on a bracket in the church but is no longer rung.

One of the greatest disasters in the village's history was the tragedy in July 1674 when a boat returning to Streatley after the Goring Fair and containing 50–60 persons, passed too close to the weir and overturned. All but 14 persons were drowned, together with one horse. This was before the first pound lock at Goring was built in 1787.

The earliest recorded bridge over the Thames at Goring was erected upstream of the old ferry in 1837. It was a toll bridge and the various charges created some rather absurd situations. A person crossing by foot was required to pay 1d, but if he drove a calf or pig over he paid only ¹/₂d. It is said one Goring man always took his pig with him when he crossed the bridge to save himself a little money. The bridge was rebuilt in 1923 and all tolls abolished.

The oldest lay buildings in the village are reputed to be a 15th century barn belonging to the Old Farm House in Station Road and parts of the Old Vicarage which may be 16th century.

A number of large houses were demolished in the 20th century and small housing estates developed on the sites. The demand for more housing accommodation indicates how Goring has changed in recent times.

The oldest inn is the Catherine Wheel in Station Road, which was the main street at one time; the inn may date back to Elizabethan times. The largest inn is the Miller of Mansfield, a name taken from an old legend concerning a miller who entertained King Henry II with a pie made from poached royal deer.

Goring lies in fine farming country providing a source of employment, particularly in the past. Notable industries no longer existing include the boat building firm of Samuel Saunders, who took over Goring wharf and built the Springfield Works near South Stoke. Later the firm developed successful speed boats and steam launches and then moved to Cowes. In 1929 it operated under the name of Saunders-Roe of flying boat fame.

The village also had a brewery, established in the 19th century, which later became Gundry and Co. The business declined and was sold in 1940.

Today, despite a certain reputation for becoming a commuters' dormitory due to the convenient train service to London, there are numerous organisations, most of which are thriving. Various river sports have their own clubs. The Goring and Streatley Regatta, one of the most important on the river in its heyday and which failed after 1914, was revived in 1992.

 GREAT COXWELL

Great Coxwell lies two miles south-west of Faringdon, and before the boundary reorganisation in 1974 was in the county of Berkshire.

Most of the surrounding farm land is owned by the National Trust, as are the Great Barn and Court House, which are also maintained by the Trust.

A Neolithic site was recently found near the Iron Age hill fort of Badbury Hill, part of which is planted by the Forest Commission. There are lovely walks around it, and a new route encompasses the Great Barn, Court House and thence the village.

The Great Barn and parts of the Court House are all that remain of the 13th century Grange, once part of Beaulieu Abbey. The Great Barn, built about 1250, is 152ft long, 44ft wide and 48ft high, and is described in a leaflet available on site. It is an impressive building and is open to the public at all times, although the nearby Court House is not. A sit-down lunch for over 250 people was held in the barn in celebration of the Queen's Silver Jubilee in 1977 and again in 1995 to commemorate VE Day.

The main village, most of it a conservation area, stretches to the south of the barn for about one mile down the main street, once called Horsleaze Lane.

The older properties are built mainly of corallian limestone rubble (the local stone, quarried from behind the village) and there are some 19th century brick-built cottages. The original roofing was of Cotswold tiles or thatch, in later years replaced by slate, corrugated iron or modern clay tiles. The majority of new building is post-1960.

Little more than 50 years ago the village had a church, chapel, school, public house, reading room, shops, a butcher, a seamstress, farmers and a laundress. Now only the church, parish reading room (opened 12th December 1901) and a small part-time sub-post office remain. The school closed in 1965, the Royal Oak public house in the early 1960s and the last shop in 1987.

The small 12th century church of St Giles, with a 14th century tower, is plain and simple inside. Note the brasses of the Mores (Morys) family, circa 1509 and the kneelers, all worked by village ladies in the early 1970s. The church registers from 1557 are now in the county archives at Reading. The churchyard is not now used for burials and a survey during the summer of 1989 identified over 75 different species of wild flowers and grasses. If seen in June or July it gives the impression of a pre-war meadow, winning a BBONT award in 1997. From the south side of the churchyard there is a distant view of the Uffington White Horse.

🍁 GREAT HASELEY

This lovely little village with its thatched cottages and many listed buildings, is situated south of the A329 which runs between Thame and Stadhampton. It nestles to the south of the ridge and is thus to some extent sheltered from the north winds. Houses on the south side of the village enjoy views of the Chilterns stretching from Chinnor to the Wittenham Clumps.

Roman coins have been dug up in the churchyard and it is thought that there was a settlement here from very early times. A document, now in the Bodleian Library, Oxford, shows that by AD 800 there was a church here, dedicated to St Peter, as it still is. Part of the font is thought to be Saxon. The village is mentioned in the Domesday Book and at that time belonged to Milo Crispin, who held it as a reward for his services to William the Conqueror.

At the Restoration of the Monarchy in 1660 there were two rectors living here, one of whom had retired in Cromwell's time because of disagreements over the services. In Charles II's reign he reappeared and tried to turn out the rector who had replaced him. At one service both rectors tried to preach at the same time; the congregation took sides and there was a great furore, hats and other objects being hurled about and fighting going on.

In the 1700s considerable building work took place in Haseley. Among the houses built were Highway Cottage, Long Row (the whole row cost £173 to build), Sundial House, Church Farm (note the windows blocked up when a window tax was imposed to help pay for the Napoleonic wars), the Crown Inn, now a private house, the Windmill and the middle part of Haseley Court.

During the 19th century the church fell into decay, but an appeal was launched to put it in order. None of the 180 different coats of arms were replaced but the Muirhead family, who lived at the Court, and who traced their ancestry back to Roger le Bigod, had their coat of arms (with Norman ships and shells) placed in a window of the south aisle. The Muirheads took their responsibilities as squires of the village very seriously and were liberal benefactors to the church.

In 1885 there was a disastrous fire in Haseley, when the village laundry at the bottom of Church Hill was destroyed. A spark from the chimney set fire to the thatched roof. Flames driven by a high wind set fire to the thatched roofs across the way and six cottages were soon alight. Someone on horseback galloped the six miles to Thame to call the volunteer fire brigade. By the time the horse-drawn fire engine arrived and got water from a quarter of a mile away, all the cottages had been burned to the ground.

During the 19th century a carrier service was begun. On Wednesdays and Saturdays the carrier went to Oxford, departing at 9 am and reaching Oxford at midday, having stopped on the way to deliver and pick up parcels. He

Sarah T. Jarvis.

Haseley Windmill

started back at 4 pm reaching Haseley between 8 and 9 pm. Transport consisted of a covered van with two horses, benches ran along the sides of the van and straw lay on the floor. Rugs were provided to cover the legs of passengers in cold weather. Candles were set in storm lanterns. On Tuesdays there was a carrier service to Thame market town.

Canon Ellison, the rector of Haseley, listed 19 activities going on in the village in 1883, including a drum and fife band, a night school, for which 2d a week was charged, and a lending library.

Now, more than a hundred years later there is still an active village life. Bell ringers continue to ring the bells of St Peter's church, cricket is played on the recreation ground, and fund raising is in progress to provide hard tennis courts. The village children, benefiting from a bequest, now have their own play area in Back Way, known as Cross Field. In 1997 Great Haseley & District Horticultural Society celebrated its half-century.

The village school has closed and the buildings are now occupied by a day

114

nursery and a small business. The shop and post office also closed, but there is still The Plough public house. A mobile library calls every fortnight and there is a bus service to and from Oxford as well as a market bus on Tuesdays to Thame.

GREAT MILTON

Great Milton is said to have been the home of the ancestors of the poet, John Milton. It lies in pleasant countryside to the east of Oxford, just south of the M40 at Junction 7. It has a wide grass-verged street and green with many 16th to 18th century cottages and houses, the parish church of St Mary (Norman and Early English), a Methodist church, a thriving primary school, a post office stores, garage, and two public houses – the Bull (1684) and the King's Head. At the edge of the village near the A329 is the renowned restaurant and hotel, Le Manoir aux Quat' Saisons.

In addition to the pavilion at the recreation ground in the middle of the village, there is the Neighbours' Hall at the eastern edge of the village. This was originally built with the intention that it should be used also by villagers from Great and Little Haseley and Little Milton, although the only joint function held there nowadays is the Neighbours' Club, a senior citizens' club meeting fortnightly throughout the year and serving all four villages.

In addition to the summer fete and harvest festival, the King's Head runs a harvest festival in early September to raise funds for the senior citizens' Christmas lunch. A tennis club caters for children and adults. There is also a Historical Society with monthly meetings on a variety of interesting topics.

GREAT ROLLRIGHT

Great Rollright is in a lovely position high on a hill, one mile from the A3400 and three miles from Chipping Norton. It is off the usual tourist route despite being set in beautiful countryside. Several farms are within and surround the village. There are now about 200 houses including a Manor House and many old properties, two of which have been converted from chapels and a number from barns.

If people from outside the area know of Great Rollright it is often because

115

they have heard of the prehistoric Rollright Stones. These consist of 77 limestone boulders set in a circle, known as 'The King's Men', a separate large 'King Stone' and a group of 'Whispering Knights'. They were first recorded in a 12th century manuscript and are believed to have been assembled during the Bronze Age for use in religious ceremonies, as others, including Stonehenge, were. The well-known legend tells of a king who met a witch at Rollright and she said that if he took seven strides and then could see Long Compton he would become King of England. Unfortunately, a small hill hid Long Compton from his view and so the witch turned him and his men to stone.

St Andrew's church is of Norman origin and the north and south doorways date from this period. The main part of the church remains largely as it was in 1450, although there has been some careful restoration. The view from the churchyard is one of the loveliest in this area. Great Rollright is one of the few churches to have had a rector abscond because of his unpaid bills immediately after delivering a sermon on the evil of debts! This was in 1851 and he was never seen here again.

Next to the church there is a thriving Church of England primary school, of which the original stone part was built in 1852. Several extensions have been added and there are now almost 80 pupils on the register. The village has a pre-school group, a club for the elderly, a football club and, of course, a WI. Our village hall was built in the 1950s by the combined efforts of a group of villagers who spent many a long hour doing both the planning and the manual work.

We have a very well stocked shop with a post office. As there is no longer a public house open to the public (although the building is still used) some of the ramblers who visit are pleased to find that the shop sells a good range of food and drink to help them on their way. There is also a farm shop and plant centre just a mile beyond the centre of the village and they have a picnic area and a restaurant from where extensive views can be enjoyed.

🍁 GREAT TEW

Visually the setting of Great Tew is its greatest asset – who could go wrong with such a sweep of hills and fold of valley? Loudon, who made the planting design, had an eye for a well placed tree and there is no doubt that the trees are the crowning glory. Such a range of species, shapes and colours to clothe the hills and soften the outlines, to settle in clumps and woodland, must have been giving pleasure for many years.

Our history is covered for about the last 900 years by the church; our wall paintings, tombstones and monuments are our link with past residents of the parish. The gardens round our church, along with the pub, remind us daily of our most famous resident and lord of the manor, Lord Falkland. He walked and talked here with his Oxford friends before being killed in the Civil War, torn between his duty to his king and an understanding of the rights of the citizen expressed by Parliament. A civilised man.

The children of our village learn in school what it was like to live in this village in the past – as a Roman farmer at the villa at Beaconsfield farm, as an Anglo-Saxon eating pigeon stew cooked over a fire in the study area, at a medieval banquet, a Tudor court, or seated in a hard wooden desk with a 'Victorian' teacher fixing you with a gimlet eye telling you to be silent and speak only when you are spoken to!

Here in Great Tew we try to plan for the future. We are encouraging more children to come to our school, adults to use our village shop. We invite visitors to explore the village – please use our new car park, it reduces the congestion – to come to our church and share our worship in such a beautiful place. Then, perhaps, enjoy the convivial atmosphere in our village pub named after our 'great man' and welcoming so many customers with good cheer.

🍁 GROVE

Grove today is the largest village in the Vale of the White Horse, its vast sprawl of housing estates seemingly never-ending. From the sparsely populated hamlet shown on an early map in the 1700s it now looks set to burst its boundaries in the 2000s.

The village is recorded as far back as 1142 when King Stephen granted a manor here to the Abbot of Bermondsey, and two local watermills are recorded as early as 1622. During the 1770s the turnpike road (now the A338) was built as a more direct route between Wantage and Oxford, and this remains as Grove's eastern boundary.

At the beginning of the 1800s the Wilts and Berks Canal cut through the village bringing with it all the colourful characters associated with the canal trade. The Great Western Railway opened Wantage Road station in 1840, two miles from Wantage on the northern boundary of Grove. To connect this with the town, the Wantage Tramway Company in 1875 laid a single track alongside the turnpike road and provided England's first steam-powered passenger and goods service. This was hauled by a succession of engines, attaining fame through an ignoble defeat in a race through Grove between the tram and the local sweep's donkey cart, and notoriety through frequent and inconvenient derailments. On one occasion a spark from a passing engine set fire to the thatched roof of a cottage.

With the outbreak of the Second World War an airfield was built over the agricultural acres to the west of the village. In August 1944 a sextet from the Glenn Miller Band came to play at a dance in the camp ballroom.

By the beginning of the 1960s the airfield was no longer used. The canal had long fallen into disuse and the three mills on the Letcombe brook suffered the same fate. Buses and lorries now provided passenger and goods transport so the tramway rails were taken up and the road widened. Dr Beeching short-sightedly closed Wantage Road station, and many older houses were demolished to make way for the new; small farmers gave up farming and sold their land to builders – the age of the housing estates had begun!

Yet Grove tries to preserve its history. Visitors come and see where the airfield once was. Although it is now almost entirely covered with housing and a new business park, it is perpetuated in many local road names. And one may stand on the road bridge and look down at what was Wantage Road station, or go to Didcot and see *Shannon*, the last of the tramway engines which is displayed in the railway museum there. Walking through the fields it is possible to trace the line of the canal, and a small stretch of it is now being restored by local enthusiasts.

Grove now has a modern parish church; three others on the same site fell down over the centuries. There is a Methodist chapel built in 1890 which now has extensions on either side of the original building, and a much older Strict Baptist chapel was completely rebuilt in the 1980s.

There are two village halls. The 1950s one became inadequate, and the 1980s one is of unusual but practical design – a good conversational gambit for those using it! Also in duplicate are the shopping centres, schools, doctors, dentists and sheltered accommodation for the elderly. There are also two graveyards, the one at the church now being full up, future customers will have to be buried half a mile away. There also used to be two ghosts, but it would seem they have moved on due to lack of interest in them and pressures of everyday living – or haunting!

Traditions too have died. The famous Duck Races, part of the ancient village feast, were stopped in the 1950s by the RSPCA as a protest against cruelty to ducks. The May Day celebrations, revived after the Second World War, in which the whole village took part, are now observed only by schoolchildren as part of the school fete. The annual summer Horticultural Show survives with the scent of the summer produce tent intact, though its venue has changed from the common to the recreation ground: but lost are the nationwide Tug-of-War Teams Competition and the AA races. However, members of societies, sports clubs, church leaders, educationalists, and even the Parish Council, manage to preserve a community spirit among this huge and changing population.

🍁 HAILEY

Standing as it does on the south-eastern edge of the old Wychwood Forest, the village of Hailey has always had strong connections with Witney, even sharing in medieval times the spoils of the annual Whitsuntide hunt. Like Caesar's Gaul, the village is divided into three parts: Delly End, Middletown and Poffley End. Delly End was once a wooded area with thickets. Poffley End, more quaintly, takes its name from 'poffle', a word in use in the 14th century to denote a small parcel of land, probably tapering to a point. Middletown links the two hamlets and all three lie in a clearing in the forest where hay was grown – a 'hay-lea' in fact.

Some of the old Hailey houses have been restored. The manor house in Poffley End was built in the 15th century and has connections with the ancestors of the famous naturalist, Gilbert White of Selborne. Swanhall Farm dates in part from the 14th century and the old School House in Middletown had the date 1649 on one of its chimneys.

However, until comparatively recently life in an Oxfordshire village was neither easy nor affluent. People depended on local charities for winter blankets and extra rations. In despair, the vicar at the turn of the 20th century opened a reading room for men which he 'confidently expected' they would prefer to the tap-room. To judge by statistics in *Kelly's Directory* for

119

1907 he may well have been disappointed: the number of Hailey businesses then included three public houses and three beer retailers – all for a population of less than 1,000!

In those days villagers made their own entertainment. An annual fair was held and Club Day was a very special date with two brass bands, morning service and a splendid dinner in the loft of the Lamb and Flag.

Ascension Day was a red letter one and a school holiday. The children had sticks especially prepared, to which were tied bunches of flowers. In their best clothes and hats they gathered at Hailey manor to play games, run races and dance. After a picnic tea and armed with flowers and banners, the young people processed to church for the service. The next day all the flowers were taken to Oxford to the patients in the Radcliffe Infirmary.

What of today? Two world wars and improved communications have brought changes in their wake, mostly for the better. Instead of rising at 6 am and walking to work in the blanket mills, the people at Hailey had a wider choice of jobs and went out into the world. The 'hay-lea' is now a very pleasant mixed village, newer homes mingling with the old. There are all the ingredients which make a complete village – church, school, post office, public house and shop. There has been a recent development of shared ownership housing (managed by Oxford Citizens Housing Association). Newcomers are made welcome and most of them enter happily into local affairs. The older activities have now ceased but an annual Peace service still takes place round the memorial on Delly Green – erected after the First World War by Mrs Phipps, then living at Hailey manor.

🍁 THE HANNEYS

The Hanneys (East and West) are two of the 'island' villages of the Vale of the White Horse. One reminder of the fact that the Hanneys were once an island is that the footpath that connects the two villages is a raised causeway, because until recent years the road soon flooded in the winter months.

The parish church of St James the Great stands in West Hanney on an ancient Saxon site. The church contains two stone Saxon coffins. The present building dates back to Norman times (1160), and over the years there have been many additions and alterations. On the north wall of the church, near the font, is a commemorative tablet to Elizabeth Bowles, said to have died in

1718 at the age of 124 (the longest recorded life span of an Englishwoman).

In East Hanney is Hanney Mission, an evangelical chapel dating back to 1862, when it was erected by the 'Frilford and Longworth Home Mission'. The Mission closed down for a time between the wars and was almost sold to the British Legion as a clubhouse. The price was agreed, the plans for alteration were drawn up, but the sale did not go through. The Mission was reopened as a place of worship about 1943.

Letcombe brook meanders through East and West Hanney, providing the power for two (now unused) mills, locally known as the 'Upper' and the 'Lower' mills. Earlier in the 20th century, the Upper Mill (correctly known as Dandridge's Mill) supplied flour to Boffin's Bakery in Headington. The horses left Hanney at 8.30 am, and did not return until 7.00 pm. The flour milling died out in 1920. At the 'Lower' mill, near Philberd's Manor, prisoners of the Napoleonic wars carried out silk weaving. There is a public footpath along the brook here, and in the spring it is particularly beautiful, with daffodils growing by the mill.

At the turn of the 20th century there were a number of shops and farms in the two villages. There were carpenters, blacksmiths, thatchers, a midwife, a harness maker, a baker, a coal merchant, a wheelwright, two carriers and an undertaker. The post office in East Hanney was kept by two sisters, one of whom delivered letters up the street and the other down! Hanney even boasted a rat catcher, whose sister-in-law was the village midwife who delivered babies for a fee of 7s 6d.

The last village shop in East and West Hanney closed a few years ago, but on a site next to the village hall is a thriving community shop and post office. The community shop is run completely by volunteers and is open every day, except Sunday. It carries a variety of goods including delicious pork supplied by a village pig farmer, and bread from a local bakery.

There is an excellent village hall, which has recently been extended. Many people in East and West Hanney have worked hard over the years to raise funds and care for the hall, which is the home of many clubs and societies.

Most of the organisations using the village hall are prefixed by the name 'Hanney', showing a unity between the two villages, which has not always been there. There used to be, on occasion, some intense rivalry between the children of the two villages. One year, the single field that separates East and West Hanney was planted with turnips, and after school (and after some arguing) the older schoolboys got into the turnip field, uprooted a lot and threw them at each other. In the morning there were turnips all over the road. The police were called but, of course, nobody had seen anything. Today, the two villages live in harmony with each other, and there have been no turnips thrown in anger for many a year!

🍁 HARWELL

It is impossible in Harwell to ignore its historic beginnings. The old Cherry Barn with its thatched garden wall was, in 1200, part of Middle Farm, known then as Bayllol's Manor. Walk down Townsend and on your right is Bishop's Manor – once the grange of the Bishop of Winchester, with records dating back to 1209. Again, go down to King's Lane bearing right at the bottom. Head for the tower of the 13th century church of St Matthew and on your left is Prince's Manor, awarded by William the Conqueror to Robert D'Oily – renamed Prince's Manor by the Black Prince.

Down the High Street is Adnams Farmhouse, which survived the Great Fire of 1852. In its farmyard, it is believed, a discharged labourer set fire to a hay rick, and left most of the houses down as far as the Crown public house and Allen's Farm in smoking ruins.

On the next street corner is Jennings Lane – he was a successful yeoman and is commemorated with his wife and their twelve children by a brass memorial in the church. Across the High Street from this corner is Gaveston Road, named after Piers of that name, Duke of Cornwall, and lord of the Upper Manor (Prince's) 1308–12. His coat of arms can be seen in the church's east window. He was executed by the barons during their disputes with Edward II.

Walking up Gaveston Road, first on your right is Loder Road. Robert Loder was tenant at Prince's Major, paying rent to Queen Mary Tudor. He was able to purchase the property, leaving it to his son, Robert. Loder Road now gives access to a modern housing estate, tucked away and discreetly infilling the land behind the houses and the back of the Crown pub. The developer planned to build houses right down to the A34 but Harwell voted unanimously against that threat to its ancient boundaries.

In 1985, at a Millennium Pageant, various village groups 'put on' the different historical events of 1,000 years: Ethelred the Unready's signing of the Royal Charter, the ten freemen, the Bishop of Winchester's Feast still commemorated each year, the levy of archers for the Black Prince's French

Wars, the wedding of a yeoman's son to a daughter of the manor, a 17th century horse fair, the Cherry Teas of the 1760s and the Great Fire of 1852, with Harwell's entry into the 20th century providing a climax.

What a climax! A march past represented two world wars with a boy bugler on the church tower playing the Last Post, while others in white coats ushered in the atomic age of Harwell's Atomic Energy Research Establishment and the Rutherford Laboratory, and the nearby JET Project at Culham.

Stand on high ground and you can see all of Harwell lying below you, the curve of the orchards stretching down and past the A34, nearly all under Grove Farm management now. Some of the famous cherry trees still belong to the Lay family of Bishop's Manor. The 'Golden Mile' of the ancient highway, so named because so many important personages travelled past the village along old travel routes such as Icknield Way, Portway, or the Ridgeway Path, is now only a collection of names on the ramblers' maps. There is a new kind of Golden Mile now and Harwell's scientific research centres attract experts from all over the world.

🍁 HATFORD

Hatford is a small parish of some 1,000 acres lying within the Vale of the White Horse. It was formerly part of Berkshire before the reorganisation of the county boundaries in 1974.

Its history goes back long before the Norman period. The earliest evidence of occupation so far is a bronze spearhead found near the river Hat, dating back to the Bronze Age. Signs of an early Iron Age settlement have also been found and there is thought to have been at least one Roman villa in the fields adjoining the present village. The manor of Hatford has changed hands many times since 1086, when the Domesday survey recorded that it was held by Payn under Gilbert de Bretevile.

Hatford was in the public eye in 1628, when the second recorded meteor to fall in the country landed in the vicinity at Bawlkin Green. It also featured in the Civil War, when the church register records the burials in 1634 of two soldiers killed in action. Hatford has also appeared in literature, since the Wiltshire thresher turned poet, Stephen Duck, who worked here in the early 19th century, commemorated life on a Hatford farm in one of his last poems.

Perhaps the most striking feature of Hatford is that it has two churches, although one is now a private residence. St George's stands on the site of the Saxon church mentioned in Domesday. It is basically Early English with a Norman south doorway to nave and chancel arch and a Norman font and one Saxon window still visible. There is a sundial carved in the stone near the doorway. One tomb in the church is believed by some to be that of Sir Robert de Hatford, reputed founder of the church and lord of the manor in the reign of Henry III, while others think it is that of Thomas Chaucer, son of Geoffrey, the author of the *Canterbury Tales*. Thomas held the manor in the later 14th century and became Speaker of the House of Commons in 1414. But whose body actually lies inside the tomb still remains a mystery.

The church also houses a mausoleum containing the remains of Rev Samuel Paynter, a former rector of the parish, and his wife and daughter. When St George's fell into disrepair, it was Samuel Paynter who had Hatford's second church, Holy Trinity, erected in 1873–4 at a cost of around £4,000. It was built in the Early English style and is particularly notable for some fine, random-coursed stonework. After serving the village for almost a century. Holy Trinity itself became dilapidated and was finally sold in 1972 for use as a private dwelling. St George's was reopened in the same year, reroofed in 1973 and reglazed in 1974 to once again assume its role as the place of worship for the village.

Apart from the two churches, there are some interesting secular buildings. Hatford manor house, adjacent to St George's church, has an 18th century frontage, but parts of the house are much older, dating from the 15th century and possibly even earlier. It stands in a commanding position at the approach to the village and enjoys an uninterrupted view of the distant Berkshire Downs and the famous White Horse. On the other side of St George's stands the rectory. The present building was put up in 1869, slightly behind the site where the previous 300 year old rectory stood. Next to the rectory and fronting the road through the village is Hatford Cottage, which was converted into a delightful single dwelling from a row of very early cottages, originally occupied by the workmen involved in building the manor house. The little green in front of the entrance to the church was where Hatford Feast used to be held until well on into the 20th century.

Despite its long history, the population has not changed much in size since the time of the Domesday survey, when it had some 120 residents. Being so small, there are virtually no amenities, but the Community Bus Service from Stanford-in-the-Vale does provide a means of transport into the market towns of Faringdon and Wantage on certain days of the week. There is no shop in the village and no pub, although there was an off-licence, until this received a direct hit from a German bomb in September 1940. One Hatford girl was killed and, ironically enough, two little boys from London, who had been sent to stay with their grandparents, in order to get away from the Blitz! Behind the site, now occupied by the aptly named Phoenix House, is a bakehouse, which has its shop in Faringdon but still supplies the villagers with bread and cakes to order.

Because Hatford lies mainly on sandstone soil, it is a rich source of sand and gravel. Sand has been extracted here for many years and it was during sand digging between 1937 and 1958 that an early Iron Age settlement was discovered. When the sand ran out in 1958 on that particular site, another pit was opened on the other side of the appropriately named Sandy Lane.

Agriculture features very much in Hatford and has probably done so since Neolithic times. There are ample springs of good clear water, even in times of drought, and the soil is rich. Hatford was one of the earliest places in the country to be enclosed, supposedly in 1577. The land is now farmed by one man, assisted by just three farm workers. Instead of a landscape divided up into strips or small fields, there are vast rolling plains, somewhat reminiscent of the prairies of the American Mid West.

HEADINGTON QUARRY

Headington Quarry village is situated on the north-eastern outskirts of Oxford city. Its name originated from the stone that was quarried there. It is now a suburb of neighbouring Headington and no longer a village in its own right, though it still keeps its individuality. One of Quarry's assets is its close proximity to Shotover. Until the advent of the eastern bypass, footpaths led directly to Shotover Plain.

Visitors can easily lose themselves among the steep, winding, narrow roads and the network of walled paths and alleyways that run behind houses and between streets. The alleys are still very much as they were in days past and it is only in recent years that they have been given names, most of them after well known Quarry people such as Coppock's Alley, Vallis Alley, Cox's Alley and Mason's Alley.

Years ago stone was quarried here and transported to nearby Oxford to be used in building the colleges for the University. The whole village, according to records, is built on a vast rabbit warren of old quarries and tip heaps. The survival of these quarries in a residential area is of great archaeological interest. Nowadays the village is a mixture of small stone cottages and modern brick houses.

Quarry boasts three public houses, the Mason's Arms, the Six Bells and the Chequers. In the 18th and 19th centuries the Chequers was the centre of the village. The first school was started in a room next to the Chequers by Catherine Mather. Later in 1864 the present school buildings were opened by Bishop Wilberforce. The school of course has been greatly improved over the years and it still teaches infants and primary children from Quarry and the surrounding neighbourhoods.

Quarry has two places of worship, a Methodist chapel and Holy Trinity church. The church was built in 1848–9. It is in the style of a 14th century church, which deceives many visitors into thinking it is much older than it is. The stone for the church was quarried from a nearby farm and was the gift of Mr Thomas Burrows, a churchwarden of St Andrew's church, Old Headington. C. S. Lewis, the famous author and his brother are buried in the churchyard.

The Methodist chapel was started when the teachings of John Wesley were felt in Quarry and a few men got together in a house near the Six Bells for prayers. For some years they continued to meet at the house but on Easter Sunday 1830 the first chapel was opened in Trinity Road. In 1860 a new and much larger chapel was built in High Street.

Morris dancing has been associated with Quarry for hundreds of years. Several dances originated in this area including many well known favourites. Tunes were handed down from fiddler to fiddler and the steps and figures to each younger generation. They were never written down until Mr William Kimber, with the help of Cecil Sharp, set about recording them. Nowadays the Morris dancers dance outside each public house on Boxing Day and at Whitsun.

Meetings are still held in the village hall for a flourishing Quarry WI, formed in 1924, but sadly the shops have all gradually closed and the post office is housed in a supermarket in Gladstone Road. The village bakery closed its doors in 1989.

The Friends of Quarry was formed in 1970 and has done much to keep Quarry as an exceptional place of interest. In 1971 Oxford City declared it a conservation area. This has helped to keep the stone walls and the narrow pathways intact for future generations and above all to retain the village atmosphere.

🍁 HETHE

On the west side of the little stream which runs through this village the ground rises steeply to form an upland ridge. This English settlers named Hethe, ie a high place, and the first dwellings were built alongside the stream. In the 15th century a family built a house on the high ground and slowly this became the main part of the village as it is today.

Like all villages, Hethe has suffered from the removal of industry to factories in the towns. The census of 1851, besides listing 50 agricultural workers, names 20 house servants, eight grooms, two coachmen, four carpenters, four tailors, four laundresses, three bakers, three dressmakers, three masons, two brewers, two sawyers, a pig dealer, a cooper, a glazier, and a straw bonnet maker. Hethe is still famous for its builders, decorators and carpenter, plumbers, florist, welder, and antiques restorer, but with the disappearance of other trades, and the halving of the agricultural workers through mechanisation of farms, the village has steadily declined.

After the Second World War the decline was reversed by the building of 34 council houses down Hardwick Road. However, the village still lost its school, its grocery/general store and its Methodist chapel, and of the two public houses, only one remains.

Besides the delightful views afforded by the hills on either side of the brook, there are several attractive buildings round the village centre. There is the Manor Farm, Hethe House (the old dower house), the rectory, and a delightful selection of thatched cottages, including the round house, the newer part of which dates from 1752.

Hethe's community spirit goes back a very long way. It is something for a small village to maintain two independent but friendly churches: Church of England in the centre of the village and the Roman Catholic church on the edge in the Hardwick Road.

Shellswell Park estate makes up part of the parish, though sadly the magnificent Shellswell House became derelict and was demolished in the early 1980s. Since then freak high winds have destroyed hundreds of the fine trees on the estate.

In 1948 the then local squire, John Dewer Harrison, who had high regard for the village folk, gave the ground floor of the dower house, Hethe House, to the village to use as a meeting place. This was used regularly until it was sold in 1986, with half the proceeds going towards building a new village hall, opened in May 1987.

🍁 THE HEYFORDS

Upper Heyford took its name from a ford across the river Cherwell, and was originally called Heyford Warren, the 'Warren' dating from the 12th century when Warin Fitzgerald was lord of the manor. The 'Upper' appeared in the 15th century, Heyford being already established as a settlement before the Norman Conquest. Manor farmhouse was built on the site of the medieval manor house, and a tithe barn has stood there since the early 15th century. New College has held the manorial rights to the village since 1382, owning the farm and most of the older cottages until fairly recent times.

Kelly's Directory of 1899 lists the following businesses: carpenter, miller, bootmaker, marine store dealer, butcher, blacksmith, grocer and post office, builder and stonemason, two public houses and three farms. Comparing this with today, we have The Barley Mow left, the Three Horseshoes having recently been turned into two houses, Manor Farm is still working, Heyfordian Coaches operate from the depot here, and there is a piano shop in the High Street. In the last few years we have seen the closure of both village shops, the post office, one pub and sadly the village school, which had been open for more than a century and had seen generations of the same families through its doors. For years there was a ban on new building in the village because of aircraft noise from the base, and this has no doubt had its effect in these closures.

Lovely St Mary's church is just below the old school and between the two, a village green. Here stands a small brick building which used to be the reading room some 70 or so years ago, which then became the infants' school. Next to this is the cemetery with its war graves, memorial and commemoration stones for RAF and USAF servicemen. The church and cemetery are kept up beautifully thanks to loyal volunteers.

128

Along the bottom of the village runs the river Cherwell and the Oxford to Birmingham Canal. Years ago we used to swim here, but it is now too polluted, and whereas once you saw coal barges, these have been replaced with holiday barges, the canal being very busy in the summer season. A water mill stood over the river here long ago.

Up the hill from the village is the air base. It originated as a First World War airfield between 1916 and 1920, became a bomber station from 1927, then a parachute training school. It was leased to the USAF in 1951 who occupied it until 1994. The base swallowed up acres of farmland belonging to Mudginwell and Two Trees farms, and it has to be decided what will happen to all this land now that it is no longer of use. The airfield is now let as small factory units and car storage on a short term basis, with some new housing due to be built. It is run by a consortium, who, along with Cherwell District Council and local village committees, are planning its future.

Lower Heyford is situated in the Cherwell valley roughly midway between Banbury and Oxford. The parish has, over the years, had a number of names. Until the mid 13th century the village was called Heyford (the ford used at hay harvest). After the building of the long bridge first recorded in 1255, it became known as Heyford ad Pontem or Heyford Bridge. From the late 14th century it was sometimes called Heyford Purcell after the prominent local Purcell family. Nether Heyford was first used in 1474 and later Little or Lower Heyford.

Heyford Bridge quickly became a place of trade and other business. A market was started in the 13th century and survived on a regular basis until the late 19th century. All this inevitably generated increased traffic which resulted in the transport links that survive to this day. The Oxford-Coventry canal was opened in 1790 with a wharf at Heyford, the chief cargo being coal to the Midlands. The Oxford to Banbury branch of the Great Western Railway opened in 1850 with one of the original stations being at Lower Heyford. Modernisation caused the cattle truck sidings to be removed but the signal box has been dismantled and transported to the Didcot Railway Museum for re-erection.

The Rousham Conservation Area, which covers a portion of the Cherwell valley north and east of Rousham Park, includes Lower and Upper Heyford villages. Rousham House has been in the ownership of the Dormer family since being built in the 17th century. The landscape gardens were created by William Kent in the 18th century. Kent made use of many buildings and features in Lower Heyford as viewpoints in his overall plan, some of which remain to this day.

Caulcott is a nearby hamlet. In the period leading up to the Second World War it had three farms, one public house, a Sunday school which was held in the school house, and church services were held in the reading room. There was one shop, and a district nurse called when needed. The children made their own entertainment. The boys would go 'clap-netting', some holding the net one side of the hedge while the others beat the hedge the other side, so catching the birds in the net. Most of the men worked on the land while the women were content to stay at home cleaning and cooking, and taking the billy-cans of tea to the fields for the men. Later on there was a single-decker bus came through the village once a week taking the women into town.

🍁 HEYTHROP

Heythrop is a windswept village high up to the north-east above Chipping Norton. It is at its best in early February when the verges which border the village street are carpeted with snowdrops, or on a warm still July afternoon when the lime trees are in full flower and the only sound is of a distant lawnmower. The chances are that walking along the street you will meet nothing apart from an occasional tractor, for Heythrop is still, as it has always been, off the beaten track and its inhabitants are few. Rarely has its population, even with the people from the surrounding farms, reached 200 persons.

The village mentioned in the Domesday survey has left few traces today apart from the chancel of the old church, into the arch of which has been rebuilt the Norman doorway of the nave pulled down in the 19th century, and faint indications of the ridge and furrow cultivation of an earlier age traceable when the light is favourable. Substantially it is still the model village built in 1873 by Albert Brassey. His estate, centred on Heythrop Hall, was the wedding gift of Thomas Brassey the millionaire railway contractor, to his third son. As in other Oxfordshire villages wealth made in industry in one generation contributed to agricultural development in the next.

Before 1873 the village seems to have consisted of one or two cottages at most, a farmhouse and the church, and had been described as decayed or depopulated at intervals since the 14th century. Heythrop Hall, built in the

130

early 18th century by the 12th earl of Shrewsbury, was one of the great houses of the county with its park laid out to the south-east in the Italian manner, but when the earldom passed to a Catholic branch of the Talbot family the owner of the house withdrew from public life and the village languished. Finally after a disastrous fire in 1831 the house was abandoned as an empty shell.

Although the golden age of English farming was already coming to an end, Albert was able with the resources inherited from his father to set out to rebuild the interior of Heythrop Hall, to restore the gardens and great stands of trees stretching down to the Banbury road, and to build his model village. There was no shop lest it should tempt the women to stand and gossip and no inn for fear of drunkenness, but the houses, constructed with stone from the local quarry, were furnished with the latest conveniences of the time – damp courses, underground water storage tanks, fed from the gutters, and outside closets with nightsoil tanks vented with soil pipes. The houses were surrounded with ample gardens and shelter belts of trees were planted to protect them from the north and east winds. The new church, built just inside the park, was sited to be the focus of the village. It was constructed to the design of A. W. Blomfield on a massive scale, with stone from the nave of the old church and from the Catholic chapel in the grounds of the Hall, in the popular Victorian Gothic style. Behind it a rectory of equally generous proportions replaced the old farmhouse. A school with an attached schoolhouse and a new lodge completed the building.

From the Hall the Brasseys overlooked village affairs. Mrs Brassey took a special interest in the cultivation of the village gardens, the best efforts being rewarded with the prize of a sovereign, quite a sum when wages were low. Forty indoor staff were needed to run the Hall and the park and gardens employed the services of a large force of gardeners, woodmen and gamekeepers.

With Albert Brassey's death in 1918 the Hall had to be sold to meet death duties, was eventually taken over by the Society of Jesus as a seminary and in 1969 was bought by the National Westminster Bank for a Management Development College. The link with the Hall broken, the village changed its character as the 20th century brought mechanisation to farming and decreased the demand for labourers. As in many Oxfordshire villages today a number of the houses are second homes or have been bought by retired people; the school has gone and the rectory is a private house.

 Holton

Holton is a small parish situated five miles east of Oxford. It was mentioned as far back as 1086 in the Domesday records, when it was known as Eltone. The area was inhabited by the Romans, but it was the Anglo-Saxons who gave the village its name.

There has been a castle or manor house in Holton Park since medieval times. The original was surrounded by a moat which was hand-dug, involving the removal of 24,000 cubic yards of rock. The present house was built in 1808 probably using stone from the original, but situated in the grounds and not on the moated island. The Biscoe family built the present house and it remained in the family until 1910 when it was sold and the estate broken up. The manorial rights had by now lapsed and in 1948 the house became a girls' grammar school.

During the Second World War an American field hospital was built in the park. It was later taken over by the RAMC as a hospital for head injuries. It closed in 1961 and some of the wards were converted into classrooms for what is now Wheatley Park school and the rest were demolished. The 18th century stables have also been converted into classrooms.

To the right of the school entrance is the headquarters of the Oxfordshire Library. In 1985 a sports hall was built on the school campus by South Oxfordshire District Council which is for school use during school hours and is open to the public at all other times. The Park also accommodates part of Oxford Brookes University, and 350 students live on the campus.

Holton church is dedicated to St Bartholomew and dates from the 12th century. The chancel was rebuilt in the 13th and 14th centuries. The whole church was extensively restored in the 19th century, the western gallery being enlarged and the stairs moved from the inside to the outside of the tower. The first organ was built in 1860, until then the music was provided by an orchestra consisting of a fiddle, a cello and a clarinet. There are three bells including one medieval example and one made in 1662.

Holton has its fair share of ghost stories. The ghost of a lady is said to walk through the park and down to the village hall. She was apparently a nanny who worked at the manor house and who dropped the baby she was looking after down the stairs, killing it. She appears in the early morning and late at night and has been seen by many people.

A few years ago two headstones from the graves of dogs were discovered on the island in the park by workmen. Pets' graves were quite common in Victorian times. This discovery probably led to the stories of headless dogs roaming the island.

The other story is of a young boy dressed in dark blue velvet with a wide lace collar who owned the manor house. He was looked after by an uncle. The boy's governess fell in love with the guardian and killed the boy, hoping to marry the guardian and get the estate. They buried him in the garden south of the moat. Years later a new house was built over the grave. When the Biscoe family lived in the house a guest was standing at the foot of the stairs one evening at about 10 pm and saw a boy run towards him, but as he went to grasp him he disappeared. The boy was also seen on the stairs and in the billiard room. It is believed he still haunts the house.

Holton today tries hard to produce a village community atmosphere. The three farms in the village, Old Park Farm, Pond Farm and Warren Farm are still being worked, but a fairly high proportion of the inhabitants are commuters. A new village hall was built in 1975 after a great deal of community effort to raise the funds. It has a licensed bar for functions and opens every Friday evening for the use of the villagers. However, there is no longer a village store or post office and the younger children have to go out of the village to school. The Old School House and Old Post Office are now residential properties.

🍁 HOOK NORTON

Hook Norton is a beautiful village surrounded by rolling countryside. It is one of the largest villages in Oxfordshire, situated ten miles south of Banbury and 25 miles north of Oxford, in a rich farming area.

The village contains a wide variety of about 800 houses, of all ages and types, and the population is at present about 2,000. It contains two churches, a primary school, a playgroup, a library, a village shop, a post office shop and many sports facilities. There are also four pubs in Hook Norton, all selling Hooky's award winning beer.

There is also a thriving pottery established 30 years ago, and an evening centre where many skills are learned and practised.

 Horspath

Nestling on the slopes of Shotover one mile outside the Oxford City boundary, Horspath is proud to remain a village. The parish boundary, along the Roman road, encloses Bullingdon Green, where gentlemen used to sport and Civil War battles were fought.

Shotover was once one of England's smaller Royal forests, and is now a conservation area and country park. The old bridle-path joining the London Road through Wheatley gave the Anglo-Saxon name Horsepadan, which became Horsepath, but in 1912 the parish council reverted to the unique form, Horspath. Medieval evidence suggests two distinct hamlets, Upper or Old Horspath and Nether, Lower or Church Horspath.

Three Oxford Colleges, Corpus Christi, Magdalen and Brasenose have owned land and property in the parish. A connection with Queen's College comes from the 15th century when student John Copcot, walking in Shotover Forest reading his Aristotle, was attacked by a wild boar. He thrust the volume down the animal's throat and 'the boar expired'. The college ceremony of carrying in the Boar's Head at Christmas resulted from this, as did the stained glass window in St Giles' church, presented in 1740 by the President of Magdalen to commemorate the Copcot Legend.

In the 19th and early 20th centuries laundresses stretched their lines across the green and market gardeners tended their vegetables for Pembroke College. Farmers also reared pigs for the college tables. In the census of 1871, showing a population of 373, 93 were employed on the land, 14 were craftsmen and there were 30 other trades, a curate and two publicans. There were 12 farmers in 1841 and only two in 1990, but the village still has its two publicans.

Horspath is not a pretty village, but it has character. It boasts 15 listed buildings including farm outbuildings and a cowhouse, the manor house, the church, and two thatched cottages, of which there were once 17, but fire has destroyed most. In 1936 the Queen's Head public house caught fire and sparks from the thatch destroyed two cottages opposite. The pub was restored with a tiled roof, as was Shepherd's Cottage, this thatch being burnt in the mid 1970s. The Chequers Inn, although dated 1624, was built in the 19th century.

The manor house, part dating back to 1513 and with a Tudor staircase, is mainly 17th century with a 19th century addition. Its ghost, 'The Grey

Lady', is reputed to wander the landings and garden. Killed by her husband in a quarrel, her body was placed in a priest's hole. Several sightings have been reported and in December 1878 a first-class shot claimed he had fired three times at the figure, and found two bullets embedded in the wall. The present owner has done much to refurbish and restore the manor to its former glory.

The church of St Giles, dating from the 12th century, is dedicated to the patron saint of beggars and cripples, whose ceramic statuette, made by a local potter in 1988, may be found in the south chapel. The church is the proud possessor of an Elizabethan silver chalice, a pre-1740 faceless blacksmith clock, a carved late Jacobean pulpit, six tuneful bells, medieval stained glass windows and interesting memorial plaques. One of these to James Salisbury of Bullingdon Green, who died in 1770, is elaborately decorated. Another is to the five children of Thomas and Esther Herbert, who died from a recurrence of the plague between 1686 and 1688. Esther, whose family founded New College, died also in 1688 aged 33.

In the early 20th century there was much change with tarmac roads, housing developments and mobile homes replacing farmland and manor grounds, the loss of the elms, the village pond and the railway. The population is now approximately 1,500 and includes people from all walks of life including those employed at Rover car works.

HORTON CUM STUDLEY

This is one of the 'Seven Towns of Otmoor', and is a busy, thriving and friendly village, with a total population approaching 500. The village is bordered by Buckinghamshire on two sides, Studley Wood – the remains of an ancient forest – on the third side, and Otmoor on the fourth.

The main building in the village is Studley Priory, situated at the top of the hill overlooking the valley. It was a priory until the Dissolution, and then given by Henry VIII to John Croke. Subsequently it was bought by the Henderson family in 1874, and when the estate passed out of their ownership in 1955 the Priory became a Country Club, and is now a hotel. John Croke built the Croke almshouses (opposite the Priory) in 1636. They were modernised in 1961, and now have four occupants.

There are numerous activities in the village. They include the church – which was designed and built by Butterfield in 1868; he was also responsible for building Keble College, Oxford. Tennis and cricket clubs use the playing field, and we are lucky enough to have two all-weather tennis courts with an adjoining well-equipped children's play area. There is also a flourishing Garden Club which attracts members from neighbouring villages, and just outside the village a recently developed golf club has been opened.

At the beginning of June each year the Otmoor Challenge takes place; this is an official 13-mile sponsored half-marathon which is run, or walked, starting and finishing at Horton cum Studley. This raises up to £9,000 in aid of charities of the participants' choice. A fete is held at the same venue – the playing field. There is also a Michaelmas fair, held in September, to raise funds for the church.

You may be surprised that in a country village there are only three farms. Two are owned and worked by long-established families, and the third until recently was a County Council farm but is now privately owned. Warren Farm, the County Teaching Farm, is also in the village, and offers opportunities for attending classes.

The village hall (recently sold) is thatched, and was owned by the Henderson family who leased the building to the WI for a peppercorn rent. In 1968 it was bought by the village and managed by a committee. Millennium funding will provide for a new hall to be built on the playing field. The village has a post office/shop and also a village green opposite the shop, although with the fast-flowing traffic the green is not used to its full potential. There is no pub as such in the village as the Kings Arms now has virtually become a small hotel. Another place of interest is the brick kiln, built in 1915 on a good seam of clay, but it is no longer used.

🍁 IFFLEY

Iffley's undoubted jewel is her famous Norman church of St Mary with its richly carved doorways, magnificent tower and tower arches. It stands on the brow of a hill overlooking the river, close to the mainly 16th century rectory, with parts dating back to the 1300s. A recent valued addition to the church is the Piper window, entitled The Nativity. Designed by John Piper and made by David Wasley, it was given in 1995 by Mrs Myfanwy Piper in memory of her husband.

The large chestnut tree by the church gate is a magnificent sight when in bloom. The glebe field, in this part of the village, together with several stone cottages and the old village school, presents an attractive and unspoiled corner.

Iffley was mentioned as early as AD 941 in the Chronicles of Abingdon and in the Domesday Book in 1086 and its name is derived from the Saxon word 'Giftelege', which means the field of gifts.

At one time, the greater part of the population was employed in agriculture and there were several farms in the village, but these no longer exist. After 1946 at least 53% of the village population were on mechanical work with no farm workers, tilers or building labourers. Many sons followed their fathers into mechanical jobs, but today there is a great variety of occupations including the professions, with a fair number of retired people.

The river and lock are great attractions to Iffley visitors who often walk along the tow-path from Oxford and pause to see the keeper operating the lock and to admire his colourful garden. The college eights start from just above this point for their Torpids and Eights Week races.

At one time there was a toll which was paid to Lincoln College to cross the bridge to the lock but this was discontinued in the mid 1950s. There was a tradition that if ever a corpse was carried through the toll it would be broken for ever and when an attempt was made to do this the toll keeper refused to let the party through and the corpse had to be taken across the water by ferry.

The old mill, featured in many old pictures of Iffley, stood nearby but, sadly, was burned down in 1908 and all that remains are two grindstones outside Grist Cottage and an inscription on a piece of wall.

The fields near Iffley lock were once rich in spring with purple fritillaries. They still bloom there, though in less profusion, and are now guarded by public-minded citizens when in flower.

The village has its fair share of ghosts and apparitions. The figure of a stately abbess has been known to appear in the old churchyard and the Rev Clarendon on his last night in the rectory heard a procession of monks as they passed through the corridors – a fitting tribute to the incumbent who had spent the longest spell of duty in the parish. Late one night in 1947 many residents were disturbed by the sound of a wooden-legged visitant clanking chains and stomping its way down Tree Lane!

Court Place, where the old manor courts were held, has housed many occupants. The *Warsaw Concerto* was written at Court House by Richard Addinsell who was the guest of John Bryson, after his London flat had been bombed. The last owner of Court House, before it was sold to the University, was Sir Alan Gardiner, the Egyptologist, who was a member of the team when Tutankhamen's tomb was discovered.

Iffley has two pubs, the Tree and the Prince of Wales, and the Hawkwell House Hotel. The village still has its shop and post office run by Morella, which provides personal service and a welcome social focus to those fortunate enough to live in Iffley.

🍁 IPSDEN

Ipsden lies in South Oxfordshire, a part of the county surrounded by a deep bend in the river Thames. It is in the foothills of the Chilterns, and is really a collection of scattered hamlets, rather than a village.

Its 13th century church stands on one of the approach roads to the village, and despite the ravages of the years, still has examples of early wall paintings within, and a very attractive brick and flint exterior.

'The Street' could be described as the centre of the village, running from the post office and stores at one end, past the Old Post House and Old Vicarage, down to Ipsden Farm with its huge tithe barn and granary, onto the A4074 Reading road.

The Church of England Aided village school had been in existence for over 100 years, but finally closed its doors in July 1989, due to a continued decline in numbers. The building now houses a flourishing nursery school.

Ipsden has had its share of characters and ghosts – only to be expected with a history which pre-dates Roman settlements in the area. Some of these have their names intertwined with village life, such as Janet Lindsey, a former postmistress whose name lives on in Janet's Grove, while Ben Remnant, killed in action, gives his name to Ben's Cottages at Newtown.

Two stones in the hedgerow opposite the school commemorate two farm workers killed by lightning. There is also a mini-Stonehenge – a comparatively recent innovation by a member of the Reade family generations ago, and also a monument near Leyend Pond which was erected on the spot where the ghost of John Reade (d1827) was seen coming to tell his mother of his death in India. Ipsden House, the home of the Reade family, boasts an ancient donkey wheel and dovecote. A well known member of the family was Charles Reade, author of *The Cloister and the Hearth*.

Braziers Park, built in the Strawberry Hill Gothic style, is home to Braziers Park School of Integrated Social Research and is also in Ipsden parish.

Modern innovations have always been slow to take hold in Ipsden. Piped water did not arrive until 1947 and electricity in 1954. Apart from a few modern houses, the village appears much the same now as it did then.

ISLIP

Islip is a 'working' village, where there are three farms, a shop, two pubs and, above all, a good number of inhabitants who take part in helping to make the village live, not just a place to have a dwelling. In the Domesday Book, Islip was Githslepe, thought to refer to the ford over the river Ray (formerly Ight or Gight).

The pre-Conquest kings hunted in Oxfordshire, and had several hunting boxes in the area. In one of these, at Islip, Edward the Confessor was born, c1003. His will states, 'I have given to Christ and to St Peter in Westminster the little town of Islippe wherein I was born with all the things that belong thereto.'

So began the enduring connection of Islip with Westminster Abbey. The living is in the gift of Westminster, and the farmland owned by the Church Commissioners. In 1464 a boy was born in Islip who became Abbot John of Westminster, also known as Abbot Islip. He built the little Islip Chapel in the Abbey, and his rebus, or heraldic device, was an eye, and a little man slipping down a tree.

On 23rd April 1645, during the Civil War, there was a skirmish at Islip bridge. The Parliamentary forces under Cromwell captured the bridge and village from the Royalists. Cromwell was helped by a local fisherman named Beckley who agreed to ferry some of his troops along the Cherwell, thus bypassing the bridge and outflanking the Royalists. Later, Cromwell gave Beckley and his heirs a monopoly of the fishing rights in Islip waters in recognition of his service. These events were remembered in 1995, the 350th anniversary, when there was a 'Rout' with displays by the English Civil War Society.

In 1678 Robert South, Canon of Westminster, became Rector of Islip. He rebuilt the chancel of the church burned during the Civil War and built a fine rectory with a lovely tithe barn attached to it. His greatest benefit to Islip was

Abbot Islip's rebus

the school which he built and endowed in 1710, with a house for the master. The school flourishes in modern buildings, and Dr South's School and the village still benefit from the provisions of his will.

The school is part of the life blood of the village. There are interesting records in its log books. In the early 1920s, Robert Graves and his wife, who preferred to be called Nancy Nicholson, lived in a cottage 'over the bridge' called World's End. He played football for Islip and for a short time served on the Parish Council. Their daughter, Jenny, was a pupil at Dr South's, and for the 18th November 1925, the log book entry reads 'Head out of school for 15 minutes this afternoon, seeing Mr R. Graves, who objects to his daughter Jenny being called by his surname, and desires that she be known as Jenny Nicholson – her name has now been altered on the register by me.'

The most famous Victorian rector was William Buckland, Dean of

140

Westminster, former Canon of Christ Church, Oxford, and the first University Reader in Mineralogy. He was a noted geologist and palaeontologist and there are many stories about his insistence on tasting everything! He regularly visited Islip in the summer and took great interest in educating the children, even sponsoring an emigration scheme for the more adventurous. The last few months of his life were spent at Islip and he is buried in the churchyard.

Monks' Cottage is thought to have been lived in by the monks who prayed for Edward the Confessor's soul in a chantry chapel which stood till about 1760 on the site of the Red Lion yard. Not described by name, but by symbol, was a cottage which in the 1930s had antlers over the front door, and its present owner says that numbers are still discernible on its bedroom doors. The antlers were a sign recognisable to some!

🍁 KELMSCOTT

The small, remote village of Kelmscott is the epitome of rural, agricultural England. It remains undeveloped, un-suburbanised and unspoilt for two reasons. First, it is at the end of a non-through road which peters out into the tow-path by the Thames. Secondly, in the main, it is in three self-perpetuating ownerships: the Church Commissioners, the National Trust and the Society of Antiquaries of London.

The older buildings are of stone and so to say in the Cotswold style, for Kelmscott lies at the south-eastern extremity of the Cotswolds. But this setting is totally at variance with the landscape of small hills, valleys and woodlands stretching away to the north-west. Here the country is totally flat as far as the eye can see and more or less devoid of woods and copses. It has nonetheless great character and charm, even if an acquired taste, with the great unbroken dome of heaven above.

The oldest building in the village is the parish church of St George, begun in the late 12th century. It was enlarged thrice thereafter before about 1550 since when it has remained virtually unaltered. William Morris, the famous poet, artist and craftsman, who lived in Kelmscott Manor nearby made sure that the late 19th century restoration of it was done with care and discrimination with the result that its medieval character was not spoiled. So it stands today, redolent of the Middle Ages. Morris himself was buried in the churchyard in

1896 under a gravestone designed by his old friend and associate Philip Webb, the famous late Victorian architect.

The second oldest building, the aforesaid Manor, Morris's home from 1871 to 1896, was finished in 1571. In about 1670 an elegant wing was added. Since then, again like the church, it has remained virtually unaltered. It is open to the public on the first Wednesdays of the months May to September and is well worth a visit. It contains many works of Morris himself and his circle, Rossetti, Burne-Jones, Ford Madox Brown and Philip Webb. The four other large houses in the village are of the 17th and 18th centuries.

The village hall is interesting for it was built to the designs of Ernest Gimson, though after his death. Gimson was perhaps the prime exponent of the Arts and Crafts Movement in architecture and furniture in England. Here everything is hand-crafted and of high quality. Again the style is the vernacular style of the region. The hall was opened in 1934 by George Bernard Shaw, and Ramsay MacDonald was present. The funds for the building were raised almost wholly by May Morris, daughter of William Morris, then living in the Manor.

Two other buildings in the village are of historical and architectural distinction: the Memorial Cottages and the Gimson Cottages (nos 3 and 4 Manor Cottages); each, though single and free-standing, contains two tenements. Both were paid for by the Morris family, the former by Jane Morris widow of William Morris in 1902 in memory of her husband, the latter by May Morris their daughter in 1915 in memory of her mother. The Memorial Cottages are recognisable by the carving on the front of William Morris sitting in the Home Mead beside Kelmscott Manor. Philip Webb was the architect. George Jack did the carving. The architect of the Gimson Cottages was, again, Ernest Gimson, the Arts and Crafts architect. These too are a remarkable example of building in the local vernacular style. Their traditional character suggests much greater antiquity than 1915.

For the rest, the cottages built since the First World War by the local Council and the Church Commissioners and the four post-1945 houses respect the local idiom and fit into the unspoilt village scene without offence. Moreover, the future is reasonably assured because the West Oxfordshire District Planners have regard for the character of the place and, in co-operation with the three major landowners, in particular the National Trust, are concerned that it remains unviolated by unsightly development.

🍁 KENNINGTON

Kennington is a long, straggly village between Oxford and Abingdon and is pleasantly situated between the river Thames and Bagley Wood. It is thought to have derived its name from Cenigtun, or the place of Cena's people and was first mentioned in a charter of AD 821.

In the early 19th century some members of the University used to keep horses in Kennington as they enjoyed driving them in tandem, which they were not allowed to do in Oxford. This is commemorated in the name of one of the popular pubs, the Tandem. The other pub, the Scholar Gipsy, is a reminder that this was the area described in Matthew Arnold's poem of the same name.

The philosopher and writer Bertrand Russell once lived in a house on Bagley Wood Road and a plaque on the wall records this.

Village life is enhanced by the facilities of the new village hall, a splendid building opened in 1989. Here one finds a library as well as a sports hall. This is also used by many village organisations and for productions of the local dramatic society. There is a new Youth Club building and adjoining the car park is the Kennington Social Club, as well as a modern health centre. Here, too, is a stone lintel with the inscription 'Sunday School 1809', reminding the inhabitants of the spot where one of the oldest Sunday schools in the country once stood.

Demolition of a war-time cold store provided space for the erection of some attractive new houses with views over the river. Otters Reach development has now pushed the number of inhabitants to over 5,000.

There are three churches in the village, Methodist, Catholic and Church of England. A great ecumenical spirit exists and many joint functions are held. Many musical events are also held, led by the Kennington & District United Church Choirs, all monies raised going to charity.

Kennington boasts an unusual open space in the delightful Memorial Field. This covers several acres of natural ground and is a tribute to members of the village who gave their lives in the Second World War. It is administered by the Oxford Preservation Trust with a local committee representing many of the village organisations.

Education is provided by an infant and primary school. Templeton College, the former centre for management studies and now part of Oxford University, is within the parish boundaries.

Open air activities are encouraged and devotees have two sports fields and the appropriate football and cricket clubs.

The new industrial estate in Sandford Lane is becoming a hive of activity with many units providing employment.

The warmth of the community spirit compensates for the change from a rural hamlet to a semi-urban development and Kennington is known as the friendly village.

🍁 KIDDINGTON

The village of Over and Nether Kiddington is situated on the A44 trunk road north of Woodstock, and the two parts are divided in the wooded valley by the river Glyme.

The village has not altered significantly since Domesday. There are only four new houses, built by the local council in the 1920s. The population is also fairly static. In 1066 it was 173. In 1951 it was 100, and at the present time it is about 110.

The village was always on the toll road between Oxford and Birmingham. The largest house near the main road, still known as 'The Chequers', was originally a coaching inn, where the Worcester Coach, the London Mail and the Blenheim called. The building close to the house was the blacksmith's and wheelwright's shop.

In the 1940s this building was given to the village on a 99 year lease by the late Squire, Mr Henry Melville Gaskell. The village people raised the money, with the help of the Oxfordshire Rural Community Council, to convert the building into a very useful village hall. Unfortunately due to rising costs and essential improvements that were required, it is no longer used.

Close by The Chequers is a stone archway, which until after the Second World War housed 'The Tap'. This was the water supply for the village. The water was carried in buckets to all parts of the village, including the council houses. On the other side of the busy A44, opposite The Chequers, there is now an import cane shop which also provides very good cream teas.

The village is composed of four blocks of typical Cotswold stone cottages, some dated 1844. On the right hand side is Gate Farm, possibly connected with the toll gate. At the rear of the farmhouse the old redundant farm buildings have been transformed into modern office accommodation for media, software and telecom firms employing about 50 people.

In Nether Kiddington, Kiddington Hall is situated on rising ground and overlooking the river Glyme and the lake. It is a great house with dormer windows and lantern roof. The grounds were designed by 'Capability' Brown.

Close by the Hall stands the strong square-towered 14th century church. There are stained glass windows to the memory of Henry Lomax Gaskell and his wife Alice. The Gaskell family lived at the Hall from 1855–1953. There is a brass of Walter Goodere, a 16th century rector of Kiddington, on the west wall. North of the church is a stone-built house which was once the priest's house, now converted to two workers' cottages. Until after the Second World War we had a rector of our own, who resided in the rectory near the entrance to the Hall. Outside the churchyard stands a very attractive 16th century dovecote.

Turning left at the Old Rectory you pass two modernised 18th century farm cottages. A little further on, at a spot known by the locals as Will's Grave, a cross used to be cut in the grass verge where the last man convicted of sheep stealing was hanged.

The estate village used to consist of the park and woodlands, Park Farm and seven other farms, farmed by tenant farmers. Of these only one, White House Farm, is still farmed by a tenant farmer, the others are now farmed by the estate.

🍁 KIDMORE END

The parish of Kidmore End covers a very wide area. The name is derived from the Celtic, 'kid' meaning wood, 'more/mawr' being great and 'end' a boundary. It was renamed Kidmore in 1894, but after representations the Council agreed in 1902 that its name should revert to Kidmore End.

Kidmore End encompasses Gallowstree Common. The tree which gave this hamlet its name was a solitary oak standing apart from woodland. It is said that the last hanging, for sheep stealing, occurred in 1825. The stump was removed at the time of the Enclosure Acts but for some time the gibbet and chains were left on a post nearby. There are, however, happier associations with Gallowstree Common. This stands with Kidmore End in the lovely part of South Oxfordshire known as 'Cherry Country' and within living memory the Methodist chapel at Gallowstree held annual Cherry Teas in July, when the tables groaned under the huge bowls filled with local cherries, from which one took one's fill ... and all for 9d! Sadly, the cherry orchards are no more, and the chapel has closed, but a walk through the lanes and woods when the wild cherries are in bloom is a delightful reminder of former days.

Kidmore End village school was established in 1862 and within a year the average attendance was 70 – this was before education became free and compulsory. In 1901 there were 143 children on the register and in this year the Bronze Medal, awarded by the Canadian Government through Lord Strathcona, was given to William Long for the best essay on Canada – a great honour for the village school.

The church festival or Parish Feast evolved from the annual treat for schoolchildren consisting of tea and games at the vicarage. In 1891 it was decided to hold a Parish Festival. On 1st July, Evensong was sung at 3 pm followed by tea on the vicarage lawn for all participants. The Festival became popular and included exhibits by children of collections of flowers and was enhanced by the attendance of the Church Lads Brigade Drum and Fife Band. These Festivals were the forerunners of present Village Days.

An ancient landmark is the Kidmore End Well, now disued but in an excellent state of preservation. Often in its lifetime it had fallen into disrepair and been threatened by demolition but public opinion and generosity saved it from such a fate, one thoughtful Parish Councillor reasoning, during war time, that 'it would be very useful should an air raid disrupt the public water supply'.

KINGSTON BAGPUIZE WITH SOUTHMOOR

Kingston Bagpuize is an old settlement lying on an ancient ridge of corals and sands between the river Thames and the river Ock. The name Bagpuize probably comes from Ralf de Bachepuise (Bachepuise is a village in Normandy). He was granted the manor of Kingston from a rich baron, Henry de Ferrers, in the 11th century. Until the middle of the 20th century it was a small cluster of houses with an inn and a forge near the Saxon site of the present manor – Kingston House, now open to the public. The village has since then grown westwards along the line of the A420 to engulf Draycott Moor and Southmoor, to become an extended village catering for about 700 households.

Early in the 20th century Kingston was a fruit growing centre, later it specialised in hop growing on the warm, well-drained soils. All of these horticultural enterprises have declined substantially but the parish still produces many vegetables and some fruits for sale in a farm centre, which has now developed into a regional leisure facility with a variety of attractions, and a garden centre two miles east of the village. The hop fields still remain but their future is uncertain. Farming in the area is mixed arable with cattle, fodder crops, maize, wheat, barley and rape commonplace. Pig farming, although a smaller industry than in the 1960s and 1970s is still important, with both extensive and intensive rearing systems. A number of equestrian enterprises have been established and Riding For The Disabled have a centre at the western end of the village in the parish of Longworth. Small industries have come to the village and a wartime airfield is now the centre of a diverse range of small firms. Many local people commute to surrounding towns.

Until 1974, Kingston was part of Berkshire but the boundary between Oxfordshire and Berkshire was then moved southwards from the Thames to the Ridgeway above Wantage. Probably the most important event, apart from the two World Wars, to influence the village, however, has been the massive increase in traffic, and the provision in 1993 of the Kingston Bagpuize by-pass. This has triggered a new phase of development in the village. In twelve months from early 1997 over 100 houses were built in the village. However, the village retains a rural atmosphere which is very much a part of this eastern end of the Vale of the White Horse.

Kingston has a range of facilities – a small number of local shops, a church, chapel and three public houses. One of these, the Maybush, lies at Newbridge on the Thames, which forms the northern parish boundary. This is in fact the oldest bridge over the Thames and in 1644 the Parliamentary army was repulsed by the King's army at the bridge. An old coaching inn, 'The George', is now divided into three separate residences. There are a few scattered old Cotswold stone houses and farms in the parish but most of the housing stock is a mix of modern building materials. The large number of thriving social clubs in the village is a hallmark of the community – tennis and bowling clubs, horticultural society, drama group and history society as well as young people's groups such as scouting, guiding and youth club. The local primary school serves the community but secondary education is provided in nearby towns. The old village primary school now houses the

147

scout troop and a new village hall provides a centre for many village events.

KINGSTON BLOUNT

The village developed at the foot of the Chiltern Hills, on the spring line. The hills provided beech trees for feeding pigs, brushwood, timber and building material. The soil on the plain is both chalky and clay, being highly productive for farming. Newcomers pronounce the 'oun' in Blount as in 'round'. It is usually taken to be lazy speech but in fact 'Blunt', used by the people born and bred in the village, is the more correct because the village takes its name from the Le Blunt family, lords of the manor in the 13th to the 15th centuries.

The nearby Icknield Way carried a lot of sheep drovers and travellers who needed sustenance and lodgings during the Middle Ages. The village expanded in the 18th and 19th centuries and was self-sufficient. It was described in 1852 as a 'large and respectable town'. It had a number of pubs, a draper, grocers, wine merchants, a smithy, a corn merchant, a butcher, baker, post office and a school. Today there remains just one pub. The shops have all closed. With the decline of farming most villagers travel to work.

Even the telephone exchange has moved. In the early days of the telephone one of the local merchants knew the chief engineer. He felt that Kingston Blount would benefit by having the exchange. He heard that the decision would be made on a particular day according to how much use the telephone system had. The gentleman arranged for many of his clients to use it that day, thus making Kingston Blount the name for all the local village telephone numbers.

The school in the village was always small. The land had been given for the building by a local landowner whose wife took an especial interest in the attendance of the children. Elderly residents tell how she walked the village in a long back dress, a black walking stick with a silver top swinging as she walked. Whenever she found a child potato-picking or stone-gathering she gave several sharp slaps to the bottom and sent them off to school. Later she would stalk into school to check that the children were there. After the school's closure, the building became a village hall, and later when a new hall was erected, a private house.

The present village hall is run by the Hillwerke Trust and is situated alongside the allotments. Many years ago the villagers had rights to collect brushwood and fuel from a part of the woods called the 'Poors Hillock'. Village rumour had it that in the 19th century firewood was not the only thing to come down the hill, but that more appetising things came down too. In those days of harsh poaching laws, villagers were taking great risks. The rights were exchanged in 1864 for four acres of land to be used as allotments by the poor of the village. The new village hall was built on a field next to the allotments and it was fitting that the old medieval word 'Hillwerke' was used.

The railway line which ran through the village had a halt at Kingston Blount and was popular as a starting point for conveying agricultural produce to the towns.

Trains apparently never went very fast for there is a story of a keen horseman challenging the train driver to a race to Chinnor from the halt at Kingston Blount. The rider won.

🍁 KIRTLINGTON

Visitors to Kirtlington today will see an attractive village, with two greens, thatched cottages and a pond with ducks and daffodils in the spring. A walk round the village can take you through 'Tinkers Ditch', along 'Molly Minns' lane and to the church via 'Betty Bulls' lane. The track from South Green leads into Kirtlington Park with its many fine trees, including three ancient cedars bordering the sports field. From North Green, Mill Road passes a disused quarry where the bones of a dinosaur were discovered and where once stone was quarried and cement manufactured. This quarry is now a nature reserve and well worth a visit, with steps and paths leading round the quarry edge down to the canal and on through a wood. At the end of the road is the Oxford Canal with Pigeons Lock, Flights Mill and the river Cherwell. The working narrow boats of the past have been replaced by holiday barges. The floodgate near Flights Mill has an eel trap incorporated in its structure.

The village is listed in the Domesday Book as a thriving community. Centuries later, in 1742 workmen began clearing the site to build the house in Kirtlington Park for Sir James Dashwood and his family, then living at the manor of Northbrook. The Dashwood family moved into the completed

Polo in Kirtlington Park

house in 1746 and many generations of the family lived there until the beginning of the 20th century.

The school log book started in April 1887 records the tea parties given by Sir George and Lady Mary Dashwood for the schoolchildren, which were the highlight of the school year. The old school, which had been converted from a barn, had 156 pupils in 1894 who paid sums varying from 1d to 4d per week for their education depending on their father's occupation. Holidays included half days for blackberrying and for the Church Temperance Fete. This building was used until 1966 when staff and pupils moved into the new school built on the same site. There are at present over 60 pupils who take an active and lively role in village life.

The church of St Mary the Virgin has been used by worshippers for centuries, the Norman arch and chancel being the oldest part. An interesting church 'character' was James Sandford who was appointed Parish Clerk in 1702 at the age of eleven and held office for 54 years, recording the births of his five children in the parish register in capital letters. At 19 he was appointed schoolmaster and taught in the village for 45 years.

One traditional event takes place each year. The Lamb Ale Festival has been recorded in many contemporary writings of the past. A piece of land was set aside to grow wheat to make a cake and barley to make beer. Early writings tell of the maids of the village, on Trinity Monday, running after a fat live lamb with their thumbs tied behind them and the maid 'that with her mouth takes and holds the lamb' is declared Lady of the Lamb, which was later cooked and eaten at the Feast. Later accounts describe 'the dray with the load of ale' being escorted into the village by the Morris dancers. The lamb was carried on the men's shoulders to different farmhouses where, after a dance, beer and money were given to the dancers to help pay for the feast. Today the Lamb Ale Festival is a weekend of celebrations with a procession and dancing, with Morris sides from many parts of this country and abroad taking part. The 'Feast' is held on Trinity Monday and there is a fair on the South Green.

For nine years the Oxfordshire Triathlon was held in the village to raise funds for a new village hall, which has now been built thanks to the efforts of the villagers. This large, attractive building by the sports field is used for many and varied activities.

Another sporting activity which takes place in the village is polo. The Kirtlington Polo Club was started in 1926 by the Budgett family. In the beautiful setting of Kirtlington Park matches are keenly contested, with the ponies skilfully guided and controlled by their riders. Prince Charles was a frequent visitor, playing for the 'Cambridge Old Blues' team.

🍁 LAUNTON

Edward the Confessor gave the parish of Launton to the Abbey of Westminser in 1065 to provide the monks with financial support. This was the village's first appearance in recorded history: yet people had been living here for many centuries – the name is most likely an Anglo-Saxon one, '*lange-tun*', a long settlement. As recently as 1940 the majority of the houses did in fact form one long street.

The monks of Westminster Abbey are credited with building the first Manor farm, and, next to it a small chapel where villagers too might worship. This chapel was enlarged and became a church dedicated to the Assumption of the Blessed Virgin Mary in 1238. The only other building remaining in Launton from the medieval period is the tithe barn, situated between the church and farm. This huge structure has recently been splendidly refurbished and re-thatched.

An unusual event was recorded in Launton in 1830. On Monday, 15th February, at about 7.30 pm, a large meteorite was seen falling to earth, accompanied by a very bright light and three loud bangs. The stone fell into some freshly dug soil. The following morning it was recovered – it weighed about a kilogramme and was the size of a cricket ball – and can now be seen in the Natural History Museum in Kensington.

Like many small villages throughout the country, Launton was badly affected by the First World War. Nineteen young men – many of them related by blood or marriage – were slaughtered, mostly on the battlefields of Flanders. Part of the parish close to Caversfield was taken over at this time to form an airfield for the newly-formed RAF. During the Second World War this airfield was extremely busy, being used to train bomber crews from all over the Empire. Three Launton men were killed in action during 1939–45. Although there were Rolls of Honour in both the church and chapel, it was to commemorate the 50th anniversary of the ending of the Second World War that a war memorial was erected in 1995 in the village.

In 1948 the whole village was supplied with mains water, and with more and more building taking place the population soon overtook the previous high point of the 1870s. A piece of land in the village has been safeguarded from development for evermore by the planting of a 'woodland on your doorstep' as part of the village's celebration of the year 2000.

Today, Launton is a very vibrant place, with many activities catering for most ages and tastes – schools, shops, pubs, interest groups and a Social Club, as well as a reasonable bus service – yet it retains a close community feeling, where people matter and newcomers are welcomed.

🍁 LEAFIELD

The name Leafield comes from 'La Felde', French for 'the field', though it was usually called Feld or Field Town until the 19th century. It was probably given this name because the site was a natural clearing within Wychwood Forest. The ancient core of the village centres round the greens to the south of Leafield Barrow, on a small island of very infertile gravelly soil, which, in contrast to the surrounding area, is probably incapable of supporting fully-developed woodland. This would have made it attractive to settlers and, together with the presence of water from ponds and wells in the Oxford Clay around Leafield, no doubt explains the siting of the village.

For much of its existence, Leafield remained remote. Two themes which recur throughout Leafield's history are the strong links between the village and the surrounding Wychwood Forest and, secondly crime. The two are closely related, partly because the forest in its legal sense of an area under Forest Law, gave scope for punishing many minor offences, but also because in its literal sense it provided hiding and protection for wrongdoers. By the early 19th century, the district had a very bad name. Arthur Young, writing in 1813 said: 'The vicinity is filled with poachers, deer-stealers, thieves and pilferers of every kind: offences of almost every description abound so much, that the offenders are a terror to all quiet and well-disposed persons; and Oxford gaol would be uninhabited, were it not for this fertile source of crimes'. It was only after the deforestation of Wychwood in 1857 and the attendant changes in social and economic conditions that Leafield's reputation for lawlessness diminished.

Leafield had a number of customs associated with the forest. On Palm Sunday, the children went with bottles and liquorice into the forest to the spring known as Worts Well, or 'Uzzle', and drank the liquorice dissolved in the water. This seems to have been a continuance of an ancient custom, based on the supposed healing powers of the spring. According to John Kibble, a local historian who wrote in the 1920s, prayers were said at the spring. The local clergy did not approve of the custom. One Leafield villager has a crucifix given to her grandmother by the vicar, as a reward for being the only child to attend church on Palm Sunday, instead of going to the forest!

In the 18th and 19th centuries Leafield was an important centre for pottery manufacture, though the industry was probably established here very much earlier. The pottery was known as 'Field Town Chiney' and was crude, everyday earthenware, with a treacly orangey-brown glaze. Broken pieces are frequently found in the village gardens.

The main landmark in the village is the church, built, together with the old vicarage, in 1859 by the eminent Victorian architect, Sir George Gilbert Scott. It is the third on this site. The first, built sometime before 1533, and the second, which replaced it in 1822, were tiny chapels of ease. Communion and other regular services were held there, but for baptisms, marriages and burials the villagers had to go to Shipton. There was a handful of exceptions, as when in 1606 Robert Jeferie was baptised in the chapel because he was 'sicke and weake'. In 1831 a local farmer, Peter Harris, gave land for a churchyard, but marriages were not celebrated in Leafield until 1853.

Across the road from the church is the village cross. It is not known when or why it was first erected, but by the 19th century it was in a ruinous state. It was restored in 1873 as a memorial to Leafield's deliverance from a smallpox epidemic.

🍁 Letcombe Bassett

Long before the Norman Conquest, here, in this small village, Saxon families lived and worked, establishing a settlement at the foot of the Berkshire Downs, close to the 'lede in the combe' – the 'brook in the valley', so that in the Domesday survey the name became Ledecumbe. In 1158 came the addition of Bassett, from the name of Richard Basset, who by that time held the manor.

In Saxon days the population was possibly 150. It is now 174. Although most people today work outside the parish, there are still three farms which recall those early cultivators of ridge and furrow.

On the east side of the village is White's Farm House, which has Norman associations – the lovely gardens here slope away to the watercress beds. The marketing of the cress was once a thriving industry, the springs rising from the hills providing the necessary pure water for cultivation. 'Bassett Cress' was one of the cries of old Covent Garden market in London.

The Old Rectory, of 17th century origins, with its large thatched barn dating from around 1400, has in its garden the mulberry tree under which Dean Swift sat while writing some of his famous satires.

Another literary association with Letcombe Bassett was made by Thomas Hardy when he wrote *Jude the Obscure*. The cottage where Jude first saw Arabella can still be found down by the brook.

Racehorse training has been carried out for many years and the village rose to fame in Capt Tim Forster's time when the Grand National was won on three occasions, with the winners returning home to a tumultuous welcome. The stables are now run by Mark and Sarah Bradstock.

The little church of St Michael and All Angels stands, as it has done for some 850 years, on high ground near to Gramps Hill, which rises to the ancient Ridgeway. It has two features of special interest: the ornamentation on the Norman chancel arch and the Norman doorway on the north side of the chancel. The bells are Elizabethan, cast in 1576. They were made by William Knight II of Reading and are the only known dated examples by him in existence.

In 1774 land was set aside for the cutting of furze, to be divided amongst the poor as fire wood. In 1977 the land was sold and the money invested. The interest still provides pensioners with cash for electricity every winter.

The village hall was once the school, designed by William Butterfield. Today the children go to Childrey for primary education.

🍁 LETCOMBE REGIS

Letcombe was first recorded as 'Regis' in the reign of Richard II, but hundreds of years earlier it had been a Royal manor of the kings of Wessex, passing to William the Conqueror in 1066. King Stephen granted it to the Abbey of Cluny in France in 1136, and later kings had a hunting lodge here. The Old Manor was the original manor house.

Antwicks Manor, once an ancient moat house, was rebuilt at the end of the 19th century. 'Boss' Croker, who had made his millions in New York, turned it into a neo-Elizabethan mansion and headquarters of his racing stables. He also invented its name. One Bonfire Night in the early 1900s, a blazing effigy of a later owner of Antwicks was carried on a cart up to the iron gates. The crowd tried to tear down the gates and, from the steps of the Greyhound Inn, the Riot Act was read for the last time in England.

The third manor house in the village is more recent and houses the Letcombe Laboratory, now owned by the international firm of Dow Elanco. There used to be a story that another owner, an Edwardian lady, was so shocked by two naked statues in the grounds that she ordered them to be sunk in the lake. In 1982, when the lake was dredged, the 6ft high white marble statue of a man was found – a 2nd century Roman statue of the hero Hercules, which was later sold for £28,000. His female companion could not be traced, but there used to be tales of a woman in white who haunted the banks of the Letcombe Brook after drowning herself for love. The Letcombe Laboratory is visited by a ghostly but friendly nun.

St Andrew's church stands on a mound at the centre of the village, near where the two streams meet. An earlier church is mentioned in the Domesday Book, and parts of the present church date from the 12th century. The east window contains fragments of 14th century glass which have recently been reassembled. An obelisk in the churchyard records the death of George King Hipango, a Maori chief who came to England to train as a Christian minister. He died here of tuberculosis when he was 19 years old, while staying at the vicarage.

There are many interesting buildings in the village. These include the church with its partly 12th century tower, thatched cottages such as Regis Cottage with its carvings of angels, the thatched Manor Farm, the two dovecotes, the Gothic gatehouse to the Letcombe Laboratory, the Georgian 'Hollies' and the Victorian vicarage.

Letcombe Regis is still an agricultural and racing village with three stables. Visitors find they need to drive carefully along the winding roads as they meet strings of horses, promenading ducks, occasional flocks of sheep, and even a sleeping dog in the road, as well as numbers of parked cars. Many people work away from the village at Harwell and the Rutherford Appleton Laboratory or in nearby towns.

The village school used to be very much part of the community, but unfortunately closed in 1997 due to lack of pupils. The Sparrow public house closed in 1998, leaving the Greyhound as the only pub. The shop and post office went many years ago. However, there are several active clubs and societies in the village, including the cricket and football clubs, the WI, the Gardening Club and the Letcombe Singers.

🍁 LITTLE MILTON

Little Milton lies along the A329 Thame to Stadhampton road, but a number of its oldest and most attractive dwellings are on the Haseley Road – a turn left immediately after the Lamb Inn. Along this road are the Old Post Office and thatched cottages with gardens a profusion of colour in the spring and summer. At the centre of the village is Wells Farm, a working farm with an associated nature reserve managed by BBONT, providing several pleasant walks.

Visitors today will find only the village post office, but in the census of 1851 Little Milton was a very active village with five shops, four stonemasons and three dealers of livestock.

Farming was the main occupation of the village with prize flocks of Downs Cotswold sheep recorded in 1934. Also recorded in the 17th and 18th centuries were wheelwrights, carpenters, cordwainers and blacksmiths, with quarries providing employment. Many of the aforesaid occupations were still carried on well into the 20th century.

The present church of St James was built in 1843/44 and has a full peal of six bells. Set on high ground the church commands a fine view over fields. A footpath beside the church will lead you down through fields and spinneys to the river Thame at Cuddesdon.

A wealth of information is passed on today through the children and grandchildren of those who lived in Little Milton during the mid 1880s. During that time the village school had around 100 pupils. When attending church services the girls had to curtsy to the vicar on entering and leaving the church. Evening classes were run for the men of the village to learn to read and write as many of them had little or no schooling prior to the mid 1880s.

Village life was far from dull and listening to villagers who were children and teenagers during the 1920s and 1930s, they had a happy and full life, every season bringing some kind of celebration in the village to look forward to.

On Christmas Eve the bell ringers rang the midnight peal and then collected their Christmas boxes. This was followed on Christmas Day by family parties and on Boxing Day the Mummers would perform around the village followed by an excited band of children. Primrose Day on Good Friday was the only day on which people were allowed to pick primroses from Haseley Cover. These decorated the church and were given to the old people as Easter posies.

On the 1st of May the children would get up very early and with their garlands and head-dresses would go from house to house singing. It is recalled that provided the men of the village went to church on May Day they were then given the day off and went home to plant their vegetable gardens.

Feast Sunday was the highlight of the year, always held on the first Sunday after the 5th of August. It began with an open air service at the Cross accompanied by the Chalgrove Brass Band, the Feast followed and an afternoon of fun at the annual fair.

The village has altered little in appearance, although small developments have appeared. At Old Field, off Thame Road, houses were built and reserved for servicemen returning from the Second World War, and bungalows for the elderly and retired. Other more recent homes are mainly occupied by people who have come to the quiet of village life, and commute daily to their work or are retired.

Annual events today are still looked forward to, such as the village Fete in June, a day which can only be described as a continuation of the old Feast Day.

🍁 Little Wittenham

Little Wittenham is a hamlet of some two dozen houses at the foot of the Sinodun Hills, better known as Wittenham Clumps. The Clumps are a favourite place for walking and kite-flying, and there is a splendid view over the Thames valley as a reward for the climb.

They are historically important too: Castle Hill is the site of an Iron Age hill fort and pottery from the early Iron Age has been found there. Unfortunately some of the trees on Round Hill had to be felled a few years ago but new ones are growing and will in time restore the well-known outline. The Clumps are now part of the Northmoor Trust. This was established in 1982, primarily for the conservation of wildlife. The public have access to the grassland and Clumps by agreement between the Trust and Oxfordshire County Council. The Council pay the Trust a 'rent' of one red rose annually for allowing this.

Little Wittenham was formerly known as Abbot's Wittenham because of its connection with the Benedictine abbey in Abingdon. It has no school or shop; the only central meeting place is St Peter's church. This little church with its 14th century tower is well worth a visit, especially in early spring when the churchyard is full of aconites and snowdrops. The nave was restored in 1862 and contains some fine memorial brasses. There is a marble and alabaster monument of Sir Walter Dunch, his wife (an aunt of Oliver Cromwell), and nine children.

Below the church, the steep path leads to the Thames. On the left the Trust are restoring a field to its original state as a water meadow. A newly rebuilt bridge over the Thames brings you to Days Lock. Here you can picnic, swim (if you dare) and watch the boats go by. The World Pooh-sticks Championships are held in the New Year. These were established by a former lock-keeper to raise money for the Lifeboat Association, and have become an annual event. Competitors from near and far drop their stick into the water on one side of the bridge and rush to see whose is the first to come out the other side, just as Winnie-the-Pooh did in A. A. Milne's book.

🍁 LITTLEMORE

There has been a mental hospital at Littlemore for over a century. It was founded in 1846 as the Pauper Lunatic Asylum, but it became a well known and highly respected psychiatric hospital. In 1997 the old hospital closed when a modern one was opened on the opposite side of Sandford Road.

Cardinal Newman was vicar of Littlemore for 18 years. In 1828, when he first walked the three miles from Oxford, Littlemore was a hamlet, with only one street but plenty of scattered cottages, mainly occupied by farm workers. There was no church. Newman's fight for a church at Littlemore took seven years, but in 1835 the foundation stone was laid by Newman's mother.

Newman was a good and sincere man and people flocked to hear his sermons. He wrote the beautiful hymns *Praise to the Holiest* and *Lead, Kindly Light* and he made the rather bleak hamlet green by arranging for trees to be planted. With help from Bloxham, his curate, he founded the

159

village school. This is now the privately run Emmanuel Christian School. He loved Littlemore and inadvertently made it famous, for while living here he turned away from the Church of England and joined the Roman faith. In 1848 he became a Catholic priest and later was made a Cardinal whilst serving at Birmingham Oratory, where he remained until his death in 1890. The modern Roman Catholic church, built in 1968, is dedicated to The Blessed Dominic Barberi who received Newman into the Church. Roman Catholics from all over the world come to Littlemore to pay their respects.

Littlemore appears to have been based on religion, for there was a priory here as early as 1120. It was called The Minchery (meaning 'nuns') and even today part of Littlemore is called Minchery Farm.

The priory was not large. There appear to have been about six nuns and the prioress. By the 16th century the building was very dilapidated and the nuns afraid to sleep there. There was little space and they were sleeping two to a bed. The priory began to have a bad reputation.

In 1517 the prioress, Elizabeth Welles, was taken for trial. She was accused of letting the building go to ruin, ill-treating the young nuns and stealing goods from the priory. She was also accused of having a lover and a baby. The baby died, but Elizabeth said that she loved the man and was making a home for him. To join him she walked to Oxford accompanied by a seven year old boy, the son of another nun.

The prioress was deposed and the nunnery dissolved in 1523. It fell into ruins but was later restored and is now a public house.

The Baptists who had been preaching in Littlemore since 1804, built a chapel here in 1807 and also ran a flourishing Sunday school in the village.

In 1873 there was cholera in Oxfordshire and it was felt that something should be done urgently, so a sewage plant was constructed on the outskirts of Littlemore. It was open-land treatment and crude sewage was systematically poured out on to the fields. When the fields were resting normal farmwork was carried out. The vegetables, it is reported, were terrific, especially the Brussels sprouts, but the smell was terrible, particularly in the evening when the valves were opened. The mosquitos and flies, too, were numerous. For some reason, the smell was stronger on frosty mornings.

However, with this sewage farm, Littlemore became noted for its bird population; lapwing, snipe, corncrake and wild duck crowded the fields. Even today, there are many birds at Littlemore, including the reed bunting, and seagulls during the winter months. A new sewage system was installed in 1920 and the bird population dropped, as also did the smell!

Littlemore today is far different from the poor hamlet it once was. Its rural character has gone and houses have been built on the farmland no longer needed for the disposal of sewage sludge. All that remains of the old village life is its stocks, which are in Pitt Rivers Museum. A village no more, Littlemore became a suburb of Oxford in 1991.

🍁 LONG WITTENHAM

Long Wittenham, a Thames-side village of a thousand people, sits on a quiet yet historic site. Archaeological remains ranging from a mammoth's tooth to an Iron Age shield, from a Viking age bracelet to a Roman brooch, have been found in the parish, in addition to a complete Iron Age village and a large Saxon cemetery. The village cross, the base of which dates from the 7th century, by tradition marks the spot where St Birinus preached and converted the pagan Saxons to Christianity.

Walter Giffard, the 3rd Earl of Buckingham, rebuilt the church in 1120. Giffard built his church of white stone from Caen, in the Norman style; it was enlarged towards the end of the 12th century by the addition of the south aisle. The lead font, one of the few extant in England, was installed about the same time. The end of the 13th century saw the carving of the smallest effigy in England; that of a Crusader knight. This was possibly commissioned by Joan of Acre, second daughter of King Edward I, in memory of her husband Gilbert de Clare – 'Gilbert the Red' – Earl of Gloucester and Hertford, who had died in 1295.

There is a legend that during the Civil War Cromwell sat under the mulberry tree in the Old Farmhouse (the tree still stands); what is true is that the churchwardens, fearing that Cromwell's soldiers would melt down the lead font for bullets, surrounded it with a wooden packing case. There it remained hidden for 200 years, when it was rediscovered and restored in 1839. The wood from the case was used to build the small table which now sits just inside the church.

From 1322 Exeter College, Oxford had the right to name the vicar of St Mary's church, which included the right to gather the tithes. From 1554 the lord of the manor was St John's College, Oxford. Over the succeeding

161

centuries more and more of the parish was purchased by the college, and certainly it is only in the second half of the 20th century that the majority of the residents of the parish have owned their own homes.

The two colleges, and other large landowners, forced the enclosure of the parish in 1809–12, and the remainder of the century saw the agricultural labourers suffering chronic poverty. Respite was apparently found in the pubs, the church and importantly, the Primitive Methodist chapel, founded sometime before 1829.

The chapel became the village shop and post office, and still flourishes today. There are now four pubs in the village, all of which provide accommodation and food. The Plough dining room was once a slaughter-house, and the Vine was a butcher's shop. The Barley Mow enjoys fame as the venue for the writing of Jerome K. Jerome's *Three Men in a Boat*.

There are a number of cruck cottages in the village, notably Church Cottage and Cruckfield Cottage, as well as many other attractive styles of architecture. A fine old pigeon cote behind the church has now been restored and is used as an architect's office. A walk through the churchyard will bring you to the remains of the village cockpit and the manor house. The village also welcomes many visitors to the Pendon Museum, which specialises in model railways and a model of the Vale of the White Horse.

🍁 LONGWORTH

Originally known as the village of Worth, the prefix 'Long' was added to describe its narrow shape. Situated on a ridge, the land drops away to the north where the river Thames forms the boundary. The soil is good sandy loam, excellent for growing most vegetables and flowers.

The oldest building in the village is the Anglican church, part of which was constructed in the 12th century. A leaflet on the table inside the south door describes the many items of interest, such as the brasses and the fragments of the monument to one of the Marten family. The monument was said to have been destroyed when Charles II came to the throne as Henry Marten had signed the death warrant of Charles I in 1649. Other distinguished persons to be born in Longworth were John Fell in 1625 and Richard Doddridge Blackmore in 1825, both sons of former rectors. John Fell later became Dean of Christ Church, Oxford and is recalled in the epigram:

> 'I do not like thee, Doctor Fell,
> The reason why I cannot tell
> But this I know and know full well,
> I do not like thee, Doctor Fell.'

Richard Blackmore was the author of the well known book, *Lorna Doone*.

Longworth village still has a few houses more than 100 or 200 years old, but during the 1980s many of the small cottages were 'developed' to make larger luxury homes. Still much of their character has been retained.

In the early 20th century, Longworth became famous for its rose-growing. Though only a small village it boasted two rose nurseries, Prince's and Drew's. The two world wars interrupted the growing and breeding and now the specialist rose breeders are found elsewhere.

Another unusual occupation in Longworth is that of the small family firm of Robert Longstaff, makers of high quality wooden toys and of folk and early musical instruments, which are sold in the UK and abroad.

Though a small village of some 550 adult persons, Longworth has a pub, two churches, a primary school, and a well run village hall. For many years the school was held behind the chapel (now the United Reformed church) but in the 1960s a new one was built on land acquired by the council for the Bow Bank estate, many houses having been erected in the early 1950s. The school serves Hinton Waldrist as well as Longworth.

🍁 LYFORD

About one mile from, and in the ecclesiastical parish of Charney Bassett, is the small village of Lyford. The name derives from a ford over the river and 'Ly' indicates a place were flax was once grown.

Lyford's link with history is bound up in Lyford Grange, the house where the Jesuit priest and martyr, Edmund Campion, in the reign of Elizabeth I was captured after celebrating Mass in 1581. He has since been canonised.

The small church of St Mary is mainly Jacobean, and was built on the site of an earlier oratory or chapel of ease. It serves a parish of only about 70 souls. There is no shop or inn, but Lyford shares all the amenities of Charney Bassett.

🍁 MARCHAM

The name Marcham is thought to come from 'merece', Old English for wild celery. Marcham was the only inland site for this plant in Southern England and it grew here because of salt springs south of the village. Unfortunately these were piped some years ago and it's now doubtful that any celery remains. Marcham is today probably better known as the 'Denman College village', and its many students can be seen strolling around the streets in the afternoon when on courses there. Denman College is the National Federation of Women's Institutes' own independent residential college.

There is however much more to Marcham, and its ancient byways are always interesting.

Turn up North Street, between the Crown Inn and the large garage, and you will see a selection of pretty cottages of varying styles, including a thatched house with a decorative thatched bird on the roof. St Nicholas's hall, built in the early years of the 20th century, is the village meeting place, and has a pair of splendid red brick lions, with shields, at its entrance.

New Road is nearly 200 years old and was cut by Mr Duffield along with a new entrance to Marcham Park (as Denman College was previously known) to keep the hoi-poloi further away from his front door. This road also leads to the church, a handsome 19th century building with a 13th century tower. There is an active Baptist group in the village with a small church on the main road.

To the south of the churchyard is the 17th century vicarage, dated 1645, with its tithe barn and attractive dovecote. The date may record repairs done after a Civil War skirmish took place nearby as parts of the house are considerably older than this. Early in the 1900s the body of a murdered new-born baby was found in this house following the hearing, over many months, of strange crying noises. Note the attractive porch with its twin 'bustle' seats.

Church Street is a quiet road to walk down, and has the Victorian rectory on the right and some of the latest additions to the village, in All Saints' Close, to the left. The building on the left as we rejoin the main road used to be a pub, 'The White Hart', but is now being converted into a private house. Turn left here and walk on along the main road passing a second dovecote and the wayside cross commemorating Marcham's war dead on the opposite side of the road.

Mill Road leads south from the village to Marcham Mill on the river Ock, a tributary of the Thames. Here we find 'green' Marcham, a haunt of butterflies and birds, and also the pound where straying animals were impounded.

Across to the east lie two old buildings, the Priory and Hyde Farm. The Priory was never a priory but a grange or farm of Abingdon Abbey, supplying food and perhaps being used as a retreat by the Abbot. Hyde Farm is a 13th century farmhouse, the oldest complete surviving domestic building that belonged to Abingdon Abbey. Next to Hyde Farm is a nursery which also sells caged birds and tropical fish.

Marcham has a post office and stores, a newsagent, a small supermarket and a carpenter. Coal is delivered, as are fish and milk. The village doubled in size in the 1960s when the new school was built, and has been increasing in size ever since. A small estate called the Farthings was built on land previously owned by Denman College. On the outskirts of the village there is a vineyard and nearby is the Doghouse, an attractive restaurant and hotel. The Ark Restaurant lies south-west of the village on the road to Wantage.

The two hamlets of Frilford and Garford are included in the ecclesiastical parish and are worth a visit. Frilford has a large pick-your-own farm and garden centre, with a restaurant, and Garford has an interesting small chapel of ease almost hidden in a farmyard.

🍁 MARSTON

In 1991 the parish of Marston was included within the boundary of the City of Oxford and the village became known as Old Marston, though the church is still St Nicholas Marston. The parish includes not only the old village but many new houses to the north, south and east, built since the late 1930s. Before then things were very different and access to North Oxford was by path along the river Cherwell or by the hand-operated Marston Ferry, and to Headington by an ancient footpath along the line of Saxon Way. In fact Marston was almost as isolated as it had been for hundreds of years.

The present line of the village street and Back Lane indicated the layout from earliest times. Each copyholding tenant of the manor had a strip of land running at right angles to the village street, many with still-existing stone-lined wells which collect water from below the gravel. Mains water did not come till the late 1920s and main drainage in 1933. Beyond Back Lane each copyholder had strips of land in the communal fields – Colterne, Sutton and

Marsh, and the use of the Cow Pasture. Brookfield, where the allotments now are, was attached to the demesne farm, Court Place. In some places the ridges and furrows can still be seen.

The Civil War and siege of Oxford put an end to the open field cultivation. Parliamentary troops under General Fairfax were billeted in the village. Earthworks were made in the fields and some time between 1646 and 1674 the fields were divided and enclosed by quickset hedges into pastures and closes. The surrender of the Royalist forces was arranged in the Mansion House, then owned by Unton Croke, a lawyer. This had been built about 1622 on the site of a previous house belonging to his wife, Anne Hore. It stands at the north end of the village in Mill Lane. After a period of decay in the late 18th and early 19th centuries, when it housed Napoleonic War prisoners and then paupers, it was altered and divided into the two present houses, Cromwell House and Manor House.

The yeoman farmers who took over the newly enclosed fields in the late 17th century, built, along the village street, substantial stone house of the 'long house' type, probably thatched. Each had its original strip or strips of orchard and garden and one or more of the outlying fields where they reared cattle, to a lesser extent sheep, and grew hay and corn. The cows would be brought back to the farms in the village for milking, along the wide grassy, very muddy street with its bordering ditch and ponds. This was still happening in the 1950s though the road was better and the ditch was underground. There were also many very small thatched cottages of one or two rooms which have disappeared in living memory, but some later brick and slate of the 'one up, one down' variety have been modernised and fetch high prices. These used to house farm labourers, often with large families. The five pubs nicely spaced through the village must have provided social life, at least for the men.

With the decline in farming and the improvement of roads, Oxford people who valued the countryside peace moved out, a process which has rapidly increased. More new houses have been built and residents now include many professional people, including university dons. One of the very distinguished was Lord Florey of penicillin fame, who shared the Noble Prize for Medicine in 1945 and whose memorial is in the church porch.

There are still builders, plumbers, a picture framer, an upholsterer, a printer, and until recently the famous Vardoc tie factory, and the Unicol office equipment factory.

St Nicholas' church has had a succession of splendid vicars, notably the Rev John Hamilton Mortimer 1904–1952, and later the Rev Paul Rimmer 1959–1990, and now since 1991 the Rev Tony Price. In 1995 the joint benefice of St Nicholas' church, Marston and St Thomas of Canterbury's church, Elsfield came into being. Mr Mortimer was a great benefactor to the village. He bought John Honour's builders' workshop to make the village reading room, where the Mortimer Memorial Garden now is with its trees, bulbs and wild flowers. He also gave land for the recreation ground beside the Mortimer Hall.

The village, now regrettably divided by Marston Ferry Road, still keeps much of its old coherence and is lucky to have a post office and shop, a great meeting place and convenience. It has become a conservation area and the fields and the Victoria Arms belong to the Oxford Preservation Trust. Hard work and vigilance try to keep the character of the village compatible with the inevitable change which time brings.

MILTON-UNDER-WYCHWOOD

Milton-under-Wychwood lies in the valley of the river Evenlode on the eastern edge of the Cotswold hills near the once Royal forest of Wychwood.

A firm of building contractors (Alfred Groves & Sons) has had a profound influence on Milton. The firm has its origins in a building business started in 1660 by William Groves, who was one of Wren's team employed on rebuilding St Paul's Cathedral after the Great Fire. The present company was founded by Alfred Groves in the 19th century and was, for many years, the main employer in the village.

Milton has had to absorb change as each decade has seen new housing development. The old-established local families and the newcomers have, together, produced a population with a wide social and age range. The village hall and sports pavilion accommodate societies for all age groups including the playgroup, Local History Society, Allotments & Gardens Association, Women's Institute, Handicrafts, Evergreens and the men's football and cricket teams. The village green has children's playground equipment, a paddling pool and a hard multi-sports area. St Simon & St Jude church and the Baptist chapel have active congregations but the Methodist and Zoar Baptist Chapels have been converted for residential use.

167

Public transport is very limited but we are fortunate in having a variety of shops and services.

There are a dentist, branch of the County library, doctors' surgery, post office and newsagent, bank, butcher, hardware shop, hairdresser, electrical shop, grocer and The Quart Pot public house. There are also other small businesses employing local people but workers commute to Oxford and farther afield. A voluntary hospital car service takes patients without their own transport to hospitals in Oxford, Banbury, Chipping Norton and Burford.

Ruins of Minster Lovell Hall

🍁 MINSTER LOVELL

Domesday Book records two manors, Minstre and Parva Minstre (Little Minstre) separated by the river Windrush, the connecting bridge once being a toll bridge. In the first half of the 19th century the land on the higher ground towards Brize Norton was chosen by the Chartist Land Company for one of its housing allotment developments, and from the 1930s up to the present day the housing in this area has increased.

In early days the sheltered valley, with the river Windrush for fish, marshland for gamefowl and thatching reed, the Wychwood Forest for protection (villagers often disappeared to live in the forest in troubled times), timber and fuel, and plenty of quarriable stone, made it an obvious place for continuous habitation. Roman Akeman Street passes through the north of the parish, there are names of Celtic derivation and a jewelled brooch (thought to have come from the same workshop as the Alfred Jewel) was found here. There have been at least two manor houses on the same site and two churches, together with a chapel and an alien cell, for the church and land in Minster was once given to the abbey of Ivry in Normandy. The name Minster acknowledges the fact that the church here was of some significance in this area.

St Kenelm's church, named after the Cotswold prince, was completed in about 1450 and is very little changed except for the removal of the chancel screen and the minstrels' gallery. Cruciform in design and Perpendicular in style, it has an unusual central crossing where minor arches support the tower, which is narrower than the nave.

William Lovell, whose effigy is to be found in the church, rebuilt the manor house and the church. The family came to full eminence with William's grandson, Francis, Viscount Lovell, who was Lord Chamberlain to Richard III, and Richard is known to have stayed at Minster Hall, as did his successor Henry VII on three occasions. After the death of Richard at Bosworth Field, Francis supported the pretender, Lambert Simnel, the Oxford baker's boy, and escaped again after further defeat at the battle of Stoke to disappear, which was the occasion for various legends, one being that he was incarcerated in a secret room at Minster Hall where he perished. John Buchan makes use of the legend in his fine historical novel *The Blanket of the Dark*. Later the house passed into the Coke family, sometime Earls of Leicester, but they rarely lived here and Thomas Coke dismantled much of the house to sell off the materials to raise money to build his great house and 'museum' at Holkham in Norfolk. The remaining romantic ruins show what a fine house it must have been.

The Chartists' housing development, called Charterville, was designed to rehouse city dwellers in the countryside, to make them more self-sufficient and to qualify them for the vote through the ownership of land. The development of 78 bungalows, each with land of from two to four acres, a school and school house, took only ten months to build in 1847, but the newcomers did not settle to the rural life and soon most of the allotments were sold off. Although it could be called a failed experiment, the bungalows remain a token to good craftsmanship.

At the turn of the 20th century Minster Lovell was famous for is rushes and river crayfish. Rushes were used for caulking barrels and the rush cutter, Mr Greengrow, who came every year from Kent, declared this rush to be the best in the south of England.

The village once had three mills. There remains only one and this has been converted into a beautiful conference centre. However, there are three pubs. The Olde Swan is widely known and contains many features of its distant past. The White Hart was once a busy coaching inn serving coaches on the London-Gloucester-Cheltenham route. The New Inn, formerly called the 'Garibaldi', was only licensed at the end of the 19th century and was formerly a Charterville bungalow.

🍁 MORETON

The hamlet of Moreton lies one mile to the south-west of Thame and forms part of its parish. It has been in existence as long as Thame, being mentioned with it in the Domesday Book.

In the past the main occupation of the inhabitants was farming – there being at least seven farms and more than 30 cottages, the majority housing the farm labourers. A decline in agriculture greatly reduced the size of the village and eventually led to the closure of the Methodist chapel, the school and the shop, which now are all transformed into attractive houses. The bottom of the decline came in the 1950s and today there are about 50 houses/cottages, plus two farms and a smallholding, all family-owned and run.

The majority of Moreton's older buildings cluster at the east end of the hamlet surrounding the green and the two ponds. They then trail thinly up to the war memorial which was erected in 1920. On from the war memorial is a small, but mixed, collection of houses, including the pub.

Although to car users Moreton is now a cul-de-sac, its roads were passable once. Until well into the 18th century, the main thoroughfare from Aylesbury to Tetsworth and Wallingford ran through Moreton. The needlemakers of Long Crendon made use of this road twice a year to send their goods via stage coach for sale in London. Before that, it was used by the Roundheads, who would have passed through carrying the mortally wounded John Hampden from the battle of Chalgrove to Thame in 1643.

Like many villages (and towns) in Oxfordshire, Moreton was troubled by pillaging during the Civil War. This era is the one that appeared to have produced the 'troubled spirit' that haunts Brook Cottage. The various happenings have been recorded by Mr Ron Mott (now an inhabitant of Thame) who was born in the cottage. He remembers his parents occasionally referring to hearing the 'Old Man's' rat-tat on the door and heavy footsteps on the brick path outside.

Until early in the 20th century, Moreton was a two-pub hamlet with the Bell at one end and the Royal Oak at the other. The former was closed in 1908 but the latter (still going strong) was renowned in the neighbourhood as having the best beer, brewed on the premises by its blind but redoubtable publican, Mr John North.

In the mid 1990s the area between Lobbersdown Hill and Moreton underwent a topographical change to accommodate a golf course. Any fears that this would have an adverse effect on the village have proved to be groundless. Although the lines of some footpaths were altered they, and the bridleways, were upgraded, old existing trees remain, and nesting boxes have been built to house the barn owls. The golf course has become host of international competitions, and Moreton has an attractive and safe walking area where countryside, and golfing, delights can be enjoyed.

🍁 MURCOTT

Murcott, linked usually with Fencott, is the smallest of Otmoor's 'seven towns'. Separated by a straight mile of road, and green belt, the two villages barely support 100 dwellings, although Murcott has its own surviving public house, the Nut Tree, an Anglican church and a Primitive Methodist chapel dated 1847, both still in use. Only two small lanes off the main road provide access to the few houses.

Much of the customary winter flooding has been eradicated by the present Otmoor drainage schemes and the advent of mains water and sewage disposal to the village. It is barely 30 years ago though, that many householders moved upstairs to escape the periodic flooding. Certainly when the roads flooded they became impassable, the waters ebbing and flowing like a tidal wave.

Because of its close proximity to Otmoor, and during the Second World War, the practice bombing ground, one cottage received a direct hit from a German bomb, killing a mother and child who had evacuated here for safety from London's bombs. There were several other bombs unloaded in the area, which left enormous craters.

Murcott House, dated 1803, would seem to have been the first cottage in the village in its original form. Many additions have been made during subsequent decades. Very few of the thatched cottages remain with any vestige of their original form. Most have succumbed to modern development.

The Nut Tree has been modernised and enlarged, but with the thatched roof and reflection in the village pond, still retains much of its rustic charm.

Fiveacres still retains its original cottage which until 30 years ago housed the village shop. Later another shop was set up, almost next door, but with modern ease of transport to the supermarkets it proved an uneconomic venture; both shops are now dwelling houses.

Murcott was essentially a farm village; apart from the three actual farms, every householder owned sufficient land to run a smallholding. The little paddocks still bear witness to the validity of the green belt area; there has been very little building off the main road. The lanes lead directly on to the moor and provide relaxing and delightful walks for the enthusiast.

🍁 NETTLEBED

Nettlebed is one of the highest villages in the Chilterns, 211 metres above sea level, in an area of outstanding natural beauty. It stands on the Roman road between London and Oxford and Queen Elizabeth I is reputed to have stayed at the White Hart Hotel, a very old coaching inn situated in the main street.

Nettlebed was famous for its brick industry. Tiles and bricks were made here from at least the 14th century onwards. In 1365, 35,000 tiles were made for Wallingford Castle and they were also made for the roofing of a hall and chamber at Abingdon Abbey in 1422–3. Bricks were also made for the almshouses at Ewelme and for the chapel in Stonor Park. One bottle kiln remains, probably of 18th century date and it was restored between 1972–74.

The church of St Bartholomew has two stained glass windows designed by John Piper and interpreted by Patrick Teyntiens. The south window is in memory of Peter Fleming (1907–1971), a writer, traveller and soldier, and the east window is in memory of Robin Williamson, a much loved and respected doctor who served Nettlebed and the surrounding districts from 1946 to 1969.

The village hall was built in 1913 and presented as a gift by Robert Fleming. The Nettlebed Working Men's Club which uses the hall has recently changed its name to become the Nettlebed Village Club. The Fleming family lived at Joyce Grove, now a Sue Ryder Home. Joyce Grove was given to St Mary's Hospital, Paddington as a convalescent home and eventually sold to Sue Ryder in 1978.

NORTH LEIGH

The village of North Leigh has a particularly rich tradition of stories and rhymes. For instance, the North Leigh Enclosure Award is dated 14th April 1759. During 1760 and 1761 feelings were running high over the enclosures and when fences and hedges belonging to James Leigh Perrot were torn down by rioters the Berkshire Militia marched from Witney to North Leigh, where several were arrested. Thus this version of a contemporary verse –

> 'They was bad what stole the geese off the common . . .
> But they was wuss what stole the common off the geese.'

A spring supplied the town well, which was situated near the Gospel chapel, and the pond which in the Enclosure Award was called Cucking Stood Pond. The name later changed to Cuckamus pond and is now Cuckamus Green. A certain Billy Wickson was blamed for the low level of water in the well and evidently the villagers were glad to see the back of him!

> 'Now grumbling Billy has gone away,
> There's plenty of water night and day'.

On the floor of the chancel in St Mary's church is a brass of Thomas Beckingham, 1431. On returning from the wars, it was said, he was told of a monster living in Fish Hill Bottom below the church. He decided to do battle with it and taking his sword he went alone and succeeded in killing it, though in so doing he lost his life. He was found next day with his feet on the monster – as shown in the brass!

In early 1996 it was agreed that the church needed a new organ. Funds were raised through many special events in the village, to buy the 1861 organ built by Father Henry Willis. It was restored in the workshops of Bishop & Sons in Ipswich. By August 1997 it had been installed and tuned, and was blessed by the Rt Rev Richard Harries, Bishop of Oxford.

🍁 NORTHMOOR

Northmoor is a very small village, of about 70 houses, in the rough triangle of land bounded by the Windrush to the west, the Thames to the south and east and the gravel lakes of Stanton Harcourt to the north. Its position has meant that the area has been remarkably undisturbed by roads or development, with the result that recent archaeological exploration has been able to find signs of continuous habitation and land cultivation going back to the Iron Age.

The village lies very low, and until a system of drainage ditches was dug by prisoners of war during the Second World War, was liable to flooding. Not only does it lie hidden off the beaten track, on the way to nowhere, but its shape is so strung out and full of gaps that it is possible for strangers to whisk through in their cars without quite realizing that they have been through a village. This impression is perhaps assisted by the fact that the nucleus of architecturally interesting buildings, that is to say the church which dates back to the 14th century, the Elizabethan Rectory Farm close by, with its dovecote, and, a little further off, the 18th century Church House, all stand well back from the road, offering only glimpses to the passing motorist.

But to the inhabitants of Northmoor, it is a very real and vital community. The farm just mentioned is a working farm, with its bulging haysheds and barns full of cattle bordering the churchyard. On the other side of the road is Ferryman's Farm, still in operation, though part time now, its cow byres visited by local children whenever there's a newborn calf to be kept in the warm. The sight of a tractor trundling along the village road, or, at the appropriate times, of livestock being herded down the street is so common here that only a townee would comment. But modern farming methods require less labour than formerly, so what used to be primarily an agricultural community is now more diverse. The largest single substitute for farm employment has been gravel extraction, carried out by the international conglomerate ARC on a very large scale.

Northmoor takes some pride in being a working, as distinct from a

175

dormitory or weekend, village. It is true that, sadly, the one-room primary school had to close, the village shop and post office is now a private house, and the Dun Cow pub closed in 1991. But there is a continuing focus for village life in the form of the Red Lion, and the recently restored church, with its crusading knight and his lady, the de la Mores, after whom the village is named.

NORTH MORETON

The manor of North Moreton is recorded in the Domesday book of 1086, and a church existed then. The manor house itself no longer exists, its site lying east of the church and roughly identified by the remains of a moat.

North Moreton retains many houses from the 15th, 16th and 17th centuries, despite a fire in 1807 which destroyed one side of the main street. Important buildings include Stapleton's Chantry, where the chantry priests once lived, the Tudor vicarage and a tithe barn. The church itself has a 12th century tub-font. The glass in the chantry is regarded by experts as one of the finest examples of late 13th century glass in the country.

In August 1603 'this little village' was visited 'with great sickness', ten people dying 'all out of one house where the plague did first begin'. 'It could never be known how it did first come' although the incumbent, far ahead of his times, made a reference to bad water being drunk. Thirty-nine people died in that month, the normal death rate for the 17th century in the parish being about five a year.

Later in the century, the village was a centre for marriages under the Protectorate of Cromwell – five times as many ceremonies taking place as in any comparable period in the 16th and 17th centuries. People came from as far as Wallingford and Abingdon to be married by a parson licensed to perform the ceremony, probably because of his Cromwellian sympathies.

The comparative remoteness of North Moreton ended in the 19th century. The coming of the railways provided both links and employment while the episcopate of Samuel Wilberforce, in the diocese of Oxford, encouraged the restoration of the church fabric in North Moreton in the 1850s.

In the following 14 years, North Moreton came under the influence of the Oxford Movement. The incumbent, Albert Barff, brought important figures in the movement such as Edward King, Henry Liddon, John Keble and

Edward Pusey to preach on several occasions. Barff's visitation returns provide an interesting commentary on local events. He noted, for example, the relationship between agricultural depression and population movements. North Moreton's population dropped from 400 in the 1841 census to well below 300.

In the 20th century, among those who lived in North Moreton were R. G. Collingwood, described in the *Dictionary of National Biography* as 'one of the most learned men of his generation', and the pioneer women-educationalists Geraldine and Eglantyne Jebb. The village firm of Thames Valley Eggs Ltd was founded by A. G. Kingham. Beginning as a farmers' co-operative in 1934 it is now part of one of the largest organisations of its kind in Western Europe.

Today North Moreton is a typical commuting village although increasing numbers of people find it possible to work from home for at least part of their time. Cricket has always been a feature of village life since the club was founded in 1858 and it is one of the oldest clubs in Oxfordshire.

🍁 NORTH STOKE

North Stoke is one of a handful of pretty villages between Wallingford and Goring. It has a population of about 200, which has remained stable for many years.

To reach the quaint village street, pass the modern buildings and former council houses on the B4009 and turn into Cook Lane, where in 1966 a few bungalows and chalets were built on what used to be allotments. After a sharp right turn, 'The Street' appears very much as it has for many years, a mixture of farmhouses and cottages. At the end of the street is the mill, over a stream called the Drincan, flowing from the spring-fed lake to the north-east of the village. Until the 19th century the mill ground corn and provided meal for the villagers' bread, but latterly it harnessed the force of the stream to generate electricity to light The Springs house. The mill later became derelict, but has now been restored and is a private home. Beyond the mill the Ridgeway Path, which passes through the village, leads along a bridle track towards Mongewell.

The old farmhouses, built mainly in the 16th, 17th and 18th centuries, have been restored or extended and are now the comfortable homes of business or professional people. How different from former times when all the inhabitants were employed in the village, either on the farms, in the big houses or in Robert Keen's North Stoke Wagon Works that was in production from 1936 until it moved to Wallingford in the late 1940s. There are still a few original cottages, though some were demolished and others extended. Until the early 1960s, there had been virtually no new building for many years.

The largest house in the village is The Springs. In the early part of the 20th century the house was occupied by Sir John Wormald, who added to the house and improved the beautiful grounds. He was a generous benefactor to the village, providing it with a village hall and an excellent cricket ground. Unfortunately, years later a subsequent owner had the cricket field ploughed up! Sir John was said to be a man who liked, and usually got his own way. On Sunday mornings in church, while sitting with his family in his front pew, he would ostentatiously turn and scan the congregation to see who among his workers was missing! The house became an old people's home in the late 1950s and since about 1970 has been an hotel. Recently a golf course has been added and is proving very popular.

The village no longer has a shop, post office, school or pub. The nearest public house, the King William, is in the neighbouring village of Ipsden, two miles away.

From The Street, a short lane leads to the 13th century St Mary's church. Inside there are interesting wall paintings and a Jacobean pulpit. On the west side of the church beneath the tower is a memorial to Dame Clara Butt, the singer, who with her husband Robert Kennerley Rumford, lived at Brook Lodge from 1922. There are still some in the village who remember, with pleasure, her rich contralto voice. When possible she entered into village life and was, in fact, the first president of the North Stoke WI. The lime-shaded lychgate at the entrance to the churchyard, was given by Dame Clara in memory of one of her two sons, both of whom died young.

The 17th century Rectory Farm House, next to the church is one of several houses built on this site, thought to be originally that of a Roman settlement.

This village has had its share of interesting characters, but none so eccentric as the gentleman who in the 1930s kept lions at The Grange, and took them for walks along the village street.

🍁 ODDINGTON

Oddington, situated on the edge of Otmoor, is an attractive village of about 115 people. It has two village greens and a beautiful church with a 13th century tower.

The churchyard, which affords spectacular views of Otmoor, contains the grave of a Maori princess, Maggie Papakura, who lived in Oddington after her marriage to a local farmer. She died in 1930. A Maori war memorial, given by her in memory of the Maori soldiers who lost their lives in the First World War, can be seen inside the church, and groups of Maoris regularly come to Oddington to visit her grave.

The church also contains an unusual 15th century memorial brass depicting a former rector. He is shown in his shroud, with maggots emerging from various parts of his anatomy! This is meant to express the spiritual humility of the deceased.

The farmhouses are all large and old; one has a fireplace dated 1659. As in most villages, there have been barn conversions and a new housing development, keeping the population steady and bringing the number of houses back to what it was before the two rows of thatched cottages were demolished in the 1950s.

Oddington is closely bound to Otmoor, which still has an air of mystery and remoteness, even though much of it has been reclaimed and grows heavy crops of corn. Large tracts of the moor have recently been bought by the RSPB, who aim to restore the wetland and encourage back birds such as the bittern.

🍁 OLD HEADINGTON

The impact created by Old Headington is one of inherited timeless character as a 'Village within a City'! So it was aptly identified by Leslie Taylor and Jean Cook in their book.

The polished axes of prehistoric man, found locally, can be seen in the Ashmolean and Pitt-Rivers Museums. There is also evidence of Roman pottery and kilns. Quarrying was a source of village livelihood, and many farms, dairy and agricultural, were scattered over the area, giving a mixed community.

Many beautiful houses, some dating from the 17th century and vernacular in character, lie alongside small attractive cottages. A feature of the village are the rubble-stone walls that surround the properties and line the crofts and lanes that criss-cross the village.

The manor house is now used as offices by the Oxfordshire Health Authority. It had previously been the preliminary training school for nurses. The old TB hospital and convalescent home have long since disappeared in a sea of laboratories, and a large modern hospital has brought social and visual dominance to the area. Undeterred are flocks of wagtails that gather on the roof garden to roost, and the song of the nightingale can still be enjoyed.

Bury Knowle Mansion, built in the 19th century, and set in an attractive park now open to the public, offers sports facilities and space to enjoy peace and quiet. The City Council acquired the property that now houses a branch library.

Granny Berry, who had twelve children, started baking bread in the farm kitchen when her husband died. The popular bakery was run by three generations, but sadly is now closed and a modern house stands on the site.

A pub rhyme, naming all the old Headington pubs goes as follows: 'A Black Boy rode a White Horse carrying a Royal Standard, shouting rule Britannia. He chased the White Hart which had a Bell around its neck. This disturbed the Fox which ran to ground at the Princess Castle.' The White Hart, the Black Boy and the Bell are still serving ale in the village, but the other public houses are now outside the parish.

The church of St Andrew, which may have originated as a small Saxon building on the same site, was founded by St Frideswide in 1004. Later rebuilt, it has had many repairs and additions, and in 1977 the 19th century roof was somewhat controversially redecorated in strong medieval colours. An underground passage is said to run from the church to the Rookery now owned by Ruskin College. The Fish Window marks the initiation of the Fish Good Neighbourhood Scheme, adopted world wide. New seating arrangements allow for religious plays, organ recitals and choral works to be performed.

From the original post office, telegrams were dispatched by horse and cart, and the shops selling fresh bread, fish, meat and vegetables have sadly disappeared. A large supermarket now supplies village needs, and a car park stands on the site of what was once a market garden. Mattocks, the famous rose growers, started their nurseries in the village.

Transport into Oxford was provided by the *Rocket*, a two-horse brake that needed two extra horses to pull it up Headington Hill. William Morris, later Lord Nuffield, initiated the first double-decker buses. Now, ironically, the village has no direct public transport.

The Friends of Old Headington, now affiliated with the Oxford Preservation Trust, have been given three awards for watching over development proposals, thus helping to preserve the character of the village, which has been recognised as a conservation area. Many of the houses are designated as listed buildings, and several new projects have been sympathetically designed and screened behind the original rubble-stone walling.

OVER NORTON

The village lies about one mile north of the town of Chipping Norton. The earliest dated record (12th century) concerns Cold Norton Priory, so called because of its bleak situation.

In 1559 some priory buildings were let, including the Chapel on the Heath, situated off what was then the main road from Oxford and which is today signposted to Heythrop. According to local legend, the priory had a secret underground passage, said to have been used in later times by highwaymen.

The chapel was eventually demolished and an inn, no longer extant as such, named the Shakespeare's Head took its place.

Other roads, or dust tracks, came into use, including the 'Woolway' from Great Rollright. This route would be taken by Cotswold sheep, famous for their quality wool. The ancient 'Salt Way' also crossed Over Norton from the west to avoid the toll area.

A family of landowners named Dawkins has been prominent in the village since the early 18th century, when James Dawkins (1696–1766) is recorded as living here. Born in Jamaica, he was MP for Woodstock from 1734 to 1747, and is commemorated by a plaque in Chipping Norton church. A later member of the family, Henry Dawkins, was also an MP. As a tribute to him and his wife, Emma, both of whom died in 1864, their four children had a memorial drinking fountain erected on the village green, where it can still be seen. Over Norton Park, a Dawkins property, consists of some 90 acres of well-wooded grounds. The present house (in Tudor style) was built in 1879, replacing an earlier one.

Some considerable interest was taken in Over Norton Park in 1891 when geological exploration was carried out regarding the likelihood of a coal seam being present. A report for Lt Col W. G. Dawkins produced a suggestion for further investigation, but no more is known about the enterprise. Previously, records of quarrying in the area of Hit or Miss Wood mention a site where stone may have been obtained for the building of Chipping Norton properties.

Before approximately 1878 there were few ovens in the village and food was generally cooked above the fire. About this time the bakery was a welcome addition to the village, selling groceries and providing a cooking service for the villagers. Yorkshire puddings cost 1d, and 1½d for pies; these were sometimes delivered by the children. In 1887 the Great Western Railway Corporation opened a single line between Banbury and Chipping Norton.

With the changing pattern of farming, the milking herds have made way for arable cultivation. A council estate has been established at Quarhill Close and private houses have been added in the beautiful setting of the surrounding countryside. In 1998 the village felt the effect of another aspect of national change – the privatisation of water supplies, renewing and improving a system which, through age, had become subject to intermittent failures.

🍁 PUDLICOTE

Pudlicote is a small hamlet situated about two miles from Chadlington. The existing Pudlicote House is built on the site of a Roman villa. The present owner, Sir Frederic Bolton, has been researching the history of Pudlicote and has copies of leases dated in the 1740s which show that the present boundaries are more or less the same as they were then, and that the land was not affected by any of the local enclosure acts. There is also evidence that this land was afforested to celebrate the coronation of Henry II and according to the laws of the forests, if anyone was found shooting game they had their thumbs cut off.

A notorious owner of Pudlicote House was John de Pudlicote, who in 1303 attempted to steal the Crown Jewels from the Chapel of the Pyx in Westminster Abbey. He and his accomplices were caught and hanged.

A number of crooked sixpences have been dug up in the fields around Pudlicote and these apparently were luck tokens. Is there a connection here with the rhyme, 'There was a crooked man who walked a crooked mile, And found a crooked sixpence upon a crooked stile.'?

Sir Frederic also has in his possession a bill of sale dated 1878 which proudly boasted of 'two rookeries', obviously in those days considered to be an advantage to the sale of the farm, by supplementing the dinner table with rook pie. The rookeries are still in existence today, but there is a very different view of their value as they take their toll of the crops.

🍁 RADLEY

The village of Radley has a church and college, a river and railway and, centrally located, a post office and a pub. Modern village life is centred around the church, the school and the village hall. The ancient office of Clerk of the Green Cloth has been revived, with royal permission, and the biennially elected officer acts as an informal Village Mayor.

St James the Great, a pretty 13th century stone church with a square tower, overlooks the timber-framed vicarage house believed to have been inhabited since the 13th century, but not always by vicars! By the font beneath a gallery, is a pictorial map of Radley embroidered by members of the WI in 1971.

In the 1930s village boys competed for the right to earn sixpence carrying the 'Young Gents' trunks up to the college from the railway station. Since then the building of large areas of housing has increased the pre-war size of the village fourfold and the rural cottages are overshadowed. Local people have access to the college's sporting facilities and often walk in the pleasant tree-filled, well maintained grounds. The summer months are characterized by the daily stream of athletic-looking young men running or cycling past the church and over the railway bridge down to the college boathouse on the Thames.

The railway bridge links Radley, where almost all the houses were built since 1920, and Lower Radley where the picturesque thatched cottages can be found. Both railway and Thames run through Radley on their journey from Oxford to London. The station, originally built to serve the college, now meets the needs of commuters but many locals use the buses which give a good service to Abingdon and Oxford.

The passing year is marked by the church's Palm Sunday procession through the village, the Good Friday Walk into Oxford to raise money for local charities, the school's May Fayre, the Fete and Flower Show, the Football Festival, the Harvest Supper and the Christmas Bazaar. In all seasons tractors can be heard working late into the evenings and the sound of a train in the cutting is a herald of rain over Radley.

🍁 RAMSDEN

A clearing in an ancient Royal hunting forest, at the crossroads of a well trodden footpath and the Roman road from St Albans to Cirencester, were the humble beginnings of an attractive and well-loved, mellow Cotswold-stone village called Ramsden. Early in the 20th century herds of cows were a common sight wandering down the high street for milking. The road was made of broken stone then and the village had its own stonebreaker who worked from a shed on the site of the top pub, the Stag and Hounds, which became a private dwelling in the spring of 1996.

In the centre of the village at the crossroads is a recently cleaned and repaired war memorial which lists all the men killed in the Great War. Once there were three places for Christian worship, a Methodist chapel, a Roman Catholic chapel, and the parish church of St James. This was consecrated in 1872 and has a magnificent spire which can be seen for miles around. Now the only centre for worship, the large festivals have an ecumenical flavour and are well supported by villagers of many persuasions. The most popular service is the candlelit carol service on Christmas Eve when there is standing room only at the back of the packed church.

Most of the village community life takes place in the Memorial Hall which is a converted barn, opened in 1949, after a concerted effort by a handful of villagers to raise funds. This became the meeting place of Ramsden Women's Institute which was started in the village school in December 1922. One momentous achievement by WI members during the Second World War is recorded in the minutes when one ton of plums was canned by hand in 15 hours, the last lid being sealed at midnight on the 1,010th tin!

ROTHERFIELD GREYS

Despite the loss of the village school and post office over the years, Greys still retains its charm and attracts many visitors to see the beautiful cherry blossom in the spring, to watch the cricket matches on the village green and to visit Greys Court (the home of Lady Brunner) with its beautiful gardens set amid the ruins of a 14th century fortress.

The estate was given to the National Trust several years ago and is open to the public from Easter each year. The village hall has recently been extended and modernised as a memorial to the late Sir Felix Brunner.

Three generations of the Barratt family owned and worked at the blacksmith's premises bordering the village green; the last smith died in the late 1980s. Much of his work can be seen around the village.

The interior of the church and the churchyard are tended by a band of willing helpers and the rector serves both the parish of Rotherfield Greys and Rotherfield Peppard. Of special interest is the magnificent Knollys tomb, dating from 1605. This shows the reclining effigies of Sir Francis Knollys and his wife Katherine, with their 16 children.

ROTHERFIELD PEPPARD

Situated on the southern slopes of the Chilterns, in that loop of the Thames that dips towards Reading, Rotherfield Peppard was long ago on the 'Pack and Prime' way from Henley to Goring, an overland route transporting goods to avoid the difficult navigation of the Thames around Reading. A settlement called Redrefeld is recorded in the Domesday Book. Later, in the reign of Edward I, Ralph Pipard was given the estate, whereby the area became known as Retheresfelde Pipard. Around that time the construction of All Saints' church began, consisting then only of the chancel which has three small 12th century windows. One of its three bells is a mid 14th century bell from the Wokingham foundry; another is 17th century, inscribed 'Henry Knight made mee 1621'.

The village is scattered on two sides of Peppard Common, a natural beauty spot deeply divided by a dry valley that in prehistoric times carried water as it wound its way down to the river at Henley. Indeed, the parish once extended as far as the Thames and had its own pump, in Mill Lane, Henley, for

185

extracting water from the river in times of severe drought. Until the water main was laid in early 1900, people relied on rain water tanks in their gardens, although some were lucky to live near Spring Wood, from whose natural spring the local bakery still drew water a generation ago.

The common has always been the great meeting place for the villagers to celebrate, a place for recreation and enjoyment, for providing pasture and firewood, blackberries and crab apples. Generations of children have sat astride its 'wishing stone', isolated in the undergrowth – perhaps originally a marker stone for those packhorses of the Pack and Prime way that crossed the common here? Not far away, overlooking the common, stands one of the oldest houses in the village, Manor House, once a coaching house known as 'The Blue Monkey' which served those same travellers on the Pack and Prime road.

Centuries ago the villagers met here on fair days, as featured in Elizabeth Goudge's book, *The White Witch*, set in this village during the English Civil War. (This well-loved author lived in Dog Lane for many years.) The Peppard Revels were held annually on Whit Monday, and appear to have been wanton and wicked!

In the 1950s an area of the common was donated by the lord of the manor to provide a sports ground and pavilion, in memory of those villagers who lost their lives in the Second World War. Earlier, in memory of those lives lost in the First World War, a fine village hall had been built. Here also is a flourishing bowls club.

For generations this was a farming community with cattle, pigs and poultry grazing and rooting in patchwork meadows. Today, sadly, the small farms have given way to vast acres of cereals and oilseed rape, devoid of wildlife – no partridge, hare or lapwing on these antiseptic fields.

Most people now commute to Reading and London for work. Until a few years ago Peppard Hospital employed many local people, on its farm and market garden as well as the wards. Starting as a sanatorium because of the 'wonderful healing air' here in Peppard, it pioneered the valuable work in beating that one-time scourge, tuberculosis.

Once on the Pack and Prime route, hence pubs such as the Pack Horse and the Pack Saddle in a neighbouring parish, also on the old drovers' route from Bristol, hence the Butcher's Arms, Peppard is now, unfortunately, on the 'avoid Reading' route to the M4.

Although there has been considerable development since 1900 (population then about 500), luckily Peppard, perched on its common, surrounded by beautiful beech woods, has not spread alarmingly in recent years, with a population of under 1,500 today. Fortunately there is still a village stores and a long-established builder's merchant-cum-DIY department. Sadly the village post office, run by the same family since 1900, has recently closed. How great is its loss!

❧ SALFORD

Salford is no beauty spot frequented by tourists. Nor is it on the way to anywhere, lying as it does off the A44 between Chipping Norton and Moreton-in-Marsh. It is a small village of just over 300 souls in the centre of the manor of Salford, which lies within the boundaries of the 1,500 acres forming the ancient parish. Small it may be, but it is today a very close-knit and active village. The school and the village shop have gone, and the Methodist chapel has been converted into a small house, but the church and pub flourish and the villagers run a history society, a WI and an active village hall amongst other activities. A local dramatic society, Salford Players, is based in the village.

As a place name, Salford is relatively common, but this version is unique. The other Salford settlements take their names from the Latin 'Salix' or willow, and presumably mean the ford near the willow copse or osiers. This Salford means 'salt-ford' and the village may have been a stop-over on the ancient Salt Way linking Droitwich to the south coast.

So Salford is an ancient village and there are still families in it who have lived here for several centuries. Among these are the Fawdrys and the well-stocked churchyard indicates the continuity of the family within the parish. Fawdrys have been farming here – though not at the same farm – over the centuries. The first mention of the family occurs in an old document as 'Ralph Fawdry flourishing in Salford 1640'. They look set to farm and flourish here for some time to come.

Agriculture, of course, was the only livelihood of the majority of villagers until the Industrial Revolution, when workers drifted into nearby towns. Before the Second World War, the parish of Salford contained ten farms. Now, with intensive farming, there are four farms and a smallholding.

Salford is part of what is fondly known as 'The Five Parishes' – Salford,

187

Cornwell, Chastleton, Little Compton and Little Rollright — and 13th century St Mary's church stands on a rise to the west of the village. It was considerably altered by George Street in 1856, but original windows, a Norman tympanum and Norman font speak of the past.

The most dramatic church event of late has been the removal on 12th September 1989 of the historic Bagley ring of five bells, all cast in 1687. Whites of Appleton joined forces with volunteer labour on that day and the tower became a hive of activity. By lunch time they had cleared all the wood, wheels and old frame from the tower, and the five bells were lined up on the church path. It was a beautiful moment, as sightseers and workers stood in the mellow September sun, gazing at these historic pieces of art. The bells were returned to their home in April 1990.

Since 1981, summertime has seen a Salford Flower Show, originally held in a field in the middle of the village, and more recently in the beautiful garden of the Old Rectory. This is now followed in the autumn by a Horticultural Show in the village hall, when competition amongst the vegetable growers is very keen!

🍁 SHELLINGFORD

Shellingford was first mentioned in Saxon times, when King Athelstan granted the monastery of Abingdon twelve hides of land at 'Scaringaford', in AD 931. The ford crossed Mill brook, one of the tributaries of Rosey brook. Drinking water was at one time obtained here from a spring and served the whole village, as well as a roadside pump. Various industries were also served by this water – as many as six malthouses, a mill, a laundry for the Kitemore estate, and an old smithy which existed from the 18th century until the early 20th century.

The largest house still standing was built in 1867 as Kitemore House and it still commands a fine view across the parish to the Ridgeway.

Several large houses in the village have served as rectory, four in all, the largest being a 16th century manor house known locally as Shellingford Castle. Sadly it fell into decay and was finally demolished. On its site the newest rectory stands, now in its turn redundant and privately owned.

St Faith's, the partly Norman, 12th century church stands nearby, and still provides services on a regular basis, although like many local churches, the rector is shared amongst other parishes.

One of the more noted rectors was John Morton, who went on to become Archbishop of Canterbury and Chancellor of England in the reign of Henry VII. He was noted as being the inventor of 'Morton's Fork', a two-pronged attempt at securing monies for the Church and Crown from the thrifty and spendthrift alike!

The local area is mainly agricultural, and as such the lifeblood of the village could be called the many farms – Home Farm and Church Farm within the village and Sands Farm and Little Newbury Farms on the outskirts, as well as Kitemore Home Farm. Many of the inhabitants of the village are agricultural workers.

Land over the centuries has changed a great deal, an enormous amount of woodland having disappeared, although there are remnants of copses still remaining. In Fishpond Copse, attached to the village, there can be seen the remains of medieval fishponds managed by sluices and banks to provide fish and wildfowl for the table at Kitemore estate and the rectory.

Although the village has now lost its shop and pub (known locally as the 'Hole in the Wall' as the customers had to stand in the yard to drink their ale, served from a literal hole in the wall!), there is still a very busy and thriving school, built on land given by one of the former inhabitants of Kitemore House. A school has existed in the village for a very long time, although it is now a far cry from the 'Penny on a Monday' for the week's tuition – no penny, no school!

🍁 SHILTON

A lovely little stream runs through Shilton, called 'The Shill', so it may be from this the village gets its name. It certainly owes its reputation for being a very pretty place to its setting in a valley with the pond in the centre, grass areas, red and white chestnut trees, a pump from which villagers used to get their drinking and washing water, a pump-stack where water barrels were filled for farm use. Close by is a well complete with ornamental stone, a war memorial, and spanning the stream as it leaves the pond is a very attractive stone footbridge called 'The Arch'.

The source of the stream rises somewhere near Westwell and runs through

Signett and Burford Bottoms (once called Mount Zion Bottom) before reaching Shilton.

In a dry season this stream almost disappears but a strong spring, called Wells Head, rises just beyond a beautiful water-meadow, and this ensures the village is never without a constant flow of water. Snowdrops and later kingcups grow in profusion here in the spring. This is one of a dwindling number of ancient unspoilt meadows. Luckily there are two 'common land banks', a small paddock and a water meadow in the middle of the village which give it 'green lungs'. Willow trees on the banks of the stream add to its beauty.

In medieval times there was a Cistercian settlement consisting of a grange, tithe barn, dovecot, fish pond and rabbit warren. The paddock is still called Conyger after the latter. The main building was used as a stable around 1910–40, and as a chick-rearing unit from 1948–51, and converted to a dwelling about 1970. The roof of the tithe barn was destroyed by fire years ago and replaced with corrugated iron. This was made into a house at about the same time.

Shilton was once very much a farming community consisting of six farms, and four farmyards right in the village. Cows were driven up the street and grazed the grass banks whilst ducks and hens wandered in and out of the rickyards. There was a baker, blacksmith, post office and for a time two shops, a band and also cricket and football teams. Alas they are no more!

The Norman church sits squarely on a hill overlooking the village – the church of the Holy Rood. It has a notable font with beautifully carved scenes from the life of Christ on its four faces. There are several 'wool tombs' in the churchyard and a magnificent copper beech tree near the gate. On the opposite side of the lane is the old school which closed in 1970 – it is now a village hall fulfilling many needs.

Also in Church Lane is the Baptist chapel built in 1830. It has a small band of faithful worshippers.

A footpath linking Shilton with Alvescot passes through the churchyard, and a bridlepath from Shilton to Burford crosses the route of the old Akeman Street and is a lovely walk. People who know this small Cotswold village well have a tremendous love for, and loyalty to it. As the old jingle says –

Bampton steeple wears a hat,
Witney steeple looks at that,
Burford steeple's ready to fall,
Shilton tower beats them all.

 SHIPLAKE

Newcomers often ask 'but where is the village?' It is true there are few houses on the main road from Henley to Reading but not many would grumble these days at having a built-in bypass.

It happened for historic reasons. The late 18th century owner of Shiplake Court, the manor house, gambled away all his money, and the house fell into such decay that it was pulled down in 1804. The estate did not support a thriving economy and little building took place for the next 50 years.

In 1858 the railway came through the parish, about a mile away from what had been the centre, near the Court and the church. It passed trough a small settlement near the Lashbrook. In fact this was probably settled before Shiplake, as it is mentioned in Domesday Book, along with its mill. The mill, which was where the lock now is, existed until 1908. It is interesting that though Lashbrook Farm, the site of the Domesday manor, is in the flood plain, it occupies a small area of higher ground which becomes an island.

Gradually summer houseboats moored on the river-bank near the new station, and they acquired gardens alongside. The gardens were then built upon to provide luxurious homes. As commuting became common, more and more houses were built within easy reach of the station and although the long steam-engined trains have given way to one and two-coach diesels it is still this part of the parish which is the main settlement. It is here that the two shops, the hairdresser and the garage are. As in most of the south-east commuter belt the pressure for new houses is great and nearly 200 new houses have been built since the 1960s.

But it is a very mixed village – there is council-run sheltered housing, and a thriving Church of England primary school. A playgroup for the very small has its home in the village hall, which, recently refurbished, hosts many other activities. Cricket, football, bowls and tennis clubs flourish. The school and the hall and playing fields form part of another area of development on the opposite side of the main road from the station.

191

Shiplake Court was rebuilt in 1894 on its beautiful site overlooking the river. Now it is a boys' public school which has flourished since its foundation in 1959. They have a great success at rowing, and in teaching the dyslexic.

Modern estate agents like to call the village Shiplake on Thames. It's not correct but most villagers appreciate the beautiful two path walk upstream from Shiplake Lock. A small tea, ice cream and postcard shop does a flourishing trade on sunny days. A world away from the social accent of Henley Royal Regatta, Shiplake joins forces each year with Wargrave, the village on the Berkshire bank of the river, for a 'fun' regatta.

The historic parish, only a mile and a half wide, stretched seven miles, from the river up to the fringe of the Chilterns. All the South Oxfordshire parishes were of this form, providing lush water meadows which flooded in winter, and the upland pasture necessary as a result. Small settlements occurred all the way along the seven miles, and one has grown to form another small village at Binfield Heath.

Shiplake has no great claims to a place in the history of the nation. Sir Francis Plowden, Queen Elizabeth's Chancellor lived at Shiplake Court, but as far as is known Queen Elizabeth did *not* sleep here. James Granger, vicar from 1747 to 1776, was famous in his day as a promoter of illustrating books by adding pictures cut from other books. His name has entered the dictionaries as 'grangerising'. Lord Tennyson was married in the attractive small church, and wrote a poem about the place. George Orwell lived here briefly as a boy. There have been a brickworks and a paper mill, though now there is little employment actually in the village: like so many rural places it is but a dormitory and retirement home. However, it is a happy community that few people leave voluntarily.

SHIPTON-UNDER-WYCHWOOD

Through the centuries Saxon, Norman, Plantagenet and Tudor hunters, all have pursued the hart, hind and hare in the now drastically reduced metes and bounds of the Wychwood Forest. William the Conqueror enjoyed such sport and set aside some 68 forests in England for his royal chases. Of these, the Wychwood was one of the four largest in the land. It is not surprising then that three neighbouring villages took the name of this mighty domain – Ascott, Milton and Shipton – all 'under Wychwood'.

Shipton is an ancient village pleasantly situated on the Evenlode river. It was a very important royal manor before Domesday and the church of St Mary the Virgin may have been a minster in Saxon times.

If calling at Christmastide, look up to the arches decorated with evergreen-covered battens, a custom still carried on from the early 1900s. Sadly, in the churchyard the gravestones now stand around the wall, or lie flat to form a path. Walk there in the spring and the snowdrops and daffodils will dance for you.

Adjacent to the church is the now restored and resplendent Old Prebendal House, which boasts as one of its 40-odd prebends John Foxe, author of *The Book of Martyrs*. The core of this fine mellow stone building is mid-13th century with later additions. It is now a beautifully appointed retirement home.

Shipton Court, which may have been the local manor house, is situated on the High Street across from the cricket ground. It was built by Sir Rowland de Lacy in 1603 and is one of the largest Jacobean houses in the country. An 18th

Village scene at Shipton-under-Wychwood

193

century couplet pays grudging tribute to three Cotswold families who seem to have been 'to the manor born':

The Lacies, Tracies and Fettiplaces
Own all the manors, parks and chases.

A number of families now share the leasehold ownership of the Court and the houses and cottages within its confines.

The village green was allotments until the late 1960s, then was bought for the village by Colonel Stedall in memory of his wife. At the top of the green is the war memorial and the fountain in memory of 17 Shipton people who perished at sea on the *Cospatrick* in 1874 when emigrating to New Zealand. The beech tree was planted in 1974 to commemorate 100 years from the sinking of the *Cospatrick* and the closing of the post office, which had been in the Wiggins family since 1845. It was the oldest-established post office in England and now it is the Old Post House looking onto the green.

Shipton-under-Wychwood has three fine, unspoiled pubs – the Lamb, the Shaven Crown and the Red Horse, as well as a cricket ground, a bowls club, and a late 19th century village hall which hosts the many and varied local activities. If Shiptonians cannot lay claim to a Cotswold home – the purists exclude us from that Area of Outstanding Beauty by some four miles – villagers are content. The houses and dry-stone walls are of the same golden oolite eggstone, the sheep are as fat, the river is as swift flowing, the valley is as green and the people – well, the people are the nicest mix of Oxfordshire natives, Home Counties' retirees and outright 'foreigners' that one could find anywhere!

❧ SHRIVENHAM

One of the most westerly villages in Oxfordshire, Shrivenham nestles in the Vale of the White Horse on the route from Swindon to Oxford. A bypass, built in 1984, ensures that Shrivenham's rural atmosphere is preserved. Elm Tree House, a gracious house built in the style of Inigo Jones, a village school built in 1863 and many lovely thatched cottages border the wide tree-lined main street. In *Tom Brown's Schooldays*, Thomas Hughes' hero set forth to Rugby school from Shrivenham station (sadly now defunct).

St Andrew's church is impressively large for a small village, with parts dating back to the 11th, 12th and 13th centuries. Its many unusual features include the central tower, 18 large clear windows, Tuscan-like tapering columns, magnificent brass chandeliers and hanging pyx. There are many memorials to the Barrington family, important landowners locally in previous decades.

The ancient manor of Beckett, mentioned in the Domesday survey as Becote, was acquired by King John in 1204. One of the four Shrivenham manors, Fowersmill was held by the de Becotes in 1367 in service of coming before the King whenever he passed Fowersmill Bridge and offering two white capons saying, 'See here, Sir, these two capons you shall have at some other time but not now!'. Obviously, to have two white leghorns flapping round in one's coach was not conducive to a pleasant journey! The manor later belonged to the Barrington family and now, the house and grounds belong to the Royal Military College of Science.

Shrivenham possesses one of the finest village halls in the county, the Memorial Hall, presented by Charlotte, Countess Barrington and opened by Princess Beatrice in 1925 as a memorial to villagers killed in the First World War. Six houses for ex-servicemen border the adjoining recreation ground, which is large enough for a football and cricket pitch. In August, Shrivenham village fete is held here. The hall is a splendid edifice for a small village. The roof covering is Cotswold stone tiles supported by a massive hammerbeam roof of very large oak members, possibly the last of the great timber roofs to be built in the country.

Fred 'Gramophone' Knapp was an eccentric village character. After seeking his fortune in America, he returned to Shrivenham to make very large garden plant bowls in concrete, and he also cast a man to stand in the garden. A lorry driver approached this realistic figure at dusk, to ask the way! Fred could recite a long poem which he had composed about some poor soul's foot trouble and he also had the family history of Lord Barrington committed to memory. Considered one of the 'long-headed' of the village, he was often in demand as a letter reader or writer.

Fred's son Harold farmed the village farm and would 'accidentally' let the ram out into the street. This creature chased anything in sight and women dived into the nearest shop at the ram's approach. Harold would follow, waving his arms but enjoying every minute of it! He heard that the Duke of Edinburgh was visiting locally and painted RAF roundels in red and blue on

195

the wings of several of his geese and paraded them in the street. He insisted on doing his own thatching with the resultant cottage looking like a rick and always managing to grow a lovely bright green crop of grass on it!

The definitive book about the history of Shrivenham was written by the Rev Edward F. Hill, MA in 1928. Frequently quoted, this volume is the most sought-after book in Shrivenham. Canon Hill's Gardens, a beautiful short road of modern houses curving round a tree-shaded village pond, immortalises the name of this highly-esteemed former vicar of Shrivenham.

SIBFORD FERRIS & SIBFORD GOWER

Between Banbury and Shipston-on-Stour, just off the B4035, lie the delightful Sibford villages, known locally as The Ferris and The Gower, with the tiny hamlet of Burdrop adjoining the latter.

In the 12th century considerable land at Sibford was given by William Fitz Roger to the Knights Templars. Today's Temple Close, with its dovecote, and Temple Mill, bear witness to their Norman connections.

The two local inns are other reminders of the past. Dated 1610, the Bishop Blaize (patron saint of wool weavers) indicates that Sibford was part of the flourishing Cotswold sheep-farming area. The Wykham Arms undoubtedly derived its name from the Wykehams, lords of nearby Swalcliffe Manor.

The spiritual welfare of the Sibfords is cared for by the church, the small Methodist chapel and the Society of Friends. The church of Holy Trinity, consecrated in 1840 when the modern parish was created, is unusual in having neither tower nor steeple.

The first Friends' Meeting House, a small thatched building dated 1680, was erected by an enthusiastic band of puritan dissenters following a visit from George Fox, the Quaker leader. This was replaced in 1866 by the present, much larger, building.

In 1839 Joshua Lamb walked to Oxford from Sibford, and resulting from his meeting with other Quakers there, the 'Great House' in Sibford Ferris, built in 1666 and later known as the Manor, was purchased for £1,200. Three years later 26 boys and 22 girls were admitted as the first boarding scholars. Girls assisted with household duties and boys worked on the 25 acre farm, from whence home-grown corn was ground at Temple Mill. Later the Manor was the home of Frank Lascelles, Pageant Master of international renown. It was whilst a visitor at the Manor that Ivor Novello wrote the famous song, *Keep The Home Fires Burning*.

There has been a village school on the present site in the Gower since 1631. The mid-Victorian building was updated in 1957 when coke stoves, bucket toilets and high latticed windows gave place to modern amenities. With its panoramic views to the south, it is thought to be one of the most beautifully situated in the country.

The Sibford Gower and Burdrop Town Estates Charity was founded in 1560, the income from the bequeathed land being equally divided between 'the poor', 'pious and charitable purposes' and 'the primary school and school master'. Much benefit is still derived from this charity.

The Lamb family have farmed in the village for over 300 years. Unquestionably the best-known member of the family was Theodore, born about 1880. The youngest of a large family he attended the Quaker school and became a skilled watch and lock mender. There is no known explanation

Sibford Manor

197

of why he spent his last 40 years living as a hermit; his home, on Sibford Heath, a shack of galvanised sheets and iron bedsteads; his transport a tyre-less bicycle; and his raiment mostly sacking. Totally honest, completely harmless and immensely strong, he eventually contracted pneumonia and died, aged 70, in Banbury hospital, the nurses respecting his request not to cut his long matted hair – he said it would spoil his appearance! Money which he had entrusted to the vicar was sufficient to pay for his funeral, attended by many paying their last respects to a long-to-be-remembered Sibford character.

❧ SOMERTON

In 1580, Somerton became home to the first charity school opened in Oxfordshire. A mullioned window from the original building is set in a wall inside the present school which dates from the 18th/19th century. The free school was endowed by Thomas Fermor, a member of the influential family who lived at the manor until the beginning of the 17th century when they moved to Tusmore. The once great Tudor mansion has long since been demolished but the family's presence is still recorded in the local church which boasts an altar tomb and brasses to William Fermor who died in 1552; and also effigies to Thomas Fermor (1580), John Fermor (1625) and Richard Fermor (1642). In the churchyard are the remains of a medieval cross.

Somerton also boasts the only turf maze still preserved in the county. Possibly of medieval origin, it can be found in the garden at Troy Farm. It consists of a series of winding grass paths separated by banks and ditches and it is approximately a quarter mile to its centre.

❧ SONNING COMMON

Just over the border from Berkshire, Sonning Common today is a far cry from the few cottages, farms and beerhouses scattered on and around 200 acres of rough pasture, with cultivated areas and woods, that existed in the 1860s. Originally part of the manor of Sonning-on-Thames, the land was used for grazing cattle and sheep. When the rich water meadows by the river flooded, animals were driven up to the higher ground, often for months in the winter.

Hog Lane (now Woodlands Road) in Sonning Common was so called because pigs were driven along it to the woods, to feed on the beech mast.

Widmore Pond, on the edge of the village, at one time supplied most of the water used locally. Dr Plot's *Natural History of Oxfordshire*, written in 1677, stated that when the pond was cleaned out, oak trees were found standing upright. In the mud at the bottom Roman coins and stag antlers were found, and the theory was put forward that it had originally been a Roman clay pit. Before 1940, local boys spent many hours sitting on the wall fishing – but the fish died out, and the whole area became neglected and overgrown. In the early 1970s members of the Parish Council organised working parties, and the pond was cleared of rubbish, landscaped, and a seat provided. Ducks and swans were installed, and the whole area has become a feature of the village, with some of the best-fed birds in Oxfordshire!

With the break up of the manor in the 1880s, much of the land was sold off piecemeal, and the slow building of an actual village began. Formerly part of the civil parish of Eye and Dunsden, it was afforded its own Parish Council status in 1951. With the building of three large housing estates in the 1960s the population increased from about 1,000 at the beginning of the decade to 3,700 by 1997.

Pressure from developers has been constant and house prices have soared. Recent attempts to incorporate the village into Berkshire, with the likelihood of it simply becoming a suburb of Reading, have been successfully repelled, and Sonning Common Open Spaces Trust has been instrumental in purchasing surrounding greenfield sites.

Sonning Common is an active, lively community, with 15 shops, three public houses, a bank, three garages, a library, health centre, dentist and veterinary surgery. The primary school has over 200 pupils on the roll, and Chiltern Edge Comprehensive covers a considerably larger catchment area. The Community Education Centre attached to the latter runs a wide range of vocational and leisure classes, and the village boasts over 30 clubs and societies, including an active amenity group.

🍁 SOULDERN

Souldern is a small village of less than 200 houses situated some seven miles north of Bicester in the very north of Oxfordshire, and just half a mile from the Northamptonshire border. Being a cul-de-sac village it is fairly peaceful and quiet and has a close-knit community, some families having lived there for 200–300 years. In more recent years the character of the village has changed with the influx of commuters and retired people.

Souldern is an extremely pretty village right on the edge of the Cotswolds and overlooking the Cherwell valley. There are many keen gardeners, many of whom open their gardens to the public for a weekend each summer and divide the proceeds amongst several worthy causes.

In earlier times Souldern was known as Sulthorn because of the many thorn trees which grew there. The first recorded burial is that of William de Say in 1161, the parish church of St Mary having been built by the de Say family a few years previously. During the Civil War, when the king was stationed in Oxford, Souldern suffered badly from the marauding bands of Parliamentary troops, about 20,000 of them being camped in the area.

Most of the houses are built of stone, some being large family homes. There is a constant supply of spring water which feeds the village pond, formerly the old town well. There is also a second well known as St Chad's Well.

Souldern is fortunate in having its own village hall, which was largely built by public subscription and many local events take place there and on the adjoining sports ground.

In 1986 a group of residents, spurred on by the Parish Council, formed a committee to plan and organise the planting of a 'harmony wood' on the outskirts of the village. Since then more adjoining land has become available and extensions have been made to the wood. This is a favourite walk for local people, as indeed are the many public footpaths and bridleways in the area.

Souldern has two pubs and a garage as well as a church and a chapel. Whilst there is employment in the village, most of those who work do so in either Banbury, Bicester or Oxford. The M40 motorway now passes less than a mile from the village and can be seen down in the valley.

🍁 SOUTH MORETON

The parish of South Moreton was part of the Blewbury Hundred in the Domesday Book. It extends from the northerly boundary with Wittenham edge to Mill brook and its tributary Hakkas brook in the south, an area of approximately 1,350 acres. It was once part of Berkshire. Part of the parish boundary brook called Tibbald was once the sheepwash where local farmers drove their sheep for dipping.

From pre-Conquest times the settlement was a prosperous place supporting four manor houses. In 1199 Robert de Sanderville held the moated manor house on the north side of the village street. The manor house of Bray, with Tudor remains, has now been converted into two cottages near to the present-day Hall Farm. The terraces of the manor house of Adresham are traceable on the south side of the street. The hamlet of Fulscot, also mentioned in Domesday, lies to the west of the village and there is a manor house where a moat can be traced and buildings and cottages supporting a mixed farm.

Malting was a staple in Elizabethan times and there was a forge and a village pound. The village stocks, last used in 1838, were situated where Manor Lane meets the main village street, known today as Cross Tree. There were many small businesses such as saddler, baker, grocer, boot and shoe maker, blacksmith, wheelwright and carpenter, bricklayer, tailor and dressmaker.

There was a paper mill and a corn mill, which was possibly the mill valued at twelve shillings in Domesday. The (corn) mill house was hired out as a hospital during the smallpox epidemic of 1799. This mill was also used as a rag store where the rags were prepared and then sent down the brook in flat-bottomed boats to the paper mill, located near to the present railway arch over the Mill brook. There are few remains as the mill was burnt down in 1825, and although rebuilt, it suffered the same fate 13 years later.

The church of St John the Baptist was built on the site of a chapel which overlooked the causeway that connected the brook crossing-point to the village. The original chapel was a stopping-point for medieval pilgrims following the footsteps of St Birinus, who journeyed from Churn Knob near Blewbury to Dorchester, where he founded the abbey. This pilgrimage is revived each year on the first Sunday in July but the pilgrims now cross the brook by the bridge at the mill and stop for refreshments in the village. The church has a rare Saxon doorway, which is blocked up, and near the gate stands a mighty yew tree reputed to be 1,600 years old.

In 1850 the Great Western Railway was built and the main line from London ran across the parish north of the village street. Gravel and sand were extracted locally and used in its construction. Some local men worked on the line and at the important goods' marshalling yards in the west of the parish.

A nameless shepherd, who tended sheep by the wayside, left £10 to parish charity. This amount, together with £1,000 sterling given by Edward Sherman Esq of London in 1863, formed the South Moreton Consolidated Charity, the annual proceeds thereof to be distributed amongst the poor of the parish. Edward Sherman had lived at one of the manors with his uncle Sadgrove, who is reputed to have boxed his ears. He then ran off to London and later became the largest coach proprietor in the country with 17,000 horses at work in various parts. The Consolidated Charity still divides proceeds among the villagers during the Christmas period.

Anchor Inn, now a private house, was once the site of much merrymaking when the Whitsun Feast was held there, with swingboats, coconut shies and dancing on the barrel to accordion music.

Hilaire Belloc, the French-born writer, lived in the village and the name of his son Peter Belloc appears on the war memorial in the church.

The parish has an abundance of footpaths and bridleways making interesting connections with neighbouring parishes, and the recent addition of the Moreton Ride, a licensed horseway which skirts the fields and links existing tracks, enables the horselover to enjoy traffic-free exercise.

🍁 SOUTH STOKE

The village of South Stoke is unusual in that three highways, which have done much to influence its history and people, pass through it. Two of these highways are ancient, the river Thames and the Ridgeway path, while the third is the Great Western Railway built by Isambard Brunel. These three routes converge as they cross the parish boundaries near Ye Olde Leatherne Bottle public house to the south and at the Moulsford railway bridge, known locally as the Four Arches, to the north.

Clearly the oldest of these is the river Thames which borders South Stoke to the west. Before the 16th century the lower land in South Stoke was marshy but then the river provided fish and the adjacent land brushwood, willows and osiers. Today one can still see, from the footpath between South Stoke and Little Stoke, remains of a series of fishponds which provided food for the medieval monks resident in the village at that time.

The Ridgeway path is a prehistoric way which was part of a comprehensive communication system long before the Romans arrived. Evidence of ancient enclosures and burial pits has been found in South Stoke, together with Roman remains and coins. The Ridgeway now crosses land still owned by Christ Church, Oxford, before it passes through the village.

When the railway came in 1838 it changed the character of the village dramatically. It is built on a wide embankment with three low bridges over the only roads into the village and there is a small culvert, known locally as the bogey hole, which was constructed for the footpath to Little Stoke. The Four Arches bridge, which crosses the river and the Ridgeway path together is, itself, a listed building.

Manor Farm, beside the church, has always been the largest farm in South Stoke and is still active. Parts of the present farmhouse date from the 16th century and it still has the original oak panelling, moulded beams and a fireplace from an even earlier date. Within the old brick and flint walls around the house are several old buildings and barns. These include a square four-gabled medieval brick dovecote, reputed to be one of the largest in the south of England, and a granary standing on staddle stones.

St Andrew's church incorporates several periods of architecture, with some of the arches on the north side suggesting Norman work. The font is Early English and a fragment of 14th century glass can be seen in the south-east window. The chancel is dominated by a memorial commemorating Griffith Higgs. South Stoke's most famous son was born in 1589, was ordained as a priest and became chaplain to King Charles I. The King sent him to be chaplain to his sister, Princess Elizabeth, when she married and became Queen of Bohemia. Later Griffith Higgs became Dean of Lichfield but during the Civil War, like his sponsor, fell from grace. He saved his head but was stripped of all his titles and returned to South Stoke. He created many charities and, in particular, an educational charity which still benefits the children of South Stoke today.

During the early 19th century the parishioners of South Stoke became increasingly disenchanted with the church vestry's conduct of local affairs. Twenty four dissenters who worshipped in Goring built their own chapel in South Stoke in 1820. Like the Goring chapel it came under the auspices of the Countess of Huntingdon's Connexion and flourished for over a century but this building has not been used for worship since 1976.

Today converted barges, other pleasure craft and energetic rowers pass up and down the river. Fishermen frequently line the banks, either in competition or just for pleasure. The public house, the Perch and Pike, still displays record catches of fish taken from the river in more recent times and large numbers of Ridgeway hikers stop here for refreshment.

🍁 SPELSBURY

Spelsbury is a small village on the road between Chipping Norton and Charlbury (B4026).

Of the 50 houses in the village about a quarter are in the region of 100 years old, while over 25 have been built since 1920. There are four almshouses, built in 1689 by the land agent of the Ditchley estate – John Carey of Wilcote. There are still charities settled on the almshouses with Wilcote connections. John Carey was buried in the churchyard – his tomb, a substantial affair, is on the south side of the church.

There are a few thatched cottages which look quite picturesque. The village school ceased to be a school in 1958 and was turned into a house. It still retains the bell turret and clock. Some dwellings have been converted from farm buildings and stables.

There is a large water fountain under a canopy built of honey-coloured and pink stone. It was built in memory of Constantine Augustus Dillon (1813–1853), who was the 13th Viscount Dillon. Until about 1953 when mains water was laid on in the village, this was the local water supply. At that time the Hon Elsie Corbett had the village sewerage system put in – both must have been of great benefit to everyone.

The church is dedicated to All Saints. There has been a place of worship on this spot for about 900 years and there is evidence of Roman work in the pillars of the tower. Parts of the nave date from about 1300 but a great deal of rebuilding has been done over the years, particularly in the 18th century.

The church has many memorials, mainly to residents of Ditchley. Lord Rochester, the 17th century poet of Charles II's Court, is interred here in the crypt and his and a number of other coffin plates are now displayed in the baptistry. Another interesting memorial is to a daughter of Charles II and Barbara, Duchess of Cleveland who married Edward Henry Lee – they lived at Ditchley for most of their married life and had 18 children.

The policy of the Rural District Council is that this should be a non-growth village. There is a small estate of a farm and a number of the older cottages, but an increasing number of the dwellings are privately owned, including the original council houses. The village is too small to have a shop or public house but there is a post office in one of the houses every Tuesday morning.

STADHAMPTON & CHISELHAMPTON

Stadhampton was not mentioned in the Domesday Book, but a village existed at that time and the first mention of it by name came in 1146. Years ago, the majority of houses were round the green where the cattle and sheep were allowed to graze for a nominal sum. At the east end of the village, the 17th century manor house lies, approached by an avenue of lime trees. In 1845 the district was hunted by the Old Berkshire Hunt, and new kennels were built in 1884 to house the South Oxfordshire Hunt. Nowadays, their premises are private properties. The Oxfordshire Animal Sanctuary, run by a charity, is housed here.

Mill Lane leads down to the mill house and Cuxham brook. The mill was still working in 1939 and continued in a small way until 1948. Several years ago, a Brook Race was held each year, and this custom was renewed recently. For many years, 'Stadham Feast' was held on the village green, with the fair people setting up their roundabouts and stalls en route from St Giles' Fair in Oxford to Thame Fair.

The oldest house in Stadhampton is Doyleys Farm House and there are still a number of Georgian houses and thatched properties round the green and other parts of the village.

The church of St John the Baptist lies at the other end of the village green and the font is the only part that survives from the original building that existed in 1146. In 1744, the curate presented the church with an oak carving of the coat of arms of Queen Elizabeth I, painted in proper colours, and which now hangs above the door leading to the belfry.

In 1957, a row of houses called Malthouse Row was pulled down to make way for the entrance to Cratlands Close, at the end of which a new primary school was built. The old school, built in 1878 of the same type of brick as was used for a great deal of 19th century building in Stadhampton, was sold in the 1970s.

There are two public houses in the village; the Crown, first licensed in 1825, and the Crazey Bear. A third, the Black Horse, with a bakehouse adjoining dated 1685 and used as a bakehouse until 1914, is now a private residence.

There is still a village shop and post office, which also sells newspapers, a daily delivery of post, doorstep deliveries of milk and a very efficient newsagent who delivers daily and evening papers in all weathers.

Chiselhampton House was built between 1766 and 1768 from bricks made locally. St Katherine's church remains one of the few complete Georgian churches in the country, with high box pews and Georgian staircase leading to the Jacobean pulpit. This church now comes under the jurisdiction of the Redundant Churches Commission. Chiselhampton Bridge also featured in the Civil War and was made of freestone from Headington Quarry. One of the oldest historical buildings still existing in the district is Camoys House.

🍁 STANDLAKE

Standlake is an appropriate name, one might think, particularly looking at the village from the air, as it is surrounded by at least eight lakes. In 1718 the diarist Richard Rawlinson wrote that Standlake was 'among streams in a moorish lakish soil' and 'situate on a dam'd standing puddle, long, deep and dirty'. In fact the Old English meaning of Standlake is 'hill by a stony stream'. Three old hamlets form Standlake as we know it today: Standlake, Brittenton and Brighthampton.

In 1228 the living of the church of St Giles was presented by Lady Eva de Gray to John de Limesaya. The 750th anniversary of this event was celebrated in 1978, when a booklet *1228 & All That* was published by the Standlake Historical Society. A new guide to the church has just been published. From 1543 until 1947 the living was in the gift of Magdalen College. Four Oxford colleges owned a large part of the village until the end of the First World War when they sold off much of their property.

In 1989 a new village hall was opened on the edge of the village. To mark the occasion a village map was made, incorporating pictorial contributions from all village organisations and the primary school children, and water colours of a number of properties. Recently, a new children's playground and two hard tennis courts have also been added at the recreation ground by the hall. Cricket is played regularly at the Oxford Downs Cricket Club, where young cricketers are also coached. The village school now has 108 children and includes a playgroup on the premises for about 20 pre-school age children. The Mulberry Bush, an internationally renowned school for severely emotionally disturbed children, celebrated its 50th anniversary in 1998.

A light engineering firm, several builders, a computer company and a light industrial estate on the edge of the village provide employment, as do the garage, shop, schools, several farms and two residential homes for the elderly. The Museum Store for Oxfordshire is situated in the village. Standlake has become a centre for tourists and holidaymakers, with two caravan and camping sites and fishing, sailing, windsurfing, boating and water skiing facilities on many of the lakes.

The lack of affordable housing in the village for young families is a problem. Standlake has few village customs; primary school children receive a 'penny loaf' on Ascension Day and income from land bequeathed by the Rev John Chambers in 1721 provides book prizes. The annual church fete is no longer held, nor barrel rolling and tug-of-war competitions between teams from local pubs, but an annual Road Race and Fun Run in aid of the church and the primary school has been organised each year since 1988.

Dr Robert Plot in his *Natural History of Oxfordshire*, 1705, mentioned that the parson, in procession on Holy Thursday, read a gospel at a barrel's head in the cellar of the Chequer Inn, which was once a hermitage and where there had been a cross. The Chequer Inn was on the main London to Gloucester road, now the Abingdon Road, but ceased to be a public house in 1789 when other routes became more important. There are now only two pubs remaining in the village out of eight in existence in the 18th century.

STANFORD-IN-THE-VALE

Stanford is a large village with attractive houses of different periods and many lovely gardens. There are three greens, Upper Green, the new Millennium Green and the central Church Green.

Church Green, with its many lime trees planted to celebrate Queen Victoria's Diamond Jubilee in 1897, is dominated by the large square tower of the church of St Denys and bordered on two sides by rows of ancient, picturesque cottages. Here, too, is the Manor House, once occupied by Anne Neville, daughter of the Earl of Warwick. The south porch of the church bearing the Arms of Warwick was built to mark her marriage to the Duke of Gloucester, later Richard III. On the other side of Church Green stands Rectory House and the former vicarage, once home to Bishop Wordsworth who wrote many well known hymns, now The Grange nursing home.

Stanford was once a farming community, consisting of eight farms. Some sent milk to London every day by train from Challow station, others kept sheep. There were two smithies, a carpenter, a brickmaking yard, a

Cottages at Church Green, Stanford in the Vale

wheelwright's yard and two sets of threshing tackle. Corn was ground at the two mills.

The population in 1913 was 300, now it is over 1,800. In the 1950s a new estate was built, part of which is called Hunter's Field, after the Hunter family who lived at the Manor House from 1816 to 1935. There are also roads called Warwick Close, Neville Way and Wordsworth Close, named after the famous people who once lived there. A smaller vicarage has been built and there is a modern village hall available for entertainments. In 1913 there were seven public houses, now there are only two. At the present time there are still eight farms in the parish and many people commute to London, Reading, Swindon and Oxford or work at AERE Harwell. There is a flourishing business park on the old airfield, west of the village. It includes a car seat factory employing over 300 people.

STANTON HARCOURT

One lady recalls life in Stanton Harcourt in the past: I was born in the village, eldest of six, in the house which was at one time the post office and bakery. Strangely enough, the present post office is next door in what used to be the old stable where Mr Alfred Batts ('Starchy') kept his horse and cart as, in those days, he was the carrier. As a village we were lucky because we had several small 'shops' where you could buy a yard of elastic, a reel of cotton and various items of clothing. There was also a butcher, two blacksmiths and a wheelwright. The school, which is now a house, boasted a headmaster and two teachers. They were very happy days. We attended Sunday school which was held in the schoolroom, then, as we grew older, we went to church but always came out before the sermon. I joined the choir at eleven and learnt why they let us out before the sermon!

Most girls – and I was one of them – were employed in service. In the late 1930s there was a great deal of activity in the village, preparing for war. We were to have an aerodrome, trees were cut down and soon, it seemed, every field around had Nissen huts. Pre-fab buildings housed the RAF and WAAF, also a small unit of the RA moved in – they manned the searchlights.

Things quietened down after the war. Some of the huts were used for families needing a home, the RAF had gone and some of the land went back to agriculture. Two hangars and a few huts still remain, and part of the aerodrome site is now an industrial estate. Gravel excavations have also been carried out there. Some land has been restored for fishing and sailing, also for waste tipping.

A field at one time sported a tennis court, before it was transferred to the green – now we don't have one at all. The same ground was also the venue for cricket matches, the Village Flower Show and Sports Day and, later, carnivals. Now it is a housing estate, over 150 houses having been built since the war. Some of the older properties have been demolished, others renovated. We have a new school which children attend until they reach the age of eleven, then it's by bus to Eynsham. Our present rector is responsible for four parishes including our own.

Now there are no cattle grazing the verges, no horse and cart with loads of sheaves; most people have at least one car per household and we do have a small bus to Oxford picking up here and around nearby villages. At one time a Welfare Clinic was held in the village hall but, due to lack of custom, this was closed; now with all the new houses in the village, there are lots of young children around again.

STANTON ST JOHN

Up on the stony ridge of the saucer of low hills surrounding Oxford, only five miles north-east of that city, with all it has to offer, is Stanton St John – the Saxon 'stan-tun' meaning 'homestead on stony ground' and St John perpetuating the name of the family who held the lordship of the manor for 200 years from the 12th century. In the 16th century, after years of dispute, the lordship passed to New College, which still owns land in the surrounding countryside and a few village houses.

Several dwellings date back to the 16th century, although 21 of the original dwellings were destroyed in 1793 in a fire which traversed the narrow village street, fanned by wind and setting alight the thatched roofs on either side. The unfortunate villagers were left destitute by the disaster and were sustained largely by public appeal. The devastation was rectified by building pairs of stone houses, slate-roofed and set well back from the road – some bearing the New College coat of arms. This crest is repeated in the church, the oldest and dominant building in the village, set in a beflowered churchyard. The interior has much of interest – carved bench ends of human heads or grotesque animals, 13th and 14th century glass, and further evidence of the link with New College through the crest carved in the Jacobean pulpit and set into a window in the chancel. Another window bears the arms of Robert Pinck, the last Warden of the College to be rector of the parish, though his successors to the end of the 18th century included Fellows of the College.

Robert Pinck DD was a devoted Royalist who suffered imprisonment in 1642 at the hands of the Parliamentary troops under Lord Saye and Sele. He is remembered today in the village because of a bequest he made in his will in 1647. He left £110 so that local children could be helped to take up apprenticeships with tradesmen living outside the parish. The money was invested and today young people may still apply to the charity's trustees for help with such things as books and tools.

The village also has reason to be grateful to Lady Elizabeth Holford who was born here in 1650. She married a rich London merchant Henry Harbin, and after his death married Sir William Holford. In her will, dated 1717, she left £500 to be invested until the sum of £750 had accumulated, when it was to

Rectory farm house, Stanton St John

be used to build a charity school at Stanton St John. Children from both Stanton St John and the neighbouring village of Forest Hill were to be given instruction and six boys and six girls to be provided with clothing and called Lady Holford's scholars.

Across the road from the 13th century church of St John the Baptist is Rectory Farm House. A plaque over the door says 'The birthplace of John White, 1575–1648, Fellow of New College, Oxford, and chief founder of the colony of Massachusetts, New England'. John White was the son of the tenant farmer, and 400 years later the house is still lived in by the tenant farmer of New College.

The village today is still a thriving community. It is fortunate still to have a friendly shop and post office. The school closed in 1984 and is now called the Holford Centre: playschools, committee meetings and adult education classes are held there. The village hall was built with funds raised in the village, and opened in 1960. Next to the hall car park and opposite the church, is a children's playground. There still remains one public house, The Star, and what was The George is a restaurant, with a bar and accommodation, named The Talkhouse. The recreation ground, adjacent to the B4027, is still in use today for cricket and football.

🍁 STEEPLE ASTON

Steeple Aston lies about nine miles south of Banbury and was an established market centre of 200 souls when, according to the Domesday Book, Henry de Estone was the non-resident rector. By the end of the 13th century the name had changed to Stepelaston, a steeple being the old name for an unfortified tower. It is not possible to know when the first church was built on the site used regularly today for worship, but part of the pillar now used for the hymns board is probably original. Additions and alterations have been made every century since and there is now an excellent organ and a peal of eight bells. There is also a memorial to Judge Page (the hanging judge) whose ghost, it is said, is put into a beer barrel every midsummer night and chased round Middle Aston pond by owls, who are the ghosts of widows of 100 men hanged by the Judge. Judge Page would not complete payment to the stonemason, Hendrick Scheemaker, because he omitted the wedding ring on the finger of the Judge's wife.

The famous Steeple Aston cope, which was cut up at the time of the Reformation, is now in the Victoria and Albert Museum for safe keeping, but a photograph of it is at the back of the church. The original rectory is now a private residence with a new rectory built in the grounds.

Brasenose College was entitled to appoint rectors to Steeple Aston, as they do now, one of the earliest being Dr Samuel Radcliffe who founded a school and master's house in North Side. The school celebrated its 350th anniversary in 1990. As the village grew a new technical school (now the village hall) was built, also an infants' school with its inscription 'Feed my Lambs' which can be seen from the road. The children still celebrate the May Day Festival with the crowning of a May Queen, Jack o' the Green and dancing round the maypole.

Under Dr Radcliffe's will two almshouses were built (1663) near the old school. These have been modernised and are well maintained under the Radcliffe Trust. Until the Second World War a Sunday dinner was sent from the rectory to each house weekly but food rationing put a stop to that.

Over 30 Grade II listed buildings are in the conservation area. Most large houses have been subdivided, including the Grange, an ornate house with some doors and window tracery (visible from Water Lane) which may have come from Kew Palace. After a battle to save an ancient hedge, 1998 saw the very latest new housing estate being built, 19 houses on land between the war memorial and the Old Forge, land which used to belong to Lawrence Field, one of the old village craftsman. In 1995 we lost our village butcher's shop, after some 200 years, and Walton House has been built in its place.

The nine footpaths are well marked and include The Tchur which runs from North Side to South Side – the word Tchur is local and means a passage between two high walls. To complete the walk round the village centre is exactly one mile. Go down Cow Lane and follow the signs round Folly Field to find the eye-catcher designed by William Kent (1740) as a feature of landscape for Rousham House. The remains of a Roman villa are hidden under a field, but for special pleasure see the huge sycamore tree in the late winter when snowdrops are out or walk down South Side at daffodil time; everywhere are young trees planted to commemorate Queen Elizabeth's Jubilee in 1977.

Buses run through the village several times a day between Oxford and Coventry. The Heyford BR station is only one mile down the hill by the canal and river Cherwell. Both the Red Lion and White Lion offer pub food, the

Westfield Farm Motel provides excellent bed and breakfast facilities, and the Hopcrofts Holt Hotel, on the extreme south-west border of the village, has a conference centre. The Hopcrofts Holt has been a staging post for many centuries. When the old thatch roof was removed, lucky-charm mud-cats were found, still in good condition. The pub sign shows highwayman Duval, with the gallows behind him, on one of his raiding trips before he was caught and hanged at Tyburn.

🍁 STEVENTON

Mention Steventon to anyone in South Oxfordshire and they will think of the village green ... probably the finest in the county, set about with ancient houses and noble chestnuts, and bisected from east to west by the raised Causeway. Along this stone pathway the feet of monks, villagers and travellers have passed for centuries, going westward to the Downs and the great Sheep Fair at Ilsley, and east towards the Abbey of Abingdon, centre of learning and religion until the mid 16th century. Unfortunately, the B4017 divides the green from north to south.

For the visitor on foot the village is an architectural delight. Start at the parish church of St Michael and All Angels, a lovely village church with beautiful timbered roof, and notice the Manor Farm opposite. This is a good square Queen Anne house, with a wonderful barn raised on arches above flood level. Nearby the partly 16th century Mill House has been carefully restored, and beside it the mill stream cascades over a miniature waterfall.

The Priory and Priory Cottage date from 1462, and surround a courtyard. This beautiful house is National Trust property and the Great Hall, dated about 1500, contains a fine hammerbeam roof and is open to the public on Wednesday afternoons.

At the railway level crossing stands one of the oldest houses in the village (number 89) and nearby is Cruck House, beautifully preserved from the 14th century, in which no original feature is dated later than 1350. Steventon is rich in timber and plaster houses, and there are several beautifully restored on the east side of the Causeway.

Great Western region trains rush through Steventon, but they no longer stop and the stone-built station and cottages have been partly demolished. The materials that built the railway were brought by the Wilts and Berks canal, which connected the Thames with the Kennet and the Avon. Now the canal, too, has gone, and very little trace of it remains.

The village, with a population of about 1,600, has a great many new houses on its outskirts and along the Hanney Road, and on the green a very handsome village hall, much used by the greatly enlarged population. Cricket is enthusiastically played on the green and a great range of clubs and societies hold social gatherings in the hall.

At the junction between the Causeway and Stocks Lane stands the North Star public house. This inn has been in the hands of the Cox family since 1842, dating probably from the mid 17th century. The North Star is named after the locomotive which hauled the first train from Paddington to Steventon in 1840. This village pub has a delightfully old fashioned interior. The village has three other public houses situated in the High Street which serve excellent food. It has its own butcher's shop, grocery store and post office.

🍁 STOKE LYNE

The stream that runs through Stoke Lyne is a tributary of the Padbury Brook, which joins the Great Ouse river on the outskirts of Buckingham.

Stoke Lyne is a small village with a population of approximately 160 people. The pub has a builder's stone marked and dated 'W.B. 1806' and is called the Peyton Arms. Until recently, the Peyton family lived at Swifts House – the estate at the edge of the village. The village was a stop for stagecoaches in earlier days, and is now only half a mile from junction 10 of the M40 motorway.

The church, dating from the 12th century, is dedicated to St Peter. A statue – probably of St Peter – can be seen above the main south door. In 1993 the west end of the church was tastefully re-designed to provide the parish with a meeting room and kitchen facilities. The vicarage, now a private house, was built in 1872. It has seen many vicars, but none so infamous as the Rev William Bryant MA who used to walk around the church tower, calling his parishioners to worship. He shot himself, in the vicarage, in 1914. His burial on 3rd November 1914 took place without the services of the Church of England.

Opposite the church is the village playing field, where three trees have been

planted by members of Stoke Lyne WI, in memory of fellow member Mrs
Agnes Salter who was chairman of the National Federation of Women's
Institutes from 1985 to 1988. The colourful display of spring bulbs around
the churchyard wall each year is another tribute to the memory of past WI
members.

Like most villages years ago, Stoke Lyne had its own annual Feast Day.
This has long since discontinued; though it has been customary, for a few
years now, to hold a village cricket match as part of the St Peter's Day
celebrations in June. We hope this will continue as part of the social life of
the village.

🍁 STOKE ROW

The map of South Oxfordshire shows Stoke Row at the epicentre of the
Thames loop, equidistant from Wallingford, Reading and Henley. It is also
at the highest point of the southern Chiltern hills (about 670 ft), reached
along steep, deeply wooded roads. This high ground is poor for farming as it
is exceptionally chalky with flints and has pockets of heavy clay and no natural
sources of water.

Because of these inhospitable characteristics the area was slow to develop,
although its name is traceable to the 1300s when it was part of the ancient
Saxon parish of North Stoke along with Ipsden.

Although historically it is bound up with Ipsden, today the two villages
have little contact. Until 1848, Stoke Row did not have its own parish
church, all its affairs being recorded in the Ipsden registers. In that year it
also became an ecclesiastical parish in its own right, but remained part of
Ipsden parish until 1952 for civil affairs. At the opposite end of the village is
the pleasing red-brick chapel built in 1815 to cater for a substantial non-
conformist element in the district.

The principal landowners for some 700 years were the Reade family of
Ipsden. Over the years they lost much of their land and influence in Stoke
Row but their name has guaranteed the village a unique claim to fame via its
world-renowned monument, 'The Maharajah's Well'. The well is 365 ft deep
(twice the height of Nelson's Column) and was entirely dug by hand although
only four feet wide from top to bottom!

The expenses of sinking it, building the honey-pot Warden's cottage and providing and planting the adjacent cherry orchard, were defrayed by the Maharajah of Benares in 1863 as a token of friendship with Mr A. E. Reade, who worked in India and who had told his Highness about the acute local water shortages. It is open to the public and has recently been beautifully restored, the Indian temple appearance and yew avenue being a source of quaint delight.

Stoke Row's brick, tile and pottery industry started up in the 1600s, probably about the time the majority of its oldest vernacular houses were built. The clay pits, where up to 30 ft of clay was hauled out, are still evident in the woods and fields and the industry continued up to the start of the Second World War. There are no kilns left on the yard site, which over recent years has been developed into units of small offices and workshops. Pottery examples can be seen at the Reading and county museums.

Besides farming and the clay industry, timber has always been (and still is) an important local pursuit. For generations it was mostly the provision of firewood in huge commercial quantities but craft industries obviously developed to meet demands. Many still remember the chair-leg bodgers and the tent peggers who in their scores made a hard living working in the local woods and barns.

Bodgers existed from circa 1840 to circa 1940 throughout the Chiltern Hills, making chair legs and stretchers from local beech for the emerging, mechanised chair-making factories at High Wycombe, until the factories there developed machine methods for the tasks.

Tent pegging, however, is unique to Stoke Row and its neighbouring villages. Like bodging it was almost obsolete in the 1930s but the threat of war revived it so dramatically that some five million pegs were made for the Forces in a period up to 1942. It carried on until about 1952 when it finally succumbed.

The outbuildings at the Cherry Tree and Crooked Billet pubs were much used for these wood-craft industries and bodging equipment is in the county museum. Today most people work outside the village but the community (electoral roll 505) is thriving and dynamic.

SUNNINGWELL & BAYWORTH

The villages of Sunningwell and Bayworth, lying on the south-western slopes of Boars Hill, three and a half miles from the city of Oxford, were in Saxon times the original site of the Abbey of Abingdon. Historically part of Berkshire, of which Abingdon was once the county town, the area became part of the county of Oxfordshire and under the control of the Vale of the White Horse District Council after local government reorganisation in 1974.

The Stert stream, which rises in the vicinity of Boars Hill, flows through the two villages and eventually joins the river Thames at Abingdon Bridge. Legend has it that the stream first appeared as a miraculous spring in answer to the prayers of a Saxon noble named Aben when he was dying of thirst. In memory of this saintly man it was decided to build the abbey at the site of the miracle. However, any work completed on one day was found demolished the next, so the abbey was eventually sited at the mouth of the stream.

At the dissolution of the abbey in 1538, the prior became rector of Sunningwell. John Jewel, a noted Bishop of Salisbury, was rector here in 1551. It was he who, to provide shelter for baptismal parties at the church, had the heptagonal porch built, in a mixture of Gothic and Renaissance styles unique in English church architecture. He also gave the church its finely carved Elizabethan altar table. Another rector of Sunningwell was Samuel Fell, the famous Dean of Christ Church, who was in the village from 1625 to 1649, and with his family lies buried in the chancel of the church. His illustrious son Dr John Fell was born in the village.

The manor house at Bayworth, built and occupied by the Baskerville family, was almost a ruin by 1722. During a dig on the site local secondary school pupils found a number of old wine bottles which came from the Crown Tavern in Abingdon, and this find was thought to indicate the cause of the fall of the house of Baskerville! Materials from the old house were put to good use in the building of the present Manor Farmhouse 200 years ago.

Sunningwell still has its manor house, built by Benedictine monks; it was occupied by the abbot and used as a hospice and resthouse, the monks themselves living in cells in the grounds. After the Dissolution, Elizabeth I frequently stayed there when collecting monies from her Treasurer, who also lived in the neighbourhood. A former owner, Mrs Una Duval, was a companion of the redoubtable Mrs Pankhurst in the Women's Suffrage Movement.

Today Sunningwell parish is part of the joint benefice of Sunningwell and

Radley. In 1972 a new school was built in Dark Lane to replace the original church school which had stood for some 100 years next to the village pond. The original premises now house the very popular Sunningwell School of Art.

The village pub, the Flowing Well, was originally the home of a bachelor rector of the parish, and is named after the source of the stream which flows into the pond opposite the church, and from which Sunningwell gets its name.

Cricket is played on a recreation ground presented to the village during the First World War, and a new pavilion was built some years ago by the efforts of villagers.

The parish of Sunningwell and Bayworth used to be mainly agricultural, consisting of five farms, Blagrove, Beaulieu, Church, Long Furlong and Manor Farm. There are no longer any working farms in the parish and many of the farm buildings have been converted into houses.

SUTTON COURTENAY

Sutton Courtenay is situated three miles south-east of Abingdon. Most of the finer buildings lie in the area around All Saints' church and the well preserved village green. A pleasant walk is along the footpath from the church to Culham village, by the weirs and over the river Thames beyond. This causeway is reputed to have been constructed in about AD 1000.

The Liberal Prime Minister, H. H. Asquith, was the longest serving Prime Minister in the 20th century, until his record was taken by Mrs Margaret Thatcher. He made his home in Sutton Courtenay at The Wharf and now lies buried with his wife, Margot, and his son Anthony, in the local churchyard. Anthony, often known by his nickname 'Puffin', was a well known film director. Asquith's daughter, Lady Violet Bonham Carter, was a frequent visitor to the village.

Also buried in the churchyard is George Orwell, the author of *Animal Farm* and *1984*. His tombstone, in his real name of Eric Arthur Blair, bears a simple inscription.

The manor house was formerly known as Brunce's Court when it was the home of the Brunce family, one of whom became Bishop of Norwich. It is a five-gabled, two-winged house which has had many additions over the centuries but originated as the great medieval hall of the Courtenay family, who gave their name to the village.

The Abbey, actually the rectory house, dates from c1300. The 15th century Great Hall has an oak roof on arched supports.

Norman Hall is one of the oldest buildings in the village. It was built c1190, in the reign of Richard I, Coeur de Lion. All Saints' church also dates from Norman times. The brick-built south porch has a room above reached by a narrow stairway from inside the church. The clock on the church tower is unusual in that it is one-handed and dates from about 1700.

A healthy community life flourishes despite the fact that the church lies at one end of the village and the school at the other in the centre of the housing estate.

Cocky, a white cockatoo, is a very popular character in the village. He is often to be seen perched on the fencing, bouncing up and down calling 'Cocky, Cocky' to passers-by in the High Street.

In the past, agriculture, a local paper mill and domestic service were the main sources of employment within the village. Now the prime employers include local scientific establishments, Milton Park and Didcot power station. There are many commuters using Didcot railway station, London being a mere 35 minutes away.

The outer area of the village has become scarred with gravel workings, and a landfill site, but this still remains a most pleasant village.

❧ SWALCLIFFE

Swalcliffe is a small village lying astride a ridge some six miles west of Banbury. Only two small, sympathetic developments have taken place in recent years, one on the site of the old Forge Garage and another, including barn conversions, to the rear of the Tithe Barn. From being an almost totally farming community, nearly all villagers now commute to work, with several dwellings becoming weekend cottages.

The church of St Peter and St Paul has stood on a mound overlooking the village since Saxon times, having been altered and enlarged around the 14th century and 'improved' by the Victorians. It still needs costly restoration and care. William of Wykeham is thought to have been responsible for the former work and also some of the ancient manor house and the great tithe barn standing near to it. The family of Wykeham were great benefactors and of considerable influence, as their monuments and gifts in the church show. One descendant sailed on the *Mayflower* to the New World.

The Tithe Barn has been renovated and now houses an interesting collection of rural artefacts. It is open to the public on weekend afternoons and bank holidays from April to October. There is an Iron Age fort and evidence of Roman occupation within the village boundaries.

The wooden village hall was built by voluntary work and public subscriptions in 1924 and equipped with a billiard table, games and cards etc. There was also a well-used reading room before the 'wireless' was so common.

The village carrier, given a note, a bag and a charge of about 6d, would pick up shopping in Banbury on Thursdays and Saturdays. The village shop sold almost anything – food and hardware. The post office was at the other end of the village.

After the Second World War, and the evacuees had returned home, the number of children dwindled and the school closed in 1948. Mains water came about 1954 – not so nice as spring water but less work; then in 1970, mains drainage, long overdue.

Today there are 200 residents, 25 of them children, but no school, shop or post office and a very poor bus service. The green and cottages still slope down past the Stag's Head and the now disused bakery, where Sunday dinners could be cooked for a few pence whilst the housewives attended morning service, and a house where Dick Turpin was said to call. The school is now a house, as is the shop though the window has not been changed. The Swalcliffe Park House, with its ancient remnant of a former building is now a residential school.

There are not many 'old' families left now to remember the past. However, the seasonal festivities continue and Swalcliffe is still a quiet and peaceful place when the traffic will allow. People get on well together and help each other in difficult times as they have always done.

❧ SWINBROOK

Swinbrook is a delightful village, with its houses spread along the roadside for over a mile beside the little Wenrisc stream, that joins the river Windrush here. As you approach from the Burford road there is a lovely view of the stream tumbling into the river and the pond, scene of a wartime landmine crater, where there are swans, geese, ducks and moorhens enjoying life in and around the meadows. The cricket field with its beautiful trees is situated here, where all through the summer on Sundays and some Saturdays the local teams enjoy their games.

The bridge crosses two rivers, the Windrush on its way down to join the Thames at Newbridge and the mill stream which rejoins it in a few yards. The old mill has not been used for many decades for milling, but the house has a lovely garden, especially in springtime, with thousands of daffodils, which visitors to the Swan Inn next door fully appreciate.

St Mary's church contains some very interesting figures, 16th and 17th century effigies of members of the Fettiplace family who lived at Swinbrook in a large house to the west of the church. There is now no trace of the house, which was destroyed almost 200 years ago, but the fishponds and formal terraces lie on either side of the footpath to Widford. The Redesdale family lived at Swinbrook House to the north of the village. Besides Lord and Lady Redesdale, three of their daughters are buried here: Nancy Mitford the authoress, her sister Unity, and another sister, the Hon Mrs Pamela Jackson. For many years they owned the estate, which included most of Asthall, Swinbrook and Widford, and all the houses and gateways were painted Redesdale Blue. There are very few houses with blue paint today, if any.

To the east of the Hall the little Swin Lane goes up Lime Kiln Hill towards Asthall Leigh, Fordwells and Leafield. On the left upstream, the Old School House is a reminder of the days when the school flourished here. As the numbers of children dropped after the Second World War and the evacuees returned home, the school was closed.

Passing the school house you come to the 'splash' where the stream crosses the road. On the side there is a small bridge for walkers or cyclists. Now the houses are spread thinly, three on the right, where a raised path shows where the stream used to come down the road. It now crosses and recrosses under two little humps. The 'Old Forge' stands on the corner of Blacksmith's Lane. It ceased to be a forge some 50 years ago.

The houses and large gardens through the narrow valley continue to be quite a distance apart until you get to the building which was a Primitive Methodist chapel. Here several homes are set into the steep hillside.

Almost at the end of Swinbrook a turning goes off right, up the New Road through the woods to Fordwells, but bearing left towards Shipton-under-Wychwood you will pass the 'Hit or Miss', formerly a public house used by foresters, farm hands and poachers. Among them were the Dunsden brothers, whose bodies were hanged on the gibbet tree on Capps Lodge Plain. They had been found guilty of various crimes at Gloucester Assizes and their bodies brought back to the scene of their crimes.

The lane to the left leads on to Paynes Farm and four cottages and then becomes a farm track up on to the downs, but on the corner is a very attractive pond which attracts lots of visitors to see the ducks, geese and other water fowl that live there. The bank below the farmhouse is full of bulbs in spring and trees and shrubs lean over the water.

🍁 SYDENHAM

Sydenham is a small village with a total population of around 300. A large part of the village is designated as a conservation area and there are many listed buildings of timber framing, brick, flint and wychert under thatch and old tiled roofs.

The place-name Sydenham means 'by the wide river meadow' and the Crowell brook has played an important part in the village's economy throughout its history. It was already settled by Anglo-Saxon times and Domesday Book records that there was land for 14 ploughs and 60 acres of meadow land. There are still meadows supporting sheep and cattle, many bearing the mark of the medieval open field system. Only a few villagers are employed in agriculture now.

Robert Monday was a prosperous yeoman farmer. He died in 1662 and left a house and 'three and twenty acres of arable land in the common fields of Kingston Blount to the poor of Sydenham for ever' together with an annual payment of £1 for the upkeep of the church. The land was exchanged for a field and allotments in the Enclosure Award and the rents are now used to help pensioners with transport.

Baroness Wenman of Thame Park gave land and money towards the building of the National school in 1849. It was enlarged in 1886 and catered for all the village children. In 1929 it became a junior and infant school, when the children over 11 years old walked or cycled to Chinnor. The school closed in 1949. The old school room serves as a well-used village hall.

A village fair has been revived over the past few years and is held in the centre of Sydenham at the beginning of June. The proceeds are given to charity and have helped restore the Early English church of St Mary, which is a picturesque centre-piece for the village.

🍁 Tackley

Tackley lies north of Kidlington, in beautiful countryside between the A4260 Oxford to Banbury road and the river Cherwell, its eastern parish boundary. Parts are within a conservation area, protecting all the dry stone walls and old limestone buildings. The modern estates have crystallised ancient field shapes and typify successive building fashions. Volunteers, led by WI members, recently set up a small local nature reserve to save an area of old grassland of county significance. There are still free-range animals about, which intrigue the children.

The church has two large and one small Saxon-transitional arches clearly visible. Situated above the village, with high chancel walls, it looks like a stronghold. It has examples of every design period, but overall remains uniformly plain. The churchyard is spectacular when carpeted with

View of Tackley village

snowdrops and supports a larger than usual variety of butterflies, insects, and plants. Elizabethan John Harborne remodelled the transepts, built an imposing three-storey thatched stable and huge pigeon house near the green, two large stone gateways and some nationally important fishponds.

After the Civil War, as it was situated between Royalist Oxford and Parliamentary Broughton, 'Tackley was like a waste place'. The present stone cottages date from after that time. One large Elizabethan manor house survived intact and is a private dwelling. The next century bequeathed two landscaped lakes linked by a tufa boathouse, and the old rectory.

The Oxford Canal follows the river on the Tackley side, and the main Banbury railway line fringes the village, bringing slates to replace thatch, a few Victorian cottages, a station in the 1920s, and some employment.

Post-war Tackley thrived with Cowley works and Shipton cement works. Since then the cement works has completely closed, while Cowley works is functional on a very much reduced labour force. New housing brought urbanisation. Many clubs reflect the interests of today's villagers. There is a flourishing primary school, an excellent Methodist chapel, a post office, and two pubs. A furniture designer and a quality printer have converted barns, with more conversions pending. Tackley is responding to modern changes and carefully mixing new with old.

🍁 TADMARTON

More than a hundred years before the Norman Conquest, Tadmarton is recorded as a royal estate belonging to the Saxon king, Edwy. Go back another 1,300 years and there is evidence of human habitation at the Iron Age camp on Tadmarton Heath. Situated at 641 ft above sea level on quick draining sandy soil, near to the ironstone which they needed for their tools, the camp must have been a place of refuge for people and their livestock in times of danger. The two barrows which are known to have been nearby have disappeared, but golfers enjoying a game at Tadmarton Heath Golf Club still have to skirt around the spring-fed pool near the site of the Holy Well.

The road over Tadmarton Heath, which bisects the Iron Age camp, follows a prehistoric way which was used by Welsh drovers up until the 19th century. Roman coins, a spearhead and human remains have also been found in this area.

It is likely that the hamlet of Lower Tadmarton, with its favourable location by a ford over the Sor brook, was an earlier settlement than Upper Tadmarton. It may be that the name derives from 'the place by the frog pool' – there still are quantities of frogs in a pool at Lower Tadmarton.

Some of the parish boundaries can be recognised as being the same as the boundaries of an estate granted to Abingdon Abbey in the 10th century – and which the abbey held, throughout many legal disputes over the payment of rent, for the next 500 years. The parish church of St Nicholas in Upper Tadmarton was built and added to during these centuries, also the manor tithe barn. These two buildings still stand in a good state of repair and are in constant use.

During the 19th century, three generations of MacDermots held the manor. The Manor Farm and house were let to tenants for most of this period. In the 1890s John Charles MacDermot reduced his family to penury through his gambling. However, the MacDermot family are remembered with gratitude by the older people in the village who receive benefits each year from a charity set up by the family in 1864.

Another landowner of the 19th century was Capt W. L. Lampet who built The Highlands, an imposing mansion on a hill between Lower Tadmarton and Bloxham. This also was let as the Captain certainly did not want to live surrounded by 'all those sheep'. He gave his family name to the pub, the Lampet Arms, which he may have built as a railway hotel when it was thought that the line would run along the Sor brook valley. The name of The Highlands was later changed to Tadmarton House.

Cromwell slept the night of 12th May 1645 in the rectory, which had long been abandoned by the Royalist parson, Ambrose Sacheverell. This house, renamed the Grange, was mostly rebuilt in gracious early Victorian style in 1842.

The village and its hamlet still have many of the 26 stone, thatched houses built in the prosperous farming years of the 16th and 17th centuries, which were registered for the Hearth Tax of 1665. The population reached the high number of 450 in the census of 1851; the number of people registered to pay the Community Charge in 1998 was 377. The 19th century building which was once the village school has been transformed into a lovely village hall.

A memorial plaque in the church to someone who lived in Tadmarton for only three years sums up the sentiments of many who live in the village to this day: 'He lived in Tadmarton only a little while but loved it much'.

🍁 TIDDINGTON WITH ALBURY

Tiddington lies midway between Thame and Wheatley, astride the busy A418 road. Drivers passing quickly through the village might see a garage, the Fox public house and a large caravan sales and service centre, as well as a few houses along the main road. Much of the village lies on the north-facing slope of the valley of the river Thame, south of the A418.

The village street has a number of cottages dating from the 16th to 18th centuries, with Tiddington House on the hill-top built in the reign of Queen Anne. There has been a steady increase in building in the village, from the Airey local authority housing of 1947, replaced with brick-built houses and bungalows in 1995, to the estate houses of the 1960s and 1970s. Other post-war dwellings, including a small estate built in the late 1980s, extend along the Ickford Road towards the water meadows of the river Thame.

St Helen's church at Albury

On the south-eastern boundary of Tiddington lies Fernhill bluebell wood and a quarter of a mile to the east, along the Oxfordshire Way, is the hamlet of Albury, once a much larger community than Tiddington. Here stands the parish church of St Helen together with the Old Rectory, the Grange and Church Farm. The original church was demolished in 1828 and the present church was built in the Perpendicular style by Thomas Rickman in 1830. The Roman-esque font with zigzag ornamentation is all that remains from the original building.

Although the population of Tiddington has grown considerably since the Second World War, these years have also seen the disappearance of many of the amenities which were important to the village. The school, the general stores with post office and the forge have all become private houses and the railway line, once a useful link to Princes Risborough, Thame, Wheatley and Oxford, has become a haven for wildlife.

In earlier times the villagers worked on the many farms in the area or for the large estate of Rycote Park to the east. At the end of the 18th century there were nine farms. Now only Manor Farm in the centre of Tiddington and Sandy Lane Farm exist as working farms, where modern machinery replaces farm labourers. Church Farm at Albury, which had for some years been a teaching farm, is now renamed Albury Court and home to a marketing company.

The village hall is the community centre of the village. Built on the recreation ground in 1953 by the villagers to commemorate the Coronation of Queen Elizabeth II, it provides a meeting place for activities organised by several clubs and groups. Coronation year also marked the beginning of the annual tug-of-war between Oxfordshire and Buckinghamshire, represented by Tiddington and Ickford respectively, and contested from opposite banks of the river Thame, which is the county boundary at Ickford Bridges. Held on the first Friday in August, junior and adult teams compete to avoid a ducking in the river. Tiddington Cricket Club, founded in 1886 with a picturesque ground south of the railway embankment, reached the National Village Cricket competition final at Lord's in 1995.

🍁 UFFINGTON

Situated in the Vale of the White Horse, Uffington is dominated by the beautiful 13th century church known as 'The Cathedral of the Vale'. It is a large cruciform building with an octagonal tower, and has eleven of the original twelve consecration crosses, the most complete series to be seen anywhere in England. The iron chandelier which hangs in the church was made by the local blacksmith in memory of the master craftsman, churchwarden and chorister, from whom he learned his trade. St Mary's has a modern font with a cover designed and made some years ago, by a local carpenter.

In the early 10th century the village was granted to the Abbey of Abingdon and it was mentioned in the Domesday survey of 1086. In 1620 it passed through marriage into the Craven family and until 1959 most of the land was held by the Craven estate.

Uffington was a thriving agricultural community. The Wilts and Berks canal, used as a means of carrying cargoes, contributed to its prosperity. Coal, wheat, bricks (made at the village's three kilns) and salt were all transported by horse-drawn barge; the salt house still remains at the wharf farm. The opening of the Great Western Railway caused the death of the canal. The railway provided transport and employment, but with the closure of the station in 1964 work became limited, as it did on the farms after mechanisation. Today, as in the majority of villages, most people commute to work. Since the Second World War a number of houses have been built and so the population has increased considerably.

'The Scouring of the White Horse' and *Tom Brown's Schooldays* both have their origins in this area. The games and merriment held on the hill, rolling of cheeses into the manger, the backsword play and the beer that flowed were all stories told by the old 'uns of the day, and recorded by Thomas Hughes. In *Tom Brown's Schooldays* he gives a colourful picture of 'Veast' held in the field behind the present school. He describes cheapjacks and penny shows, men in white smocks and women in red capes. People came from miles around to join in the fun. Strangely, history does repeat itself and people by the thousand still descend on the village each year for the well known White Horse Show.

In 1972 the Thomas Hughes memorial hall was built and is in constant use by the numerous organisations. The 17th century reading room known as

Tom Brown's School is now a museum where remains of Roman pottery can be seen, found during the building of Craven Common housing estate. Having both a sports field donated by the Craven estate and a recreation ground, Uffington people are fortunate in being able to enjoy many sporting activities. Three shops have now been reduced to one, this being a general store and post office, and where there were five public houses only two remain.

WARBOROUGH & SHILLINGFORD

The villages of Warborough and Shillingford lie approximately eleven miles east of Oxford, on the north side of the river Thames between Dorchester and Wallingford. Shillingford Bridge, with its three arches and balustrade, was built in 1827 to carry traffic between Thame and Wallingford on the road that had been turnpiked in 1764.

Warborough post office

Beautiful scenery can be enjoyed from boat or foot between Shillingford and Days Lock, and if the climb to Wittenham Clumps can be made, a poem will be found carved into a beech tree in 1847 by Joseph Tubb, who camped up there for a fortnight so he could complete his work.

The Tubb family lived in Warborough and Shillingford between the years 1800 and 1984. Initially Benjamin Tubb, farmer and maltster, bought a house, and 20 years later in 1820 his brother James settled in the area too. James was a friend of William Cobbett, who among many other involvements was a radical reformer and later Member of Parliament, and he mentioned James Tubb in his *Rural Rides*.

The charming village green in Warborough is off the main thoroughfare and has a wonderful outlook towards Benson and on up to the Chiltern hills. Throughout the year either football or cricket are played on the green. Records suggest that cricket has been played there for at least 130 years. The cricket club has at various times been associated with each of the five local hostelries, the Cricketers, the Nelly's, the Six Bells, the Kingfisher and the Shillingford Bridge, so it seems hardly surprising that their motto is 'Win or lose, we enjoy our booze'!

Up until 1987 Warborough and Shillingford's post office was situated in the centre of the village in a pretty black and white cottage. It had opened in 1840, the year the penny post was introduced by Rowland Hill and 15 days after the first issue of the penny black. Remarkably the position of sub post-master was held by a member of the same family for all that time. The last incumbent, Theo King, joined his aunt after his return from war service and took over as sub post-master after her death. He served the village in that capacity, and many others, for 41 years. Although now a private residence a plaque on the garden wall reminds us of Mr King's many services to the village.

The parish church of St Laurence was built in 1666, having a three-stage tower and, most unusually for Oxfordshire, a leaden font, similar to, but with a much simpler design, the one in Dorchester Abbey. Close to the church is the Georgian vicarage, a beautiful large building typical of that era, though no longer used as the vicarage. There are two village halls, one being the St Laurence Hall, once the village Church school but now the parish hall. The Greet Memorial Hall was taken out of farming use by the Greet family, who used it for theatrical plays renowned locally and in London, and handed it over to the parish in 1930.

🍁 WATERPERRY

Waterperry is on the Buckinghamshire border, with the river Thame for its southern boundary and the Holton brook for its western boundary. The ground is low-lying, generally about 200 ft above sea level, rising to 234 ft to the north. The soil is rich loam with a subsoil of gravel and clay, and it provides excellent meadow land and pasture.

Bernwood Forest is north-west of the parish, where rare butterflies can sometimes be found during the summer.

Waterperry has one street, with a mixture of new council houses and ancient cottages which are mostly of the 17th and 18th century. They are built of coarse rubble or brick and some are timber-framed.

Waterperry House owes its graceful Queen Anne frontage to Sir John Curson, who had it rebuilt in 1713. The Henley family bought the estate in 1830 and it was sold to Magdalen College in 1925. Seven years later Waterperry Horticultural School was opened by Beatrix Havergal, the principal, as a residential horticultural college for women. Miss Havergal was known as the 'Strawberry Queen' at Chelsea Flower Show, where for many years she won the gold medal prize for her exhibit of Royal Sovereign strawberries. She retired in 1971.

The house was then taken over by the Fellowship of the School of Economic Science. It is now run as a horticultural and garden centre. The school organises the annual 'Art in Action' festival in July, where craftsmen and women from all over the world exhibit their skills.

The church of St Mary was built in the pre-Conquest period. It comprises a nave of three bays, chancel, south aisle and south porch. The west tower with its weather-boarded bellcote is of wood, supported on oak pillars within the church. In the nave there are some high-backed pews on which the candlesticks remain and with the original hinges on the doors. Most interesting are the early 14th century windows with excellent tracery on the north wall.

The ghost of Waterperry is the Grey Lady, who walks the footpath from Holton to Waterperry House. Two people living in Waterperry in the past 20 years have encountered her while walking the footpath.

🍁 WATERSTOCK

The little village of Waterstock lies in a loop off the A418 between Wheatley and Thame, and is completely surrounded by open farming land, some of which has recently been converted into a golf course, and through which runs the Oxfordshire Way. Waterstock lies in a bend of the river Thame and the name meaning 'Waterplace' indicates Anglo-Saxon origins. Many of the fields show ridge-and-furrow strip cultivation and in 1279 there were probably about 200 inhabitants, but after the Black Death the population decreased to 51 persons over the age of 14. Today there are about 80 inhabitants.

St Leonard's church, Waterstock

233

St Leonard's church is very much the hub of the village and, as well as regular church services, meetings and concerts take place there. The earliest church record dates from about 1190, though it was largely rebuilt in the 15th century, since when there has been much rebuilding, with thorough restoration in the 19th century. If you look inside, much of the history of the church and village is revealed. Notably remnants of medieval glass were recovered after the Reformation and have been inserted above the armorial Ashhurst window. This window, together with monuments, records the important families of the Oxfordshire gentry who inhabited the manor house and made up the squirearchy, a feudal system which only released the last of its patronage and grip in 1957.

The grounds of Waterstock House are adjacent to the church and the manor house was finally pulled down after the servants' quarters were converted into the present substantial residence. The stone-built stables are probably contemporary with the 1787 house. They are the home of the Waterstock Equestrian Centre.

By the entrance to Waterstock House is the Pump House dated 1898, a little building reminiscent of a Saxon tower from which many of the villagers collected water until mains water came to the village in 1951.

Opposite the church are Church Farm Cottages and the Old Rectory, a substantial stone-built 18th century house, the only other 'gentlemen's house'. It was the home of Manoug Parikian, the celebrated violinist until his sudden death on Christmas Eve in 1987. He is buried in the churchyard.

On the bridleway leading to Waterperry, Waterstock Mill stands on a small island on the river Thame and was mentioned in the Domesday survey (1086). Almost certainly on this site, the 15th century timber and brick house with its watermill was rebuilt in the Elizabethan period and converted in 1957 when it was sold. Beyond the mill is the delightful little Bow Bridge built by Diana Ashhurst in 1790. It is a single-arch brick bridge curving outward and can be seen best from the riverside, much frequented by anglers. Swans and moorhens and the occasional flash of a kingfisher give added pleasure.

The single street is flanked by cottages built of stone or local brick, some retaining the small buildings in the gardens, originally privies or pig-sties. At the further end of the village, Home Farm is a 17th century timber-framed house with its ancient thatched barn and 17th century granary, and the 18th century Park Farm can be seen beyond.

The oldest buildings are the two thatched cottages thought to date from the late 13th or early 14th century and from the 16th. Orchard End has proved to be a medieval cruck house, its smoke-blackened beams showing that it was originally a two-bay open hall.

Waterstock retains a mellow, lived-in feeling with many of the inhabitants working from their own homes, and much of the traffic consists of farm vehicles and horses. As you walk through this unspoilt village there is a sense of unity and permanence reflecting a strong community spirit.

🍁 WATLINGTON

Watlington is ideally situated, on the spring line at the foot of the Chilterns and surrounded by countryside, much of it National Trust property. Many people who have moved here in the last 25 years agree, and it seems now more like a dormitory town for London or Birmingham than a large village.

Centuries ago Watlington was a market town as important as Wallingford and Thame, on the ancient Icknield Way and near drovers' roads from Oxford to London, but it did not develop much, probably because there is no convenient river. There had been a castle or monastery near the church of St Leonard, but the villagers moved away from it and nearer to the spring line around the time of the Black Death.

More recent times showed a thriving community, with a regular market, varied tradesmen and a large number of women lacemakers, but these homeworkers lost their livelihoods when machine-made lace became available.

There used to be numerous pubs, some of which were run by the wife, while her husband earned a supplementary wage on a farm or latterly at Morris Motors (which might have been built at Watlington had Mr Morris and Lord Macclesfield been able to make an amicable deal!). Now Watlington has only three pubs and a social club, and modern life exerts its pressures on the place. Traffic is a major problem with the B4009 cutting through the centre narrow crossroads – one of the very few B roads to have access to a motorway – and there seem to be continuous battles to keep open the library, cottage hospital and some shops. Market stalls are seen in the streets again, providing a useful service and reverting to the old ways.

🍁 WENDLEBURY

The village of Wendlebury lies in the north of the county, two and a half miles to the south of the market town of Bicester. There has been a settlement on or around this site since before Roman times. The remains of the Roman town of Alchester are just to the north of the village. The older houses are constructed from local stone, some of which may have been removed from the Roman ruins.

The village lies on the old Oxford to Bicester road, which was made a turnpike road in 1793 (in the 13th century the road south from Alchester was known as 'Buggestreet'). The village was bypassed in 1949 by the A421 trunk road. The aspect of the village has been changed with the completion of the M40 London to Birmingham motorway.

The only pub still open for business is the Red Lion, which stands in the centre of the village opposite the stream. This early 18th century building has been used over the years as the manorial court, the blacksmith's and a coaching inn. The other pub, called the Plough, lay at the south of the village opposite where the village hall now stands. It is now a private home.

Until the late 19th century there were at least five farm houses and most of the men living in the village were employed on the farms. Many of the wives and children helped in the fields during the harvest and sheep-shearing time. The stream also provided income, the cress was harvested and sold in the local markets. All of the farm houses are now private homes, including the barns which formed College Farm, once owned by Christ Church College of Oxford.

The manor house in Church Lane is 17th century with an 18th century frontage. This has been divided over the years, with once as many as three houses. The smaller house at one end served the village as the washhouse and in the yard can still be seen the cobblestones that formed the draining area for the coppers. The old rectory is perhaps the largest building in the village, this has now been converted into flats. The field at its front, which is where Rectory Close now stands, used to be the playing field for the village where cricket matches were played and the May fair held.

The church of St Giles lies at the top of Church Lane. It is believed that it was built in the early 13th century. It has had a very chequered history, due mainly to the fact that it is sited on unstable foundations and a clay subsoil. By the middle of the 18th century it was evident that the church was about to collapse and, after morning service on Tuesday 24th March, 1761 the assembled churchgoers started to pull it down. The restored and rebuilt church opened again just over a year later, the cost to the parishioners was £400.

Unfortunately the problems had not been solved and by 1900 the tower was in such a poor state that the parishioners feared to attend church, as large lumps of masonry were liable to fall at any time. A great deal of the church was again rebuilt and the tower removed. The cost this time was £1,400. Three bells from the original tower, one of which is badly cracked, stand at the back of the church and on the wall, behind the Norman font, is a picture of the church as it was with its tower. Just outside the door of the church are the remains of the village stocks.

The population of Wendlebury has fluctuated over the years. The present population is over 300. In 1981, when the village held a party on the day that Prince Charles and Lady Diana were married, every child of school age and under was given a commemorative crown; there were exactly 100 children. Unfortunately the village school was closed in 1959. The post office and shop was originally situated in what is now Post Well Cottage, Church Lane. It later moved to the Main Street but it too has closed.

🍁 WESTON-ON-THE-GREEN

Weston-on-the-Green is not only 'on the green' but also 'on the road'. It is just south of Akeman Street, the Roman road from Corinium to Silchester. In later years the roads to Bicester and Northampton were both turnpikes, with a tollgate at Weston. In 1847 a William Marriott was fined five shillings and costs for preventing the Rev A. H. Matthews (the magistrate) from passing him on the turnpike by driving on the wrong side of the road. Now, with the building of the M40, heavy traffic misses the village, and what had been a busy trunk road is now a relatively quiet minor road.

Weston is a typical English village of stone houses, many with thatched roofs, a manor house, a church and also a recently restored duck pond. The village school, which closed in 1984, was the only thatched school in Oxfordshire.

It has always been a farming community and in the 19th century many women supplemented the family income by lace-making. Some of their lace was sold by a splendid woman called Dinah Tuffrey, who acted as the local carrier and pedlar, walking to Bicester and then taking trains to places further afield where she sold local produce, and bringing back goods to the village.

In the 18th century the church had fallen into disrepair and was restored by Norreys Bertie, then the lord of the manor. While on his Grand Tour in Italy he commissioned an altar piece from Pompeo Batoni – it is still in the church today. The Berties' tenure of the manor ended in 1918 when Richard Bertie was killed in Palestine four days before the end of the First World War. The whole estate was sold in 1919 and the manor house is now an hotel.

In addition to Weston Manor Hotel there are two pubs, the Chequers and the Ben Jonson. Both are thatched buildings and the Ben Jonson seems to have been the centre of activities at the annual Village Feast in September. As the *Bicester Advertiser* put it in 1879, 'a number of amusements of the itinerant kind' arrived at Weston either before or after St Giles's Fair in Oxford. In addition to this celebration there was the Weston on the Green Club Feast which took place in early summer. It seems to have been a savings club affiliated to the church and at the feast there was a service with a sermon and a sit-down dinner. Sadly, the chapel, which was built by the Methodists themselves in 1838, closed in 1993.

North of the village on the B430 is Weston airfield, built in the First World War and now used by a civilian gliding club and by the RAF for parachute training. It is a common sight, in good weather, to see parachutes dropping from the sky, some of them free-falling from a great height.

Weston today is a pleasant, friendly place, with a shop, village hall, several farms, a civil engineering plant hire firm, agricultural contractors, a sculpture casting workshop and an architect's office. A flourishing new business park has been built opposite the airfield.

🍁 WHEATLEY

Wheatley village lies in a valley six miles east of Oxford. Finds from a Saxon cemetery were discovered in 1883 and are housed in the Ashmolean Museum. A Roman villa was unearthed in 1845, and although nothing remains now, fragments of pottery, tiles and coins dating from AD 260 to 378 were found. These people lived on the higher land, but subsequent settlement was in the valley alongside the stream which flowed along the main street. The stream was crossed by stepping stones until 1858 when it was contained in a culvert beneath the road.

Many of the old houses and cottages have survived, particularly in the High Street which is still the heart of the village. Of special note is the Manor House which is medieval in origin, was considerably enlarged in 1601 by Thomas Archdale and had mixed fortunes until its restoration in 1939–40. Opposite is a fine group of buildings, including a former packhorse inn, the George, which dates to before 1548. Several inns survive today, a legacy from the age of coaching when Wheatley was on the main road from London to Oxford, which crossed Shotover Plain, the descent into Wheatley being a favourite haunt of highwaymen.

An important occupation for Wheatley people was stone quarrying and the stone was used in the building of Windsor Castle, Merton College, ecclesiastical buildings and local cottages, most of which were erected between the 13th and 18th centuries. The quarry was notorious for its bull baiting and cock fighting activities. Wheatley was also famous for its ochre which was ground at the local windmill and used to paint Oxfordshire wagons in their distinctive yellow colour. However, most people worked on the land, but the arrival of the railway in 1862 linking Wheatley with Oxford, High Wycombe and London brought more opportunities for employment. William Avery's timber yard was established in 1881 and was Wheatley's largest employer until the 1950s.

During the 18th and 19th centuries Wheatley had a reputation as a disorderly village owing to the coaching trade, the quarry industry and a changing population. The Rev Edward Elton described the village as a refuge for all the worst characters in the neighbourhood. The village lock-up built in 1834 by Cooper, a local mason, was used to incarcerate offenders overnight before sending them to the Oxford Court. It still stands today near the edge of the old quarry and is a pyramid-shaped stone structure with a padlocked door, the floor space being about six feet square and with a headroom of about eight feet.

St Mary's church was designed by G. E. Street and consecrated in 1857. It replaced the chapel which stood in the centre of the village and this site is now occupied by the War Memorial. The Congregational church, now the United Reformed church, was converted from a tannery barn, the Rectory tithe barn became the Roman Catholic church, and the Granary Evangelical church was once a stone barn too.

239

Today the Merry Bells provides the chief social centre and the hall is used for many village events. It was built as a Temperance Hotel for travellers and local men and boys, and donated to the village in 1888 by Mrs Miller of Shotover House, who was saddened to see so much hardship, some of which was caused by drunkenness.

During the past 50 years Wheatley has expanded and the population has risen from 900 in the 1880s to around 4,000. There are several shops, excellent schools, a post office, bank, library and numerous village societies catering for everybody's needs. A traditional event is the annual May Day celebrations with the crowning of a King and Queen and maypole dancing.

🍁 Wigginton

Wigginton has always been a small village (the present population is about 200) and having no resident large landowner, nor at times a resident rector, has been and remains, rather independent. The church of St Giles is at least 600 years old, is well maintained and had the same resident rector for 50 years until the 1970s. There is a Roman villa which has been excavated on two occasions, but now sleeps under cultivated fields once more.

In the 19th and early 20th century Wigginton had a forge, a cartwright, a cobbler, a tailor, coal merchant, undertaker, a working mill producing flour, and until the mid 1940s the baker cooked the villagers' Sunday roasts for 3d! Farmers and labourers made up most of the population and the children were educated at the village school built on land given by the then resident rector.

Water and electricity were brought to the village through the generosity of local landowners. The railway line from Banbury to Chipping Norton which called at nearby Hook Norton was used by villagers to shop in Banbury, Wigginton offered £20 towards the cost of a local halt for the use of villagers but this generous offer was refused. However, the line was one of the casualties of the Beeching Axe and part of it is now a BBONT nature reserve.

Many trees have been planted by both the village people and local landowners and the village is well maintained. Not being directly on a main road, traffic is not a problem and the village still likes to keep to itself, the people look after each other and the old are well cared for.

Wigginton still has three working farms, but the rectory is now a private house and the school is the village hall. Recently houses have been bought by townspeople but there are still old village families of long standing. A 100 year old Methodist chapel is still in use.

✿ WOLVERCOTE

The village, north-west of Oxford, was known as Ulfgarcote in Domesday after Ulfgar, the Saxon. The name Wolvercote came into being in 1185.

Situated on the edge of the wide expanse of its common and the open stretches of Port Meadow, the inhabitants have always jealously guarded their rights and stoutly defended their environment against the repeated efforts of Oxford City to enclose the land in order to meet the needs of its growing population. Even to this day the goose is their special emblem and the Women's Institute banner, permanently displayed in the village hall, shows a goose girl on the common. Some of today's older residents, when children, herded the geese back and forth across the common to the river's edge. Grazing rights continue to this day and at least once a year the Sheriff of Oxford rounds up the horses and cattle on Port Meadow and Wolvercote Common and impounds them. Those owners who have no right to pasture their animals there must pay a heavy fine before they can be released from the pound.

Wolvercote's location near to the city of Oxford also accounts for its place in national history. At the time of the Civil War, Charles I established his headquarters and Parliament in Oxford and during the siege required fodder for his horses. He made a written agreement with the tenants of land at Wolvercote and 61 freemen to provide hay for the King's stables. One of Wolvercote's two mills was used by the King's armourers to grind sword-blades. In the spring of 1644, when King Charles made his escape from Oxford by night, he and his 3,000 men took the unguarded track across Port Meadow and through lower Wolvercote to Yarnton and Bladon to the north. Wolvercote people showed their loyalty by keeping this move secret and the King was able to leave in safety.

Dominant over the village is the paper mill. There has been one there for three centuries and until recently it was owned by the University Press, its quality paper being used for bibles. At church harvest festivals, rolls of paper or paper sculpture were displayed in addition to fruit and vegetables. The river, necessary for the mill to function, has also played an important part in the life of Wolvercote. The picnic place, near an old toll bridge, is one of the most beautifully-sited in England; to the south, across the meadow, one sees the magnificent skyline of Oxford with its ancient towers and spires.

On a summer afternoon in 1862, Charles Dodgson (otherwise known as Lewis Carroll) together with his friend Duckworth, Alice Liddell and her sisters, came by rowing boat with a picnic basket on board. It was then that Dodgson began to tell the children a story. That was the start of *Alice in Wonderland*.

Wolvercote, described in 1817 as a 'rather extensive village', was never a place of wealth, most of its inhabitants living in simple hovels or earth-floored cottages, none of which survive. Nevertheless, a few finer houses of earlier centuries remain, much restored, and the village is now a conservation area. In the 19th and 20th centuries came extensive development and all of Wolvercote became part of Oxford City in 1928. The original, low-lying village, which was subject to winter flooding, grew up round the mill at the edge of the common. It is now separated from the church and school (which are situated on higher ground in Upper Wolvercote) by the canal and main railway line. The built-up higher area has no visible boundary between it and neighbouring Summertown in the north of Oxford and its large population has as its main focus the city rather than the village.

That there is no rift between the two parts of Wolvercote may partly be attributed to the well-placed village hall built in 1932 which acts as a focal point between the two and helps to nurture a sense of community.

🍁 WOODCOTE

Woodcote is situated on the edge of the south Chiltern hills, approximately 500 ft above sea level. Proof of its early existence amid woods and hills is evident from a map drawn by John Spede in 1605, before the days of modern contour maps. Beech woods are still within walking distance, with rolling arable fields beyond. There are three ponds within the parish boundary and even within living memory one of them was used as a source of drinking water!

Good roads connect Woodcote with nearby villages and a main road goes to Oxford and Reading. A lot of building development has taken place since 1970. Nowadays many people commute to work, but there are light engineering units at Wards farm. Woodcote also has a car repair workshop, a private bus company, a garden centre, two churches, three schools, a post office, and several shops. The community library is friendly and very well stocked and nearby is the community run tea room. Further education classes offer many subjects, day or evening, and the villagers enjoy good care from the health centre.

There are many societies or sports clubs to join from pre-school nursery and playgroups to special activities for the retired and elderly. Many of these have their base in the village hall. Residents are kept up to date with local activities by a free monthly 'Correspondent'.

Every year a traction engine rally is held in Woodcote or its environs, attracting steam rollers, vintage cars and motor cycles, crafts, stalls and displays from all over Britain. Village life need not be dull.

🍁 WOODSTOCK

Woodstock was a favourite hunting place for nearly all the kings of England from Saxon times to the late Stuart period.

It was Henry I who built a manor house in what is now known as Blenheim Park. Edward the Black Prince, son of Edward III, was born here, Henry VIII was a frequent visitor with his first wife Katharine of Aragon, and Elizabeth I was imprisoned in the Manor for almost a year.

The story of Fair Rosamund is often told to visiting friends – she was a daughter of Walter de Clifford and mistress of Henry II. He brought her to Woodstock and built her a bower outside the walls of the Manor House and protected it with a complicated maze. The legend goes that Queen Eleanor, arriving at Woodstock unexpectedly, found a ball of silk attached to the King's spur. She followed it through the maze to the 'bower' where she found Rosamund whom she poisoned with a cup of wine. This has never been proved, but Rosamund did die in 1175 and she was buried at the Convent in Godstow. There are still traces of the Nunnery on the bank of the Thames opposite the Trout Inn. Fair Rosamund's Well can still be seen in Blenheim Park from the Grand Bridge.

Medieval Woodstock was a very small place with forests on all sides. The villagers were very poor – some were craftsmen but many scraped a living from the land. By the year 1450 Woodstock had become a market town having been granted a charter. The inhabitants became free burgesses and were allowed to send two representatives to Parliament, and the town was granted a staple for wool.

In about 1500 gloving became a Woodstock industry which gradually increased through Victorian times when there were many small factories producing gloves. Many were sent out to be hand-stitched by women and girls in their own homes. Gloving only started to decline after the last war when cheap Japanese imitations became readily available. It is still, however, a tradition that when a reigning king or queen visits Woodstock, a pair of gloves is presented to him or her, and when Queen Elizabeth II came here, the Mayor presented her with a pair of white kid gloves.

At one time families lived in the same house for generations, and all the shops were owned by local people, but today with high rents and properties fetching enormous prices this is no longer the case. One exception is the Banbury family who still have a drapers' shop in Oxford Street and have lived there for generations.

Many buildings are most attractive and date from the 16th, 17th and 18th centuries. Fletchers House is a notable example, a 16th century merchant's house which is now used as a county museum. Lots of interesting exhibitions are held there.

The Church of St Mary Magdalene was badly damaged by Cromwell's army and very badly restored in 1877. It is worth a visit to see the attractive and colourful kneelers worked by many members of the Woodstock WI together with a group of 'Friends of the Church'. We are rather proud of them.

In the nearby village of Bladon is the church of St Martin where the grave of Winston Churchill still proves a place of interest to those who also visit his birthplace of Blenheim Palace. A small gateway close to the church leads to the grounds of the Palace and from here a very pleasant walk may be taken round the estate.

🍁 WOOLSTONE

Overshadowed by the White Horse, the little village of Woolstone lies at the foot of the downs, its history going back into the Bronze Age.

Largely an agricultural area, the use of a steam plough led to the discovery of a Roman villa. Excavated in 1884, two mosaic floors were revealed.

It is known from Saxon charters that the Great Spring of Woolstone has been flowing for 1,000 years. Though it no longer supplies the whole population, it is still a great deal more pleasant to drink than the piped supply from the main source.

In 1195, the priory of St Swithun, Winchester built the church of All Saints. The walls, chalk and sarsen, have weathered well, and it possesses a Norman doorway and an unusual lead font. The Stations of the Cross, cast in fibreglass, makes a beautiful addition to the side chapel. The sculptor, Ulrica Seton Lloyd, lived for many years at Woolstone Lodge.

The village has a number of cottages dating from the 17th century and some very attractive thatch. It became a conservation area in the early 1970s.

The population has dwindled from around 300 in the 19th century to the present day when it is in the neighbourhood of 130. It is recorded that Mr and Mrs Breakspear had 21 children in a small cottage at lower town end, and all but one survived. Some of the cottages housed more than one family, so there must have been considerable overcrowding. Life cannot have been easy for the inhabitants. Water was supplied from wells, or the Woolstone Brook, and the first to pipe water were the Craven estate who owned the spring in 1862. It was brought to Manor and Woolstone Farms first, and to the Lodge in around 1910.

Before the Second World War, there was a shop in the village, a laundry, and even a cobbler. Now there is only the 16th century inn, which does a brisk trade.

The village school, given by Lord Craven in 1874, closed at the end of the 19th century. It became the parish meeting place and was at one time a lending library. Now it has passed into private ownership.

The arrival of George Butler in 1822 was a notable event in the village history. He saw action under Sir Robert Calder as a boy, and is listed on his memorial in Uffington church as Captain RN. It was he who converted the original corn mill to what is now known as Woolstone Lodge. His son William Butler became the tenant in 1871 until his death in 1917. The Lodge became the focal point of village life, and his four daughters, none of whom married, virtually 'ran' the village. They played the organ in the church, gave Bible classes, were responsible for the Girl Guides, and were in charge of the lending library. The Butler memorials are in Woolstone churchyard.

It seems appropriate to mention here William Noakes, one time tenant of the inn and churchwarden. Having a disagreement with the Butler family, he built the somewhat unusual tower to overlook their property. There he inscribed his initials and those of his brother and the date. The tower is built in red brick, with coloured inlay, very much in the style of Keble College, and it forms a strange contrast with the thatched building next to it.

The sharp bend on the road to Uffington is always known as Miss Newman's Corner, after the old lady, once a court dressmaker, who lived there. A regular church attender, Miss Newman was a familiar and much loved figure with her dog. Miss Newman's spaniels were always black, and they were always called Tessa!

WOOTTON & BOARS HILL

The name Wootton derives from the Anglo-Saxon word meaning 'the township in the wood' – Wood-tun. The origin of the village goes back nearly 1,000 years, when a group of Saxon farmers made a clearing in the woodlands below Boars Hill, which in those days covered all the lower slopes of the hill and much of the valley below.

Until the 20th century, practically everyone in Wootton and Boars Hill made a living from the fields which stretched from the parish boundary with Dry Sandford to the foot of Boars Hill ridge. The heathland on the top of the ridge was used for grazing sheep. Hay could not be grown satisfactorily in Wootton, and had to be grown and fetched from meadowland near Donnington Bridge, and carted up Hinksey Hill to Wootton. At the time of Domesday (1086) the population was small, no more than 20 men and their families; even in the mid 19th century it was only 300–400.

There was no church in Wootton until the 14th century, when a chapel of ease to the mother church at Cumnor was built. This chapel, and the parish of Wootton and Boars Hill, remained dependent on Cumnor for practical purposes (eg burials) until 1735, and the old track northwards over the fields of Wootton to Cumnor (now a bridle path) is evidence of the route by which the people of Wootton once had to carry their dead to Cumnor. It was not until 1885 that Wootton became a separate parish.

During the 16th and 17th centuries there was a village pound for stray animals, near the present day Waterworks Crossroads, and Whitecross may have been named after the 16th century village constable, Thomas White. This was the era of prosperity for the yeoman farmers of the village – the families of Mayo, Richards, Bond, Badcock, Broughton and Busfield. The community was largely self supporting, growing their own food, making cloth from their sheep and the flax cultivated in 'Flexfield', and brewing their own ale in the farmhouses. The smithy was near the village green.

The turn of the 20th century saw great changes on Boars Hill, when many large houses and gardens were built. Residents like Sir Arthur Evans, the archaeologist, and Lord Berkeley transformed the appearance of Boars Hill with their tree planting and development.

Sir Arthur Evans became interested in the local Scout troop and in 1914 built a Scout hall within his 100 acre Youlbury estate, 70 of which were used for scouting purposes. The army and airforce used the estate during the Second World War and in 1947 the Scout HQ bought 36 acres.

The 1920s and 1930s saw the most startling changes in the village. Abingdon airfield became operational in September 1932, and this, together with the beginnings of the Amey Group development and the expanding motor car industry in Oxford led to a rapid increase in the population, resulting in new housing and shops on the southern and western edges of 'Wootton Village'. In the early 1950s the community centre was built, within reach of Dry Sandford and the 'new' Wootton; a Roman Catholic chapel in the Cumnor Road was founded in 1952, and in 1959 Wootton school was rebuilt.

🍁 WYTHAM

Viewed from the embankment of the busy A34 bypass, Wytham appears an idyllic village. The Great Wood, once the haunt of highwaymen, is a splendid 'back-cloth' and also provides an indication of stormy weather to come, hence the old rhyme:

> When Wytham Hill wears a cap,
> Farmers all, beware of that!

The site on which the village stands has been inhabited since early times. The name Wytham is generally interpreted as meaning 'the dwelling at the bend of the river', the river being the Seacourt stream, which winds its way through the water meadows to join the Thames.

Wytham retains some aspects of a feudal settlement, for with the exception

247

The White Hart, Wytham

of the inn, the church, rectory, and two houses built on glebe land, the entire estate has one landowner, at the present time the University of Oxford. The estate was bequeathed to the University under the will of Colonel ffennell, the last lord of the manner to live in Wytham Abbey.

Before it was sold in 1920 to Raymond ffennell, Wytham Abbey was the seat of the Earls of Abingdon. Despite its name, the Abbey has no ecclesiastical connections, and until the middle of the 19th century was known as Wytham House.

It was the 5th Earl who had the old Norman church pulled down and in 1811–12 rebuilt the present church. He used materials from the ruined Cumnor Place, former home of the ill-fated Amy Robsart; the archway over the churchyard gate is one instance. There are some interesting examples of stained glass in the church from the late 14th to the early 20th century. Some of the old glass came from the earlier church, as did the 17th century altar table and chest.

Not all the residents of Wytham have added to its good name. In the early 18th century, the miller John Mauge murdered his sweetheart Annie Kite, and was hanged for the crime. The event is commemorated in a ballad, a copy of which is now lodged in the British Museum, entitled *The Wittam Miller*.

248

The University has brought many benefits to Wytham, not least the careful modernisation and maintenance of the 17th or 18th century houses, with their roofs of tiles or thatch. The wild life in the woods and surrounding fields is protected, and made the subject of careful research. For this reason, visitors to the woods must obtain permits from the University.

🍁 Yarnton

To many people, Yarnton is a blur of houses as they speed along the A44 between Oxford and Woodstock, but to the people who call it home there is much beyond this stretch of tarmac.

The first people known to have lived at Yarnton were some of the earliest farmers in the British Isles and many pottery fragments from the Neolithic era have been recovered during the gravel excavations.

By the medieval period, the village of Yarnton, or Eardington as it was then known, had moved further away from the flood plains of the Thames to the area round the church.

As in many early settlements, the history is linked with that of the church. A chapel belonging to Eynsham Abbey was mentioned as early as 1009. The 13th century church, dedicated to St Bartholomew, has gained much from two great benefactors, Sir Thomas Spencer and Alderman William Fletcher. Of particular interest are the two beautiful tombs in the Spencer Chapel to members of the family of Sir John Spencer of Althorp, the 17th century bells, and the stained glass, much of it English medieval, some of it Tudor.

Beside the church stands the lovely Jacobean manor house, originally built by Sir Thomas Spencer around 1611 and completely restored in 1897. Since 1973, it has housed the Oxford Centre for Hebrew and Jewish studies, a non-denominational academic institute attached to the University which maintains an important research library and archives.

The fields down by the river, known as Yarnton Meadows, were the last survivors of the method by which much of the meadow land of the county was allocated under the open-field system of farming. Mowing rights were determined annually by the drawing of lots, a practice carried out by the Meadsmen. These 'Lot Meadows' have been adopted by BBONT to ensure their preservation. They have never been ploughed, and each summer are ablaze with an unrivalled show of wild flowers and unusual grasses.

Well-maintained footpaths offer several interesting walks in the area – down to the Thames, past the new lakes left by the gravel workings (already home to several species of water birds), across the fields and along the canal or along Frogwelldown Lane, following the route of Charles I's retreating army as they fled from Oxford to Bladon.

Situated conveniently close to Oxford, there is a regular bus route through the village. Villagers are served by two hostelries (The Grapes and the Red Lion), a large garden centre, a primary school, post office, shops and a GP branch surgery with its own dispensary – all very valuable services. In recent years a small enthusiastic group restored and re-equipped the playing field in Rutten Lane as a children's play area. This much-appreciated amenity, now known as Yarnton Park, is very well used. Adult team games now take place on a playing field behind The Grapes.

Many new houses have been built over the past few years, the population has increased to around 3,000 and, although many people commute into Oxford to work, the various clubs and organisations flourish and grow.

🍁 Index

251